Fifteen Minutes to Freedom

The Power and Promise of Havening Techniques®

Compiled and Edited by Harry Pickens

Havening Techniques is a registered trade mark of Ronald Ruden,
15 East 91st Street, New York, New York. www.havening.org.

Harry Pickens is a Certified Havening Techniques® Practitioner.
Contact him at haveningforhumanity@gmail.com

Published by:
Havening For Humanity
Louisville, KY

Designed by Danielle Baird

ISBN-13: 978-1-5425-8117-2
ISBN-10: 1542581176
First Edition

All practitioners, trainers, and participants featured in *Fifteen Minutes to Freedom:
The Power and Promise of Havening Techniques®* have given the editor written
consent/permission to include their stories in this book for learning purposes.

DISCLAIMER
Although the authors, compiler, editor and publisher have made every effort to
ensure that the information in this book was correct at press time, the authors,
compiler, editor and publisher do not assume and hereby disclaim any liability to
any party for any loss, damage, or disruption caused by errors or omissions, whether
such errors or omissions result from negligence, accident, or any other cause.

This book is intended as a reference manual only, not as a substitute for the medical
advice of physicians. The reader should regularly consult a physician and/or mental
health professional in matters related to his/her health and particularly with respect
to any symptoms that may require diagnosis or medical attention.

Fifteen Minutes to Freedom

The Power and Promise of Havening Techniques®

Compiled and Edited by Harry Pickens

Contents

Introduction 9

Part I: A New Way Of Healing

1. What are the Havening Techniques®? 16
2. Fifteen minutes to freedom: *Kate Truitt* 22
3. From trauma to triumph: *Holly Shaw* 50
4. Helping people create the lives they desire and deserve: *Eugenia Karahalias* 63
5. Dissolving the chains of addiction: *Ross Hyslop* 74
6. Animating the process: *Tam Johnston* 92

Part II: Releasing The Pain Of The Past

7. A tool, not a therapy: *Tony Burgess* 105
8. Sculpting your own neurology: *Carol Robertson* 126
9. Touching the future of health care: *Kimberly Ann Davis* 146
10. Phantom limbs, chronic pain, and PTSD: *Chris Meaden* 162
11. The sky's the limit: *Bill Solz* 169

Part III: Helping Those Who Help

12. Rapid relief for survivors, soldiers, and first responders: *Irene Hajisawa* 185
13. Vigilance, veterans, and 'voodoo': *Malika Stephenson* . . .196
14. Healing the healers: *Joanne Harvey* 203

Part IV: Self-havening For Self-Transformation

15. I became my own case study: *Louise McKay*. 212

16. No pain, no meds: *Elizabeth White*. 233

17. It was meant to be: *Lynn Demers* 246

18. Me 2.0: *David Chametsky* 252

Part V: Becoming Your Best Self

19. Optimal performance in poker, golf, and life:
    Stephen Simpson. 263

20. Transforming stress into serenity: *Bonnie Park*. 274

21. From broken down to breaking through:
    Steven Travers 282

22. Seeing miracles every day: *Donna Ryen*. 293

23. Even skeptics spread the word: *Michele Paradise*. 302

Part VI: Real Problems, Real Solutions

24. Building the toolbox: *Susan Cortese*. 313

25. The root of the issue: *Ira Scott* 321

26. What matters is what works: *Doug O'Brien* 334

27. Get a taste of it: *Olf Stoiber* 344

Part VII: A Safe Haven For Humanity

28. Havening the world: *Paul Emery* 357

29. A community of healers: *Louise and Michael Carmi* 365

30. From inner peace to world peace: *Kathryn Temple*. 374

31. Healing, havening, and humanity: *Ulf Sandstrom* 384

Part VIII: An Idea Whose Time Has Come

32. Tracking a global movement: *Feliciana Tello* 403
33. Curiosity, patience, and persistence: *Ronald Ruden* ... 408
34. Changing the world: *Steven Ruden* 420

Postscript 434

Getting the help you need: *How to find a
Havening Techniques® Certified Practitioner* 436

Helping others heal: *How to get trained
in the Havening Techniques®* 437

About the author 439

Introduction

Stories of a Quiet Revolution

It happened. Again. For the fifth time this week.

Yesterday afternoon, between 3 and 4:15 PM, I witnessed a miracle. She walked into my office on the verge of tears. Afraid. Upset. Reactive. Stuck.

"I'm not enough," she said. "I've never been enough. I'll never be enough. I've been dealing with this for decades. Therapy, counseling, prayer, energy work. And I still never feel that I'm enough. What is wrong with me?"

One hour and fifteen minutes later, she is glowing. Radiant. At peace. The pain, the sense of struggle, the sadness, the desperation—dissolved. And the old belief that had haunted her for at least forty years—gone for good.

And it's not coming back.

How do I know? Because I've now witnessed this very same phenomenon occurring over and over and over again, probably a hundred times in the last 18 months.

I know, I know. You're thinking—too good to be true. Real change just can't happen that fast. Absolutely impossible.

And if you would have shared this story with me two years ago, I would have thought the same thing. In fact, this is the single biggest problem with the remarkable process that took my client from despair to delight in seventy-five minutes flat. Every single day, somewhere in at least 21 countries around the world, somebody experiences a shift—a positive, permanent, profound shift—that most of humanity doesn't believe is possible. And yet, there are so many stories:

A veteran who has suffered with PTSD (Post-Traumatic Stress Disorder) for four decades is set free.

A woman who can't stop grieving the sudden death of her fiancé five years after his passing finds an inner place of peace—at last.

An elderly man whose joint pain has not responded well to medical intervention walks without his cane for the first time in months.

And the miracles keep happening—one person at a time.

A Revolution Unfolding

You see, a quiet healing revolution is spreading slowly but surely across the planet. This revolution is taking place not through the latest discoveries in pharmacology, or through new insights in how to manage the symptoms of emotional, physical or psychological dis-ease.

This revolution is taking place one person at a time, through a simple process that uses the power of touch, attention, and imagination to heal emotional pain that often has seemed intractable and unresolvable. This process was developed by a Harvard-trained medical doctor who was seeking to understand the neurobiological mechanism underlying the often remarkable results commonly seen in the domain of energy psychology.

Originally labeled Amygdala Depotentiation Technique and now called Havening, this simple yet powerful procedure is

poised to transform how humanity thinks about and addresses myriad physical, psychological, and emotional issues—from
PTSD to phobias to chronic pain to the consequences of every
imaginable kind of trauma.

This revolution cuts to the core of the cause of much of
humanity's suffering, and provides a simple yet profound
cure that literally rests in the palms of our hands. And, for
the very first time, you will be able to see the revolution unfolding just as I have, through the stories of many who are
part of the charge. The voices contained in this book belong to the students, practitioners, and trainers—the quiet leaders sharing the power of Havening with the world.

How I Found the Revolution

I first learned about Havening the morning of February 14,
2015. I was on the phone with my brilliant friend and colleague
John Morgan, discussing my core passion, which is teaching
people how to live with greater fulfillment and freedom. In my
coaching practice, I had been using many powerful tools with
great success, including EFT (Emotional Freedom Technique)
to help my clients dissolve the inner blocks to living their best
lives, but I was frustrated. Although there were quite a few solid
research studies clearly demonstrating the positive impact of
EFT and other energy psychology modalities in helping people
heal, no one had yet identified a neurological mechanism of action that made sense to me. I wanted to be able to explain what
was happening IN my client's brains TO my clients.

John asked me if I had heard of Dr. Ronald Ruden, or his
book, *When The Past Is Always Present*. According to John, Dr.

Ruden had figured out the very thing I was seeking. Little did I know that this conversation was about to change my life.

I found Dr. Ruden's book on Amazon and ordered it. It arrived three days later. I read it immediately. I was beyond intrigued. Seeking to learn more online, I discovered that Dr. Ruden and his team would be presenting a training five weeks later, towards the end of March 2015.

Honestly, I didn't have the cash on hand to go, particularly considering the added expenses: travel to New York from Louisville, plus the shuttle to get to and from the Roslyn Hotel, plus the cost of a hotel room for two nights. However, my inner 'yes' was so solid that I maxed out my credit card to invest in my own learning and growth. This would prove to be one of the wisest investments of my life.

In the meantime, I was experimenting. I used what I learned from the book to clear a limiting belief that had plagued me for years. I tried it with one client and helped her dissolve the pain from a childhood memory that had haunted her for decades. I helped a friend let go of the pain of a difficult relationship that ended abruptly. I was discovering that this process really did work. And I had not even attended the training yet!

I arrived at the Roslyn Hotel that Friday evening in March, 2015, filled with eager anticipation. The training was powerful. I got to meet Dr. Ruden and his twin brother Steven, who continues to play a major role in spreading the word about Havening around the world. I both witnessed and experienced powerful and rapid transformations that I would have previously thought impossible. I immediately signed up for the certification program.

The rest is history.

Since that Valentine's morning, I have been part of this gentle revolution in healing. I've now had the opportunity to help hundreds of clients and students use Havening Techniques® to reduce and eliminate the toxic impact of negative stress, boost resilience, optimize wellbeing, and break free from the pain of the past. And I am fully engaged in helping to share the good news about this remarkable set of tools for emotional healing.

This book represents the latest chapter in my personal Havening journey. The Havening community is tight-knit, generous, brilliant and compassionate. I have rarely been part of a professional community filled with so many humble superstars, so many people who are making a real and tangible difference in the lives of others while exploring the outer edges of what's possible in the realm of emotional and psychological wellbeing. I realized one of the most powerful ways to spread the word would be to collect and share the stories and experiences of many of the outstanding students, practitioners, and trainers I have met over this past 18 months. Their voices are unparalleled in conveying the power of Havening Techniques®.

I hope that this book will inspire you to explore Havening for yourself. The possibilities inherent in Dr. Ruden's simple yet profound discovery will astound you.

Enjoy.

Harry Pickens
December 29, 2016
Louisville, Kentucky, USA

PART I

A New Way Of Healing

CHAPTER 1

What are the Havening Techniques®?

"When an event or experience is perceived as traumatic or very stressful it becomes immutably encoded, often with life-altering consequences. However, recent research from the field of neuroscience has shown us how it's possible to modify this encoding. The Havening Techniques are methods which are designed to change the brain to de-traumatize the memory and permanently remove its negative effects from both our psyche and body."

— Ronald A. Ruden, M.D., Ph.D.

The Havening Techniques represent a breakthrough in the rapid and effective treatment of stress-related physical and psychological conditions. Havening uses touch, attention and imagination to trigger electrochemical changes in the brain that alter how memories are processed.

The result of this simple procedure? Reduced stress, increased resilience, higher levels of achievement, and emotional, psychological and physical healing.

How does Havening work?

Dr. Ronald Ruden devoted over a decade to research the process of traumatic encoding: how the amygdala electrochemically 'marks' specific memories so that present-moment sensory input 'triggers' the fight/flight/freeze response.

His quest resulted in a breakthrough understanding of the process of depotentiation—how the processing of these memories can be changed on the synaptic level so that the discordant emotions previously activated no longer 'invade' the present moment. The Havening Techniques represent the practical fruitage of Dr. Ruden's research. His 2011 book, *When The Past Is Always Present,* comprehensively articulates his discoveries.

Why does Havening matter?

According to Dr. Ruden's model, Havening facilitates rapid, gentle and permanent electrochemical and physical change in the cells of the amygdala. Since this process of depotentiation occurs on the level of the individual neuron, the corresponding transformation can be nearly instantaneous. Skillful application of Havening Techniques therefore can produce significantly more rapid and efficient results than purely cognitive approaches to healing trauma.

Havening requires neither intake of drugs or use of special equipment. The transformation resulting from the successful application of Havening Techniques represents a new paradigm in the practical application of neuroscience to facilitate emotional and psychological healing.

What is the neuroscientific foundation of Havening?

The Havening Techniques emerged from Dr. Ruden's extensive research, building on the juxtaposition and synthesis of his experience as a physician, his Ph.D. in biochemistry, and his curiosity as to the neurobiological mechanisms underlying the efficacy of energy psychology protocols. This research and Ruden's conclusions are summarized in *When The Past Is Always Present*.

Constant experimentation and refinement, forged through clinical experience with over one thousand patients and clients before introducing Havening protocols to the general public in 2013, ultimately led to the development of an exquisitely simple, easy-to-apply and infinitely flexible set of tools that may be adapted and integrated into any therapeutic philosophy, healing profession, and scope of practice.

Research into the efficacy of the Havening Techniques continues on an ongoing basis. One study, documenting the impact of single sessions of Havening, has been published in the Health Science Journal (http://www.hsj.gr/medicine/impact-of-a-single-session-of-havening.php?aid=7273). More clinical trials are currently underway, with publication dates beginning in 2017.

What can Havening do?

In the hands of a skilled practitioner, clinical experience indicates that Havening Techniques® can help:

1. Heal amygdala-based disorders, including panic attacks, phobias and PTSD.

2. Halt and reverse the long-term psychological and physiological impact of Adverse Childhood Experiences.

3. Heal the emotional and psychological residue left by traumatic experiences.

4. Remove inner blocks to goal achievement.

5. Enhance performance in sports, business and the creative and performing arts.

6. Build real-time resilience.

7. Reduce the impact of chronic negative stress.

8. Reduce emotional reactivity while broadening and building capacity to respond and adapt to challenge and change.

9. Relieve present-moment emotional discomfort.

10. Reduce and eliminate the emotional roots of chronic pain.

A global movement

Havening is rapidly spreading worldwide. Over 150 Certified Practitioners in 21 countries are helping their clients reduce stress, build resilience, optimize wellbeing and heal the pain of the past.

Read on to discover how leading practitioners are using this powerful tool to change our world for the better—one person at a time.

To learn more about Havening Techniques®, go to havening.org.

About the interviews

Each of the following chapters originated as an interview conducted by phone or Skype. I have done my best to preserve the essence of each interviewee's authentic voice, while editing the transcripts to ensure clarity and readability.

Nonetheless, you will notice on occasion the kinds of non-traditional sentence structures and grammatical imperfections that occur commonly in spoken conversation.

CHAPTER 2

Fifteen minutes to freedom

Dr. Kate Truitt, Ph.D., M.B.A.

Dr. Kate Truitt is a Licensed Clinical Psychologist and trauma specialist in private practice in Pasadena, California.

Harry: *Kate, how did you first discover Havening?*

Kate: I was very lucky to be introduced to Havening in the summer of 2014 by our colleague Bill Solz, LCSW. At that point I myself had been living with PTSD for over 6 years and had given up hope of changing certain symptoms and behavioral patterns that plagued my life. You see, in 2009 I experienced a traumatic event that led me to develop PTSD. My partner of 10 years died suddenly. It was a week before our wedding and I had been invited to a Welcome to the Family bachelorette party with his sisters. When he didn't answer my calls to pick me up at the end of the evening, I knew something was wrong. I took a taxi home and came home to a dark and locked house. I had left my keys at home so I had to break in to the house and when I found him, he was non-responsive. I was unable to resuscitate him. It was a terrifying and traumatic evening that left an indelible imprint on me.

As a clinician, I had already been doing trauma work for over a decade at that point. I was utilizing Eye Movement Desensitization and Reprocessing (EMDR), Trauma Focused-Cognitive Behavioral Therapy (TF-CBT), Cognitive Processing Therapy (CPT), and the Trauma Resilience Model (TRM) in my private practice. I had been living and breathing trauma treatment in my work with patients. But this was the first time that I had an acute traumatic experience that resulted in a clinical diagnosis of a traumatic stress disorder.

I went the traditional route for my own treatment. I knew fantastic practitioners in all these areas I had trained in, so I reached out to them and for years I tried to heal.

I had what's referred to as an intractable memory. That's a memory that just can't budge and feels permanent. It has been encoded in the brain in such a manner that the brain will not release it. This memory was causing me turmoil in my daily life.

Luckily, I had friends and family who loved me and would handle the chaos of my emotional world. It felt like I was living and breathing in a crazy space. Somebody would leave my house and would agree to call or text and tell me they got home safe in 30 minutes. If they didn't call or text me in that time, I would go into a panic. I would call them repeatedly while mentally spinning stories about their horrific deaths.

I remember one time I drove to my parents house 2 hours away because they got home, fell asleep and forgot to call me. I didn't know they were home safely. Every day I was constantly reliving the trauma and my powerlessness to save him. I couldn't break the patterns so I just adjusted my life around it, but living this way was exhausting.

My late fiancé passed a week before our wedding. June 13, 2009 was the night of the trauma. I lived with this memory until I found Havening in October 2014.

Earlier in 2014, I was in Jacksonville, Florida at a treatment center conference where I ran into a colleague, Bill Solz, who had already trained in the Havening Techniques. We started to talk about trauma work and he mentioned the techniques to me.

To be honest, It sounded too good to be true. But I was desperate. It had been over 5 years at that point and this was something new that was based in neuroscience. I have a Master of Arts in Psychology with an emphasis in psychophysiology and view myself as a neuroscientist. Brain science is extremely important to me. So I thought, okay, it's based in neuroscience; it's new, but I'll try it because I'm desperate.

I flew out to New York and during the very first breakout group of that conference everything changed. On that beautiful October day, Dr. Steven Ruden, one of the founders and developers of Havening, happened to sit down at my breakout group and said "does anyone have anything to work on?"

I told him "I have this issue and I've tried everything else. What do you think?" I still remember that sparkle in his eye and his smile. He just looked at me, like "we've got this."

Just a few minutes later, that memory that I had literally spent well over $10,000 trying to alleviate changed.

Fifteen minutes later that memory was different. It was completely different. In my memory, above the body, where it had been, I now perceived a glowing light. And my late fiancee's name was John; I called him Angel, Johnny Angel, and my mind just manifested that image as we did the work. I was able to walk myself through the experience of that night with no activation. Instead my mind kept focusing on the warm glowing light and I felt peaceful. I was shocked, to say the least. I was also incredulous.

It wasn't until I got home and had a trigger that would normally spin me into that panic cycle that I really knew that something had shifted. I got two steps into that panic cycle and it was like my panic brain circuitry just collapsed. The neurons had nowhere to go. In that moment I burst out laughing with relief. I have never experienced that cycle of behavior again.

All in only fifteen minutes.

H: *Fifteen minutes to freedom.*

K: Fifteen minutes to freedom! Even to this day when I talk about it I just get this glow because my goodness, who knew? And I took that leap of faith, 90% of me thinking this isn't going to work and 10% thinking maybe. Now I just know Havening is going to change the world.

H: *Clearly it is. Thank you for that story. Kate, who are your typical patients?*

K: I specialize in treatment of PTSD—post-traumatic stress disorder.

I have over the course of the last 10 years developed a large private practice working with adult survivors of childhood sexual abuse that has since expanded to survivors of any abuse.

That's the bulk of my patientele, although I do work with individuals who have any sort of blockage that is amygdala based or fear based. And quite frequently that will lead back to difficult or stressful experiences that their brain encoded traumatically.

I also train clinicians who specialize in addiction, couples therapy, eating disorders, as well as individuals who work with children and adolescents. Because, as you know, stress, trauma and depression impact all of us.

H: *What led you to work with patients who have experienced such significant degrees of stress and trauma?*

K: I started by researching eating disorders. A bit of my personal story is appropriate here. I was a model for about 10 years. I lost a dear friend, a fellow model, to severe anorexia. That is when I left my modeling career and began my journey to become a clinical psychologist.

I always felt my focus would be eating disorders but the more I worked, researched and engaged clinically, the more I realized that obviously an eating disorder is a coping skill. I was treating symptoms but not really addressing what was hurting the person, which was the early life experiences that were causing their eating disorder. So my practice and research shifted into the etiology, what was causing the problem so I could treat the person.

H: *What place does Havening occupy in your full repertoire of tools and interventions? Has it now become the foundation of all of your work?*

K: I'm chuckling because when I think about everything I have learned and applied and integrated over the years, everything is so much more effective and more helpful because I teach everyone how to haven and I incorporate it with everyone.

If I use any other technique we are using Havening alongside it. If we are doing talk therapy we will start Havening while we are talking through it to increase the associative processes. And if an event arises, and someone remembers something that is distressing or painful, we will go right into Havening to release it. It is the foundation of my practice now. And my patients walk out in this grounded calm and open space from every session, no matter how deep the work.

H: *Yes, I've noticed that as well. When you complete a Havening session, the patient is in a more grounded, clear and peaceful state, no matter where they began. Tell me more about your experience of Havening with your patients. What are the specific advantages you find with Havening as opposed to the many other trauma techniques that you've been trained in?*

K: What I love about it is that it's adjunctive. It's not something you will use in place of a particular school of thought. It's beautifully integrative and powerfully so.

We can have someone who is psychoanalytic, or CBT oriented, someone who is mindfulness based, does NLP (Neuro-Linguistic Programming), or uses hypnotherapy and they can each bring it into their practice and really make it their own while relying on the foundational principles and techniques of Havening.

Dr. Bessel van der Kolk, who is one of the foremost trauma experts in the world, if not the foremost, talks and writes about how nothing can be accomplished without a safe place. If we can't have a safe place then we can't heal trauma. Havening provides that safe place electrochemically for the patient.

When I go work with my patients, some of these people have never felt safe in their entire life. And, with Havening, all of them demonstrate the capacity to create the electrochemical representation of safety within themselves. And their body has never felt that before.

H: *Dr. Ruden spent nearly a decade trying to decode this process of traumatic encoding. Havening developed out of his research and he came up with a powerful neurobiological model. Based on your own understanding of neuroscience which predated your exposure to Dr. Ruden and Havening, how does his model resonate with your knowledge? Do you think Dr. Ruden got it right?*

K: Yes. I think he got it more right then I was ever aware of. That was one thing that really encouraged me to fly out to New York. As you know, there is the 3 DVD set training course that comes with the purchase of any 2-Day training.

Before flying out to NYC for my initial Havening Techniques training, I started watching them. Now, mind you, I had already written a 200 page thesis on the defense cascade, which is all about information processing in the amygdala and trauma responses. And then I went in and did my own research in information processing and traumatized individuals using quantitative EEG and EEG. That was my thesis for one of my master's degrees.

The point is that I have been investing heavily in learning all about the brain, information processing, trauma, and psychophysiology. That's what encouraged me to go to New York. When I read his book the alignment with my own studies was remarkable. He references the same articles I referenced in my research. He references the same books. He references the same people. He is an MD and also has a doctorate in neuroscience, so he has been living and breathing this stuff for decades. It's in alignment with everything I have come across with doing trauma work for only 10 years and he has 40 years on me. Dr.

Ruden's work has allowed me to go much deeper with the work that I do in my practice.

H: *From your perspective, what exactly does Havening do that other tools and modalities can not do as easily or readily?*

K: Havening allows for the depotentiation of the traumatically encoded experiences in the amygdala. What that means is we can now go in and target the neurons that are holding the traumatic experience active in the brain. We can empower the brain to release these experiences that are serving as a trauma filter for present day information processing.

Posttraumatic Stress Disorder is a misnomer because it basically implies that we are living in a past experience. When a patient walks in the door they are there because of their current symptoms. So it's a present day disorder that is being run by the information processes in the present day that were designed and developed from past experiences.

As I explain it to my patients, your brain has a trauma filter in it now and we have to clear out that trauma filter. That's what Havening does. It allows us quickly and effectively to take a traumatic experience and release the traumatically encoded components so it becomes just another memory.

What that does for the brain is that now this specific memory will not activate the entire physiology of fight, flight, or freeze when the individual encounters a stimulus similar to one in the traumatically encoded experience. It will no longer burn out the adrenal system or cause the person to reach for food or alcohol or sex to soothe their nervous system because of the impact of that earlier trauma. So the individual is back in a place of empowered control. I've never seen anything like it.

H: *Hence the gateway to true client empowerment. What was most challenging or difficult for you as you integrated Havening into your current work?*

K: The integration into my work has been simple. My patients are in pain and I have a tool that alleviates that pain and results in huge positive systemic change. They trust the techniques. I have experienced the challenge in supporting other clinicians to feel comfortable using the technique. When I explain the science to my patients and start showing them the Havening touch and they have the initial experience with it, then everyone's on board. They can see that it works and they take it home and start using it immediately. I haven't had a single patient push back.

But for clinicians, especially in psychology, we are taught that this is not a touch based field. Havening is a touch based technique. We have facilitated self-havening, where the clinician models the touch while the patient provides the touch, but even that can feel uncomfortable for the clinician.

When we look at EMDR, initially before we had the tools, you would sit in very close proximity to the patient and move your fingers back and forth in front of their eyes or tap on their knees. So that was touch based and EMDR has provided a portal into a whole new world of psychosensory work.

H: *So the clinician's hesitation is because of the existing paradigm that they are living out of?*

K: Exactly. Transcending that has actually been the harder thing. I do a lot of adjunctive work with other clinicians and they witness the huge shifts their patients experience in a very short period of time. They'll send someone to me that has a trauma come up or experiences trauma; I will do two or three sessions with that person just to clear them and the amygdala and then send them back. Those are the clinicians signing up for the training. They see the transformative effect of the technique and say, "I don't want to have to refer my patients out to you to do that."

H: *Of course.*

K: "I want to create that change." They sign up.

H: *So once they have the tangible experience with the patient, like you did, then it breaks down any resistance or discomfort they might have experienced with a touch-based technique.*

K: Exactly. And when I go to do a lecture or presentation and I intro the techniques I have everyone do a little self facilitated havening, then they say, "I want in. I want to help my patients do that." But the dominant paradigm right now is that people are nervous and don't know how to effectively integrate it into their own practice.

H: *How do you approach the issue of touch with patients who are coming from a history of sexual or physical abuse where touch was used in a way that violated them?*

K: I always lead with the neuroscience. I break it down. "This is what's going on in your brain." That way they understand that they are not crazy, these things happen and their brain develops these mechanisms. Then I introduce the Havening touch based purely on the neuroscience, so that the touch cannot be misconstrued as anything other than a tool that is part of a neuroscience based technique.

Then when it's time to do the reprocessing and engaging the touch, I first model it for them. I have them apply the self-havening touch to themselves. Then I talk about the pros and cons of me facilitating the touch and them facilitating the touch and doing facilitated self-havening.

And the cons being that, for me facilitating the touch, I will be in close proximity to them and will be applying the touch. The pros being that by me facilitating the touch they will have exponentially increased delta wave activity and they will have the opportunity to focus on the work rather than managing the motor cortex while focusing on the work.

So basing it all on the science has created the receptiveness. They know that this is pure science and everything we are doing is based in literature to support the fastest and most gentle healing process.

After all, that's what they want. They want relief—don't we all when in pain?

H: *Yes, and the combination of both fast and gentle is profound and significant.*

K: Havening is the only tool I've seen that with.

H: *What are some of the specific conditions you have been able to successfully address with Havening?*

K: The easiest are panic attacks and phobias. As you know those are amygdala based disorders, so we can find the key stone event and heal those.

I've seen fantastic shifts with long term major depressive disorder, so that people who have had depression across their lifespan have just been able to release and move forward. That's where that stress based disorder component of depression comes in.

I also see success with generalized anxiety and obviously PTSD. With complex PTSD, I've seen incredible transformations working with individuals who were completely and utterly hopeless, came forward with horrifying things that happened in their childhood, and survived and are living in this chronic cycle of trauma. By the time our work is resolved they would say they are cured. That's their language, which is unbelievable to me.

I also do a lot of work with intractable pain; in other words, pain that doesn't have a physiological cause. I am so impressed with this work but, as we know, the amygdala encodes pain.

I do a lot of work with individuals who have chronic high stress and have had multiple cardiac events. I work with them to help alleviate the stress so that their nervous system calms down. We have seen blood pressure drop in incredible ways. I have a lot of cardiologists now that refer to me. Havening is such a multifaceted tool for so many things.

H: *We spoke a good bit before about the fact that you have shifted your practice where at one point you had a number of different tools and approaches you were using in terms of addressing trauma. Now Havening is part of everything you do. I'd like you to speak a little bit more about the specific distinction between EMDR, which gets to the same end result as Havening in terms of clearing the traumatically encoded memory but gets there in a very different fashion, and Havening and why you've chosen to transition more and more to Havening.*

K: I started training EMDR back in 2004, which was 12 years ago. It blew me out of the water. It was amazing. It was the new hot thing and for a very good reason. That being said, there were very certain patients that I was very reticent to use it on and with good cause.

One of the side effects of EMDR is "opening somebody up" and even though they have containers and safe places and all these protocols in place, to close somebody back up before a session ends wouldn't always work.

Sometimes we'd open up an associative network in the brain and that person's left spiraling in it. My practice is working with complex PTSD so I have a lot of personality disorders. I work with a lot of self-injurious people. I have a lot of people who struggle with suicidality. To open up somebody and then send them home with a good chance they might end up in the ER, whether it be for twenty-seven stitches from a self inflicted wound or suicide attempt, is pretty scary to me.

And yet, I also knew that in order to really do the healing work we had to be able to get into the limbic system because talk therapy doesn't work for trauma. Their prefrontal cortexes shut down. So I would use EMDR a lot of the time but it was nerve-racking for me with a lot of my patients.

H: *It was nerve-racking because specifically of those associations?*

K: For a number of reasons. One was we could be working on a highly traumatic event and we get half way through the session, the session ends and we haven't finished the reprocessing.

Traditionally EMDR requires eight to ten sessions to reprocess a discrete trauma. So you'd send them home in the middle of it, but some of the defense mechanisms that were previously helping them process it may have shifted or may not be available anymore.

Or, you may be working on a traumatic experience and they don't have a tool to use between sessions to calm themselves down. They've become activated in it.

I would also experience patients who would dissociate in session. They would have a really severe abreaction, and there wasn't a way to support their system in calming down and to keep doing the reprocessing because now they're in a completely dissociative state.

They rip off the headphones, the bilateral audio, they toss the buzzers, they're not going to look at any light and they've just completely capsized on themselves. I have to rely on all of my training just to help them ground. Thank goodness I had a bunch of other tools.

But it was scary in those moments. I would ask them to go into the hardest thing in their lives and to relive it and to do that repeatedly, recognizing there was incremental change every single time, which was great.

But there were some things that were a little too big or some people whose lives were so intense that I would have to spend eight months doing resource development before we could even begin trauma reprocessing. A lot of times that would lead to attrition because in their eyes we're not actually doing the work. Not recognizing that this resource development is a really important part of working, no matter how often I would say that, they would still walk away from treatment saying I wanted to work on this trauma, not feel better about these other things in my life.

EMDR is still a fantastic tool. I still utilize many components of EMDR with Havening. I still utilize a lot of the protocols and I find them very effective. And, I've found there are certain things with Havening that are transformative and the key one is that I can get through more experiences more quickly without any loss in thoroughness or impact.

Here's an example. Tonight I had a patient I was working with, just before our call, and we're working completely content free. She brought in a list of fifteen different highly traumatic experiences and I don't know a single thing about any of them. I've been doing forty-five to sixty minute sessions, reprocessing each one in its entirety.

So it would've been more extensive work, you know each trauma taking eight to ten sessions possibly. Sometimes you can collapse across, but it has basically been one session per item. Sometimes now because we've done four or five sessions, we're doing two traumas in one session because of the exponential growth effect of Havening. We work on one and she heals across all of them regarding a certain feeling, state, or cognitive flashback.

And it's gentle. Even though she's abreacting, she's crying, she's shaking, in some ways she's acting out the trauma, this is called a traumatic discharge. We want that. That's a good thing because of the Havening touch releasing the GABA and the serotonin, her system's actually very calm. Even though she's in the middle of it, she's still present with me, I can still engage with her, and I have a tool to ground her immediately with, the Event Havening, if the Transpirational Havening, which is a deeper more complex neural work, gets too much for her to handle. I know I have a tool that can immediately stop that processing and pull her back in the present moment within minutes.

H: *So the process itself allows for a greater grounding.*

K: Yes. My patient also has something to take home in between sessions. So if she were to somehow get activated by something (and a lot of my patients have really, really severe complex PTSD, so they do struggle with nightmares the first two or three sessions or may still have panic attacks), they have a tool that they can use immediately to stop it without reaching for a benzodiazepine.

H: *Yes.*

K: So they're empowered to do their own healing. The final piece is that it is just so much quicker. One of my patients came and spoke at the training that I gave. She came and gave an amazing testimonial and answered questions from everybody.

We'd done twelve sessions worth of work and she was a survivor of really severe childhood sexual abuse. Her perpetrator lived in the house and she was perpetrated upon sexually almost everyday. And it took us only twelve sessions. We terminated! Our work was done! I don't know anything else that can do that. She was back at work. Vibrant, vivacious, empowered, no nightmares, no panic. I can go into the neuroscience of all of it for you but basically every symptom marker that we know for PTSD was no longer there.

You tell me something else that can do this in twelve sessions. She's up there saying 'this is the most amazing thing ever; every session I walked out feeling clearer and stronger'. That was the thing with EMDR. People would leave and they would be wrecked. They would get to the end result but it was agonizing sending them back into their world in a place of pain and distress.

H: *Thank you. That's a beautiful and lucid explanation of the distinction.*

K: You're welcome.

H: *Are there other cases that you'd like to share?*

K: I did have another patient that comes to mind. I did some EMDR with her, and we ended up putting pause on the EMDR because her current home state was too chaotic and reflective of the violent, abusive home state that she grew up in.

Even though the current home state was now safe, she, as we know many of our patients do, recreated the chaos of her childhood in her present life—repetition compulsion disorder. This was a patient who is highly highly dissociative.

I remember one session in particular, this was probably ten years ago when I was working with her. I was in a clinic that had a play therapy room. There was a dollhouse in the room and for whatever reason, I don't recall right now, we ended up going in that room to do our work. I think the usual room I worked in had some work being done on it. And so we went into that office, she saw the dollhouse and went into a complete dissociative state, regressing down to about five years old. It was pretty intimidating to me to be honest.

H: *I can imagine.*

K: We had been doing some EMDR and had been working on a memory at five years old. The dollhouse never came up in the memory we were working on, or obviously I would have never brought her into that room.

H: *Of course.*

K: Basically she regressed back to the state of the last memory we had been working on. This was at an outpatient clinic, and it took me maybe four hours to ground her, get her centered, collected and back together again. After that experience she was terrified to ever do EMDR again. She had never had an experience like that in her life but we had removed those protective defenses and she didn't have the strength even though we had built her containers and her safe place and had done all the resourcing.

It was a low fee clinic, so we were able to work together for a really long time, and she had been doing really incredible work. We had done all the protocols that EMDR required for somebody who has severe PTSD. I was seeing her two to three times a week. So she had really strong structure around her. But after that incident, she'd never had anything like that happen before, so she refused to do it ever again.

Over the years, she'd sent me e-mails on how she's doing, as some patients do, which is always a gift. She's been doing a little better but still ever since that time had some regressive states. She tried TFT (Thought Field Therapy) with somebody and got some benefit just from the tools because she could take it home. However, she was still very scared to go back and do any actual reprocessing. And I don't blame her.

When I completed the Havening training and was looking for case studies, she came to mind. I had continued working with her for about a year after that incident with the doll house. By the time we wrapped up, she was in a strong place and she was ready to go independent and not be in therapy anymore.

I reached out to her and said, "we still have some work to do. Would you be willing to try this technique?" She had actually just been in a car accident. So she says, "Fine. But we're only working on that."

I say okay. That's acute trauma, that's perfect. We'll work on this one thing and just do the Event Havening. I knew we were not going to go into any old memory networks. She came in and we reprocessed the car accident and in ten minutes it's cleared completely. She had been scared to drive, and hadn't been driving in the past two months because of the car accident. But you know how this stuff works. It's just so fast. She opens her eyes and says, "that was amazing. I'm fine."

We had scheduled for ninety minutes, since it had been awhile, so we would have extra time if we needed it. I said 'so we still have eighty minutes, what do you want to do?' And she could've just said, "I'm good. Thanks so much, that was great, let's do talk therapy or whatever, this is what's been going on in my life."

But she looks at me and goes "I want to go back to that memory." I knew immediately what she meant. "I trust you. We did a lot of good work with EMDR and we talked a lot about tabling it and that was the right choice. It was not for me. But I'm wondering if this can do something else. I've never felt this calm and clear in my life after ten minutes of doing this." So I say, "okay."

I was a little nervous, to be honest. I started Havening her, applying the Havening touch. She had quite a bit of delta wave activation in her system from the work related to the car accident. Then we started working in baby increments of that memory at five years old. Just touching on tiny peripheral elements.

Within that eighty minutes we reprocessed that entire memory down to a zero, and there were many many components to it. As we got lower on our experience of the memory, got down to a 2–3 on the SUDS scale, I started bringing in some Transpirational Havening and she started collapsing entire memo-ry networks.

I remember she opened her eyes when we were done and it was one of those moments. I have yellow walls in my office and I've had this happen seven or eight times with different patients. She looks around and she says "Your walls are yellow, they weren't yellow when I walked in." And we know what that is. That's the serotonin shifting. That's that dopamine decrease in the thalamus and the amygdala so they're no longer having that hypervigilant lose the forest for the trees experience. All of a sudden she's taking in regular sensory data.

H: *Remarkable.*

K: It was just transformative. And that was one session. So we did seven more sessions and she all of the sudden starts making these huge sweeping life changes. She moves out of her boy-friend's house (her boyfriend had been abusive). She changes her job. She goes back to school. Everything's changing.

She disconnects from her family completely, draws strict boundaries, even calls CPS on her dad. I didn't know this was a component back when we were first working together, but she brings it into a session. She says, "well you know I have a niece. I'm worried that my dad interacts with the niece." She knows I'm a mandated reporter so I ask "do you want to make this call together?" Her reply blew me away, she told me "that's why I'm bringing it in, I've never brought it up before because I was too scared to have CPS show up." She knew the system because she'd been in the system. All of a sudden she says, "I'm taking my niece, I'm going to bring her to my house, I'm gonna get custody." I'm thinking, "Who are you?" This is amazing.

H: *Yes, she reclaimed her power fully.*

K: Yes, and the nightmares were gone. The panic attacks were gone. The self injury was gone.

After my final session with this patient I called up Dr. Steven Ruden and asked him if I could become a trainer, because we need more. We need more. If Havening can do this, we need more.

H: *How many sessions after the original ninety minute session?*

K: Seven. Seven ninety minute sessions over the course of several months. I don't do ninety minute sessions traditionally but with her I did them because we were working through really heated pieces. Granted, she'd done a lot of therapy so she was primed, she was prepped. She was ready for it. So she'd get these insights and all of a sudden after ten years of therapy, she'd say, "Oh I always knew that, but now I feel it." That's the gift of Havening, that experience of feeling that truth in the body rather than just knowing the truth.

H: *The possibilities that are emerging as a result of the introduction of this technology and the neurobiological understanding are poised to transform how we not only deal with trauma, but how we help people heal in every way.*

K: In every way. I think one of my pure aha moments, especially working with her and knowing the impact of complex trauma on brain development, was that I could actually start to tailor the specific Havening techniques that I was using to address very specific discrepancies in her traumatized brain.

I can start to recognize this statement, when she says this: "When I bring up my mother's face all I see is black." That means that her interior cingulate gyrus or her cingulate gyrus does not have certain receptors online. And her periaqueductal gray area is too over activated so that we can't reach into the other aspects that the periaqueductal gray area is involved in that are tied into attunement and attachment. So we can start tailoring the interventions that way. I think this was one of the first techniques that I could do that with in such a hands on and active manner in my treatment planning and my intervention. That was cool.

H: *Brain surgery in the palm of your hands.*

K: That is just the coolest thing ever to me.

H: *I was talking to Carol Robertson the other day, a Havening trainer in Scotland. She said "I teach people how to sculpt their own neurology." And I love the sculpture metaphor. It seems that you're talking about this as well as you identify that this part of the brain is not online for this reason. You're using Havening and the other tools to help the patient re-sculpt in real time that particular aspect of their neurology. That is truly remarkable.*

K: It is. Yes, remarkable. No better words.

H: *How do you see Havening impacting mental health practice say ten to twenty years in the future?*

K: I think it's going to change the world, Harry! Not only because the rapidness of the results we get but because it can be self supplied and because we can teach the foundational principles of it to students. I teach it to all my parents and they use it with their children. So we have the capacity to actually start changing the future by implementing and incorporating this technique into everybody's lives. It goes far beyond what we are going to be doing in our clinical offices now.

H: *So you've answered that Havening can be used by people who are not counselors, psychologists, therapists and so forth. Where does a person begin with using Havening for self care? Is it teaching the touch? How far can an individual who is not trained in that way go with it?*

K: Initially I teach them the applied touch, the Havening Touch. Then I move them through the basic distraction technique. So it's for anybody who has anything activating. So the child can come home and say "I got bullied at school today mom and it was upsetting to me", and mom can sit there and apply the Havening touch to little Sally and they can hum Twinkle Twinkle Little Star and imagine playing fetch with a puppy, etc. That releases the stress of the bullying event while creating a resilient landscape which protects the brain from encoding that bullying experience.

I go to that level with all of my patients whether it is self applied or applying it to someone else. Even when I do lectures, whether it is with lay people or my clinical colleagues, the Event Havening is my go to because there's really no way to screw that up. And that's the beauty of it. You are giving your system GABA and serotonin and you are going to feel good.

I don't teach people to actively do the exposure component. That's because in my own experience as a trauma specialist we never know the layers that may be underneath something. I've had patients who I teach the technique to and they say I want to do this on my own and then I get a call from the ER because they put themselves into a panic attack. So I don't teach that independently until I've been able to assess their ACES (adverse childhood experiences). How vulnerable and sensitized are they, as well as the current level of resilience in their brain.

So until we have done a lot work, if their ACE score is really high and their brain is vulnerable, I make sure that they are resilient first and then move into the Event Havening where they are actually processing traumatic experiences.

H: *How far do you go in terms of teaching basic Event Havening to people who might present as okay but might have layers of trauma underneath that?*

K: I teach it to them as a self care tool. Something happens and you feel activated and feel reactive and angry or agitated or frustrated. Then I say to start applying the touch, start going into distraction and just do that immediately. It's an immediate intervention for day to day stresses. That in itself will have a retroactive effect to gently calm their nervous system.

The more you haven across the field the more balanced your system is. But I don't have them actively go back and do trauma reprocessing independently. They don't go back and look for it and then actively immerse themselves in it. The difference is the exposure component. I don't want them doing exposure therapy on themselves because we don't know where that could take them. Everyone leaves their intake session with me knowing how to modulate their nervous system.

H: *Continuing with this theme, are there other specific situations where it would not be advisable as a clinician or someone in self care to use Havening?*

K: Not really. The main thing that I tell my patients is that the core of all of this is safety. So if you're using the technique on yourself you want to feel safe and comfortable using the touch. Now I have had some patients who were uncomfortable applying specific touches, so they would just do their hands and not their cheeks. But it's the patient's choice as to whatever resonates and what's comfortable within. If the person who is going to be havened, the receiver of the touch, has expressed they are safe and comfortable receiving the touch then you are okay to proceed.

I tell the couples that I work with that if you are in an argument don't walk up and start Havening your partner, because they may not want to be touched by you. The touch actually won't work unless they have a sense of safety. The system will reject it. Those are the main things.

The other thing is with the touch, the cadence has to be fairly specific. If it is too fast, too harsh, if it's hard then it won't have the same effect and can actually agitate the system. So having an understanding of how to effectively apply the touch is very crucial. Other than that there really is not a time that it's not okay. Even if you are just sitting in LA traffic and you're stopped and don't know why and you just start doing havening then you will feel better because of the GABA and serotonin. Then hands back on the wheel and start driving.

H: *I do it in my daily life all the time.*

K: I'm sitting here doing it now as we've been talking.

H: *Me too.*

K: As we know, it just becomes integrated. It's incredible that my patients will come in and sit down in my room and it becomes a Havening space. They will be talking and then the next thing you know they're Havening and not even realize it because the brain wants that place of safety.

H: *Speaking to your peers, other psychologists, clinicians, counselors and people who are mental health professionals, what would you say to them? What advice would you give to anyone who is in that group and looking into the possibility of adding Havening Techniques to their toolkit?*

K: I would say there are three main reasons why you should add Havening to your toolkit.

Number one is that it is an effective, adaptive tool. And because of the electrochemical environment that Havening creates in the mind and the body, traditional psychotherapy will be more effective because it removes that amygdala filter from the psychotherapeutic process.

So they resonate more fully within the individual and you just get to deeper levels more quickly in a safer way. It breaks through resistance in a soft and gentle manner. It helps the person move through resistance. It helps them feel safe going into scary places. It is the most effective tool I have ever seen for gently and effectively healing complex PTSD.

Number two, the patients get to take it home. They have something that they can use in between sessions effectively and feel powerful doing so. All of a sudden they have an incredible tool to use when they are going into a rage or panic attack or they can't sleep. I treat a lot of insomnia. Now they have an immediate intervention that is fast and effective.

Most of my patients haven two to five minutes three to five times a day. That's just ten to thirty minutes a day to massive shifts in the way the body is processing data. They want to do it and seek doing it.

So, all of a sudden they are Havening and say, "I didn't even know I was Havening," and they feel so much better. They have an immediate tool and as the clinician to give them that tool you are empowering them so that in between your sessions they know that they have something that they can use and feel secure and safe using that they know will work.

And finally, third, Havening provides a space of safety not only for our patients but it also creates a safe haven within the clinician, the provider, because we are also receiving delta waves, which is the fundamental tool that Havening is based on. So we are being Havened and even though we are empathetic and present and engaged with our patient, we are not encoding anything.

This is really key as a trauma specialist. I know for all of my colleagues, we each share with our patients very difficult life experiences and very painful things. That's why people come into our offices, because life is hard and it hurts. Most of my colleagues and I'm sure most of yours are very empathetic people; we carry that pain and we are experiencing it with our patients.

Trauma can happen first person, it can happen to us, second person we see it, or third person, we hear about it. Havening protects against second person trauma and vicarious traumatization.

Even better, you walk out of the door at the end of the day and you are not carrying the weight of everything. You walk out and think 'I've had a fantastic brain massage all day while doing incredible work with my patient, now I get to go home with my family without taking any of this home with me.' That is incredible, especially as a trauma specialist. I get to go home and live my life and know that I did incredible work and don't have to carry the weight of their trauma with me.

H: *Thank you, Kate.*

CHAPTER 3

From trauma to triumph

Holly Shaw

Dr. Holly Shaw is an associate professor of nursing at Adelphi University who also has a private clinical practice as a trauma specialist in Sea Cliff, New York.

Harry Pickens: *Holly, how did you first discover Havening?.*

Holly Shaw: It was very fortuitous. I had specialized in bereavement, crisis and trauma for about three decades. I was involved from the beginning (in the eighties) as the diagnosis of PTSD came about through the work of the International Society for Traumatic Stress Studies. At the time we were a very small group of professionals focusing on trauma work around the country and then gradually we expanded internationally.

In my bereavement practice I focus on communities, children and young families who suffer from un-anticipated loss. I was working with a family of two little girls and the dad died while in hospice care. I saw the mom, I saw the girls, I saw them together, I saw them separately. The mom had a remarkable work situation as a dental hygienist with this fabulous boss who did and said everything right.

I always said, 'I've got to meet this guy someday,' because I work with many families and I had never heard about an employer who was so supportive. Also, the office practice sounded oriented towards mental health and built around generally healthy and integrity-laden practices. Of course the dentist was Steve Ruden, co-developer of the Havening Techniques®.

I lived in the community in which he practices and I needed a dentist, so I began to use him. At the time, I had a dental phobia. I would go to the dentist, but it was excruciatingly upsetting for me, really awful. Havening was just emerging and at some point Steve said "I've got this new thing, let me try it on you," and in seven minutes or so he cured a life long dental phobia. So I was hooked.

HP: *Right there in the dentist chair.*

HS: Yes. Steve started to tell me about this burgeoning Havening technique, and I would read manuscripts in very rough form. Steve and I would meet, often every week after hours, because we're so close, geographically, that I could walk to his office. We would review the papers and collaborate. And Havening now begins to emerge from a totally different theoretical and neurobiological perspective. We used to laugh that I would leave the dentist office not having had a dental visit, but my head would still be exploding because this was such a revolutionary idea!

HP: *Holly, would you give me a sense of the nature of your current work—what your teaching, mentoring and clinical practice look like?*

HS: I've been practicing as a trauma specialist for a long time and have been involved in academics as well as clinical and consultation work, presenting nationally and internationally.

I've taught for many years part time and full time at Hunter College which is part of the City University of New York. Now I teach at Adelphi University which is a private university on Long Island.

I teach undergraduate and graduate nursing and public health students and also we have an emergency management program. In graduate school I teach mainly in theory development and some of the core graduate courses. In undergraduate, I teach public health, mental health, psychiatric mental health nursing and other courses, professional courses that go along with that. I teach theory in the classroom and also teach in the clinical area.

I also present on the topics of crisis intervention, bereavement and trauma in professional settings for staff development programs and professional conferences. I do a lot of crisis-intervention based work at hospitals, community-based centers, mental health centers, and universities.

HP: *And your private practice?*

HS: My private practice is in the little community that I live in. People come from that community or from other places around and outside of New York City. I see individuals, children, adolescents, and adults around various issues, but mainly trauma, chronic or acute illness. And then half of the practice is professionals who either in their personal lives or in the course of their work have encountered a traumatic situation.

HP: *Thank you. How has the use of Havening Techniques transformed your practice?*

HS: Before that I was using EMDR as well as a lot of complementary modalities. But in Havening I found I could more directly address certain symptoms.

At the end of the 90's I trained in EMDR and it really did change my work a lot. It was the first time I could relieve symptoms in a very meaningful way, not just alleviating but actually eradicating some symptoms. It changed my practice enormously because I was regarded as an expert in trauma and I did great work, but we couldn't change that encoding.

So somebody could be in treatment and develop a lot of insight and understanding, know that it wasn't their fault that they were sexually molested at age five, and understand the impact on their self-image and their relationships. But you couldn't take away that yucky feeling inside. EMDR could do that.

I had a very successful practice in EMDR. I used it with most of my clients, because most of my clients had trauma issues and at that point EMDR was also evolving to include performance enhancement and lots of other applications. It was a blessing and a wonderful tool, but obviously it wasn't perfect. The work could be somewhat arduous, but the results were really excellent.

HP: *But you don't use EMDR so often now? Do you use Havening in its place?*

HS: Yes. Once I became adept at Havening I have no longer used EMDR. I continued to rely on EMDR as I developed expertise and Steve Ruden and I collaborated. However, I soon realized that Havening was more effective, led to an easier process and was extremely productive.

HP: *You've had at least three decades of clinical experience grounded in solid theoretical understanding. You've worked with many thousands of people, and you have access to an incredibly wide array of tools and techniques and procedures and theoretical approaches.*

At this stage in your professional work, particularly your private clinical practice, what place does Havening occupy in the larger array of tools and techniques you have at your disposal? In other words, do you use Havening with a vast majority of clients? Do you use it as one of your primary tools?

HS: It varies. First of all, we've learned that the old strategy of talking about the bad thing that happened is not necessarily therapeutic or helpful and is sometimes even contraindicated. In a situation where the details are graphic and horrific and a person feels humiliated, for example in some cases of sexual abuse, where you don't want to talk about it much, in that kind of case, Havening is a real go-to.

However, it's sometimes different for me in an acute situation that occurs in adulthood or a situation that happened in childhood. The situation in childhood we can haven that and have those symptoms be remitted but the cost of living with that for 15, 20, 25 years, and going to therapy, for some people every week for 15 years and talking about this has caused secondary, either co-morbidities, or just other kinds of issues that Havening alone might not correct. So we might still want to work on that.

I do use Havening very often.. I see a lot of professionals, nursing, medical, and legal professionals who have very severe anxiety problems, sometimes which started during childhood, sometimes more recently. In these cases they might have had a certain neurochemical landscape in childhood but the landscape and physiology have molded and shaped around the prominence of anxiety. Teaching them strategies to mediate that is extremely important.

I always explain the theory of what we're going towards and that's enormously helpful and I also teach them to do self-havening. Self-havening is a wonderful tool that clients can use. It helps to sustain whatever progress we've done but also is adaptive. I also teach couples to haven each other which is really very valuable.

And there are other implications for the broader application of Havening Techniques, again not only in my clinical practice and as a teacher, but also as a global consultant interested in the Public Health impact of trauma and all of the associated adversities. Especially because I was consulted often on very large—scale high profile situations. I would be called in to casualties, especially school emergencies, because of my focus in adolescent health. At the time, we could do wonderful supportive work but still couldn't erase the impact of the encoded traumatic memory.

When Steve and I began to talk about this, I thought of prevention models and early intervention, not just about individual case work. For example, I read an article in the Journal of Traumatic Stress Studies about PTSD. This was a European study with a very large sample of motor vehicle accident patients, looking at who would develop a post traumatic stress disorder. The single strongest variable was the level of anxiety in the emergency department.

HP: *Wow.*

HS: There was not an explanation for it at the time, although at the time, many years ago, it was thought that there might be a genetic predisposition to anxiety disorders. So, the person with the higher anxiety is going to be manifesting that. Immediately I thought, does that mean that if we can get the anxiety level down in the Emergency Department we can prevent PTSD? Since nurses are first responders in the ER, what a powerful intervention that would be to use a simple Havening experience to actually prevent PTSD.

So, this is where my thinking has gone. For example, working in refugee camps, can we teach people to do this not only for themselves, because that is very exciting, but also with each other, for each other? I began to experiment in my own practice teaching parents, teaching couples. Steve and I would have many conversations in those early years about applications far beyond just an individual kind of practice setting. My goal is to bring Havening to nurses worldwide in every setting. Nurses can incorporate Havening into all clinical work. Almost every hospitalization and many out patient encounters involve traumatic or upsetting aspects. Havening can prevent and treat dysfunctional responses to that experience as well as improve pain management, optimize stress reduction and comfort measures, core aspects of nursing. We seek to reduce unpleasant symptoms and to enhance comfort and well-being; Havening can be an outstanding integrative and complementary modality and falls well within every nurse's scope of practice.

HP: *Could you share a few specific cases?*

HS: Sure.

CASE ONE

Here's a story that reflects one of our earliest Havening experiences. A young boy who was about 19 or 20 had been in a terrible, tragic car accident. Others were killed and, of course, he had lots of issues around that. He had been a passenger in the car, not a driver, and felt the kid who was driving was impaired.

As a result of the accident, he had to drop out of college. His catastrophic injuries were treated in the rehab center, which was in many ways similar to a nursing home. He had fractures in both legs and in an arm, he had scars, and he had a lot of constant pain and disability.

He was in this setting with old men. His body ached and slept and felt like an old man's body. His body image transformed from a student athlete in his freshman year of college to that of an old man. He couldn't perform sexually; when his girlfriend would come visit, he had no libido at all. So in addition to the other issues: having to take time off from school, being hospitalized, dealing with his injuries, being isolated from his friends who were at college and feeling really alone, he suddenly felt (and in some ways, looked) like an old man. It was very unsettling.

He was one of the first kids Steve Ruden and I havened together. He was in a lot of pain, so that was one of the first targets we focused on, but he also had intrusive recollections and flashbacks of the accidents plus the very severe body image and self image changes that caused him to experience himself as an elderly man who was disabled. We used Havening successfully to deal with all of those issues and symptoms. I saw him several times: in the hospital, in rehab, and then at home.

He also had what I would describe as dysfunctional marijuana use. He was having very confusing and unsettling responses to smoking grass or drinking, but that's what his friends did. He had also been using harder drugs but was no longer using once he was in the hospital.

After he was released from the hospital, when his friends would come home on vacation, they would expect that he would hang out with them and party (doing drugs and smoking marijuana as they did together in school), so that was an underlying issue to begin with. And, drug use intensified his neurological symptoms. So since he really couldn't do that anymore, this was another way that he felt like an old man.

He still had cravings, so he would smoke or drink but then get sick from it—a terrible, terrible situation. I used Havening for the cravings, and it completely eliminated them and at the same time, left him feeling well and relaxed.

Once after he left my office, he actually called me on a Saturday night and he said, "I can't believe it! I have no craving. My friends are all getting high, and I don't mind hanging out with them, but I have no desire to do it." He used to say he felt high from the Havening. It was almost a similar high without any of the side effects. That was one of our earlier Havening experiences.

CASE TWO

I recently saw a former student of mine for the first time since 2010. Now a successful midwife, she recently had a horrible work related situation occur. She's very astute and does mainly home deliveries.

In anticipation of an obstetrical emergency, she arranged for the mom to be seen and admitted to a hospital where she was well known and highly respected. She accompanied the mom and dad in the ambulance. However, the EMTs took them to another, closer hospital, and the baby died.

She felt traumatized by the experience. Though she did nothing questionable, there was an implication by the hospital that she was at fault. She was just horrified, traumatized and grief stricken when she called me and said "I know you can help me, please will you see me?"

She's an immigrant to the US, foreign born, and the hospital administration, in order to resolve themselves of the responsibility, were blaming her. The main accusers on the hospital side were very powerful strong men.

As we Havened it became clear that this was a familiar experience, from a cultural point of view, being intimidated by strong, powerful, condescending and punitive men.

At the time that she called me she had been suffering for about six weeks. She was unable to work, was not able to sleep and was really in very bad shape.

After two Havening sessions she immediately went to work, began to tell all of her moms about Havening. That was a remarkable (but not unusual) situation in that the Havening completely ameliorated her symptoms. She has since participated in a Havening Training for professionals and we are collaborating about bringing this remarkable modality to antepartum, L & D, post partum families.

CASE THREE

Two years ago I participated in a Nurses of the Middle East Conference held in Jordan. An Israeli nurse and her patient were presenting a very complicated case. The patient was crushed between two buses with catastrophic injuries.

The recovered patient, an American graduate student and professional presented along with the nurse who had cared for her through a very long hospitalization, many surgeries and many complications. Certainly, this was a heroic tale of great recovery. But as she was talking I could see she was still suffering from trauma.

Afterwards, although I didn't know her or the nurse personally, I said, "That was a wonderful presentation, and, I can see you're still suffering. I know a modality that might be helpful in alleviating some of these symptoms. Would you like to try it?"

She responded, "I kind of figured that this was what I've gotta live with. It hasn't gone away in five years, although it is better than it was before. Sure, if you have something that might help, I'll try it."

She and the nurse came to my hotel room and we did Havening. The result was dramatic! Before, she had experienced the taste of blood from the accident that she could never get rid of. Right away she said, "I don't taste it anymore! I don't smell it!" She was completely relieved of troubling symptoms and powerful, intrusive sensory flashbacks.

Her nurse started to cry (from joy) because she knew the burden that she was carrying that they both just expected would never go away. And, as most people do when they experience this kind of sudden change, she said, "Well this is great for now, but what do I do when it wears off?" Of course we know it's not going to wear off. She was a little skeptical, of course.

Later, I checked in with her and she said, "I can't believe it, you're right. it's not coming back". That was two years ago.

Last year, I did a presentation on Havening at the same conference and she also had me come to Israel to speak to nurses. Now, we're arranging a major training.

HP: *Remarkable stories, Holly. Thank you. As a registered nurse, and a teacher, mentor, and trainer of nurses and nurse practitioners, would you speak to the value of nurses learning and applying Havening Techniques®?*

HS: For nursing, it's just such an easy, comfortable, natural modality for us to use, unlike with our social worker and psychology colleagues in New York who are not allowed to touch their clients (they are limited to facilitating self-havening).

Touch is a fundamental aspect of nursing and our rich history of "the laying on of hands." Nurses touch people all the time and use touch as a healing modaliy.

Although we don't teach it so much now, the use of tactile connection has historically been very strong in nursing. So, from every viewpoint and every area of nursing I think that this is a modality that is enormously helpful and completely applicable. I've been able to use it not only in my clinical practice but with nurses in many places in the world and in different kinds of settings. I just think it's essential to get this practice into nursing hands because it's so powerful and impactful and such a nice complimentary modality for nurses and nursing.

For nurses the theory and the elucidation of the theory has to be impeccable, and I think we're reached that point now, so I've been able to use it in some very exciting and transformative ways. Primarily with nurses who are suffering from trauma or compassion fatigue, various aspects, and then are able to use it informally with patients.

HP: *Thank you. One final question: For someone who is a healthcare or mental health professional, it may be a nurse or counselor or therapist or social worker or psychologist who's looking into Haven-*

ing but have not yet made the commitment to get the training, what advice would you give them?

HS: Well, I would suggest that they try it. It's hard to believe without trying it, reading anecdotes, or knowing someone who's had direct experience, because the results just sound too good to be true. I think that the theoretical explanation is powerful but it doesn't really have as much of an impact until someone has seen the results. It sounds compelling enough to try, but until you've really seen what can happen, I think it's very hard to believe that this is real, and as effective and truly miraculous as it is. So I suggest that they try it. Read a liitle, learn a little, but come to a Training, where you can learn from experts, practice with colleagues and master this relatively simple but powerful approach. Then they will know for themselves how remarkable a tool this is.

HP: *Thank you!*

CHAPTER 4

Helping people create the lives they desire and deserve

Eugenia E. Karahalias

Eugenia Karahalias is a Licensed Clinical Social Worker and healing arts practitioner in private practice in Suffolk County, New York.

Harry: *Eugenia, how did you first discover Havening?*

Eugenia : Through a colleague, Bill Solz. Bill was passionate and excited about it. He's a social worker, like me, who I've known for several years. We travel in a lot of the same circles and sit on clinical committees together. I saw him do a couple of demonstrations and he invited me to his office for a more thorough explanation of how Havening worked. I was hooked immediately.

H: *You're a social worker but you also use a number of complimentary modalities. Tell me about some of those other modalities and how you integrate them into your work.*

E: I am trained in Hypnotherapy, EMDR (eye movement desensitization and reprocessing), Energy/Emotional Balancing, Havening Technique® and NLP (neuro linguistic programming). I am a Reiki Master Teacher Practitioner and Magnified Healing Teacher and Practitioner. I use these different modalities and techniques in addition to psychotherapy to assist individuals in removing blocks so that they can unleash their full potential.

H: *Who are your typical clients? Do you have a specialty?*

E: I work with clients from adolescence to mature adults and from all backgrounds. I specialize in the treatment of addictions, anxiety, bereavement, depression, improving performance, PTSD, pain management, phobias, relaxation & stress release. This includes a lot of trauma work. I find that I am seeing younger and younger clients who are dealing with trauma related anxiety. I'm also a credentialed alcoholism and substance abuse counselor and have worked in this area for about 20 years. I find that the high rate of recidivism with substances is because they are using drugs and alcohol in order to escape the trauma from their earlier years. When these individuals stop using, the trauma is right back in their face again. So you have to address that. You have to help these folks so that they don't continue to go back to drugs and alcohol to escape.

H: *I was just in a conversation earlier today with a group of people who work with new young mothers in recovery from some kind of addiction. We were discussing how often the addiction is a way to escape the feelings stemming from the trauma. And only when you heal the trauma does the urge for the substance begin to fade. That's your experience as well?*

E: Yes, more often than not. I'm talking about the individuals who have a chronic relapse history. They just keep relapsing over and over again. I believe it's a huge disservice to leave recovering addicts in such a vulnerable state. Better to address the core issues behind their substance abuse. That's an area where the Havening Techniques® can be utilized for a much greater outcome.

H: *That makes sense. Eugenia, many people are skeptical when they first hear about Havening because it seems too good to be true. Were you skeptical at first when Bill told you about it? If so, what changed your mind?*

E: I wasn't skeptical about the method or the science behind it. What I was skeptical about, if you can believe it, was the name Havening. Now I understand that Dr. Ruden is using it as a verb and it's to create a safe environment, a safe haven, but initially the name put me off. So I probably could've been involved with Havening a few months earlier, but it took time for me to get over my association with that word. And now, of course, I embrace it completely and I can't think of any better way to help folks feel better. The results are tremendous.

H: *I'm remembering that Dr. Ruden originally called it Amygdala Depotentiation Technique, which is a much more scientific term but not quite as simple or user friendly as Havening. Once you did experience Havening Techniques, why do you choose to use them so frequently since you have all these other tools at your disposal? What advantages does Havening offer your clients?*

E: Many. First of all, the client is not re-traumatized as they're going through the healing process by using Havening. You can also work with clients content free. And that's what I love about it. The other thing that I like so much about it is that it's quick, effective, and long lasting. I'm going to give you an example from my own life. Just recently, I was helping facilitate at the training in Vancouver that Dr. Steve Ruden led. He asked for a volunteer, somebody who had a phobia. I shot my hand up in the air and he chose me. I've had claustrophobia over the years, sometimes more intense than at other times. By the end of our 20 minutes of Havening it was completely eradicated. In the past I had used hypnotherapy and EMDR with some success. Havening was the one technique that eradicated it finally and completely. I love the other modalities and I continue to use them. But for some reason, it was Havening that completed the shift.

H: *How has Havening transformed your practice? Do you use it with every client?*

E: Just about. I would say in 95% of my case load, I use Havening. Another way that Havening has transformed my practice is that I am able, at the very first session, to teach my clients how to self haven. So now they go home with a tool that they can begin using immediately.

H: *Yes. And you mentioned that you use Havening with 95% of your clients now. It's become one of the most frequent tools you've used. I've heard that from almost everyone I've spoken to who has become a Havening practitioner, no matter where they started modality-wise. They may have started out as hypnotherapists, as trauma therapists, as psychologists or social workers or whatever, but they end up using Havening more and more often. I have a good friend, now a Havening practitioner who is one of the top EFT (Emotional*

Freedom Techniques) practitioners in the US and she also now uses Havening almost exclusively. Why do you suppose that is?

E: Because it's so quick. You know, we live in a quick fix society. People want to see immediate results. And you get immediate results from Havening.

H: *That's for sure. And although everything can't be solved immediately, there's nothing like walking in with a big problem that seems insurmountable, like you with your claustrophobia, and then 20 minutes, an hour later, you're good to go. Or even if you're not good to go you feel significantly better and you have a sense of possibility that you didn't have before.*

E: That's correct.

H: *Was anything particularly challenging for you as you integrated Havening into your own work?*

E: Explaining the science, because the neuroscience is intricate, and I like to keep things simple. But the good news is that we have so many skilled and talented people who are a part of this Havening journey. And Tam Johnston is one of them.

H: *Yes, I love her video—What Is Havening And How Does It Work? https://www.youtube.com/watch?v=VD6PcEWDJbo. She helped all of us by creating that. I'm so grateful to her.*

E: Absolutely. So when I see somebody for a first session, I do my in depth psychosocial interview and get a good history, plus I teach them a little bit of self-havening so they can start utilizing it for self-soothing and emotion regulation immediately. Then I send them home and I follow up with an e-mail so they can see some of these wonderful videos that our folks have come up with. In that way, they get a better understanding of it. Tam's video is 20 minutes long, and so thorough. You could watch it a couple times and really get a great understanding about how Havening works. Then they come back and they're ready to do the deeper work.

H: *And do you find that them having the scientific understanding makes it easier for the client to do the work?*

E: No, not necessarily. I don't think that they need an in-depth scientific understanding. I do think it makes them feel a little bit more comfortable. I choose which clients would benefit from it. I deal with a lot of people in the medical field, so it's nice for them to understand the science because they're a nurse, they're a doctor, they're a physical therapist or an acupuncturist.

H: *Thank you. As a clinical social worker with your own therapeutic training, what are your reflections on the use and issue of touch? It hasn't been standard practice to use touch in this way with clients and patients. How do you discuss it? How do you introduce it? How do your clients respond?*

E: I refrain from touch. It's all self-administered.

H: *Is that your preference or client preference? Your thoughts about that?*

E: Well, I am a licensed clinical social worker in the state of New York and it's taboo to touch our clients and therefore I don't. I will be doing Havening on myself (mirroring) as they're doing Havening on themselves at the same time. And it works just as well.

H: *What are some of the conditions you've been able to successfully address in your practice with Havening? You mentioned depression and anxiety earlier.*

E: I've had several people come to me through no fault cases from automobile accidents who were really in a diminished capacity; very fearful of driving, very anxious and jumpy even as a passenger, if they were a driver during the accident. And Havening worked remarkably well in those cases. I've had much success with rape survivors. Early trauma from neglectful childhoods, adult children of alcoholics where there was a lot of chaos growing up in the family. A lot of healing resulted with those clients as well.

H: *What are some of the most interesting experiences you've had as you've used the tool with your clients? Are there any case studies or stories or examples you'd like to share?*

E: There are so many. I had five women in a row who came to me after their second motor vehicle accident. They were pretty much fine after the first one, but the second one was the straw that broke the camel's back. As a result, a lot of stuff surfaced from their childhoods and we were able to go back and address those events that were causing them to feel powerless and helpless. All five were very powerful women, professional women with high-powered careers, functioning at a very high level. When that second accident happened, it was as if the rug was pulled out from under them. They could not understand why they were crumbling. And that's why Dr. Ruden always talks about doing a very thorough history taking, and this is exactly why it's so important. In each of those cases we uncovered early childhood trauma. We went back, did the work, cleaned it up, and now these women are functioning well. They're back out there living their lives.

H: *That's remarkable and encouraging. I remember Dr. Ruden discussing the importance of going back to the originating trauma. He said, "Everything downstream will get cleared, but until you get to that originating trauma, you're not going to completely eliminate the problem."*

E: And it's not just the big "T" traumas that we're going after. It's cumulative small "t" traumas that really have the deleterious impact on people's spiritual, emotional, mental and psychological well-being. It's the body, mind and spirit connection. You've got to be in alignment. I also think having a spiritual connection is very important. When you allow yourself the ability to become still, you connect to your higher source. You connect to your own higher self and to a universal collective consciousness. I think that spiritual piece is an integral component of Havening because Havening can soothe and calm you and allow you to be still so you can hear that inner voice.

H: *So in your experience Havening becomes a tool, not only to assist in emotional healing and psychological development, but also a tool to clear out the fog that gets in the way of really listening to your inner wisdom.*

E: Yes, exactly.

H: *Eugenia, how about the impact of Havening on physical appearance and energy?*

E: I remember being at a training and hearing Dr. Ron Ruden say it's like an instant face lift (laughs). And I do see that with my clients. Wrinkles automatically disappear, along with the furrow between their brows. I have experienced seeing client's faces relax so much, it's like wiping 10 years away in just one session. That's because the huge burden that they've been carrying has been lifted. And one after the other of my clients tell me, "I feel lighter, I feel lighter!" They say that over and over again. And it's so wonderful to see that after they open their eyes, that their sparkle is back. They absolutely DO look younger!

H: *That's so true. I have on two or three occasions told clients after a session to get up and go look at themselves in a mirror. They come back and they're astonished! They're astonished because of the releasing of that cumulative stress or the stress of whatever incident they came in with. And then there is the soothing, calming power of touch, whether you're administering it or the person is self-havening. Our body and brain is hardwired to respond to loving touch with relaxation and ease. And we're enjoying this simple, soothing touch for up to an hour during a typical Havening session. It's beautiful.*

E: It certainly is…and most of the time it's occurring in less than an hour.

H: *Exactly. How do you see Havening impacting mental health practice, particularly in terms of trauma, 10 to 20 years in the future? We're just in the infancy of this getting out into the world.*

E: Well I see it becoming an evidence-based practice that will be insurance reimbursable down the road. With all the research that's being accumulated now, I think we're heading in the right direction. This could happen within the next five years or less.

H: *Please say more about how Havening can be learned and used by people who are not counselors, therapists, psychologists, coaches. Tell me more about how regular people can use Havening or learn it to help themselves, like parents or teachers.*

E: Well I think it's similar to the way people are going into schools now and teaching mindfulness to children. We want to teach children how to self-regulate their emotions and Havening is an excellent tool for this. I think this is probably the number one problem that we have here in the United States, the lack of self-regulation skills. What if we could start teaching kids how to skillfully regulate and manage their emotions at a young age? On a global level, everyone says, we want peace, we want peace. THIS is the way to achieve it.

H: *Thank you. What advice would you give somebody who's looking into the possibility of learning Havening?*

E: I have a hypnotist friend on the West Coast. She's also an NLP practitioner. I showed her a little bit of Havening. She sees that it works. She told me there was no way that she was taking any more trainings because she's had it up to here with trainings. She also has a mentor that she's studying under that takes up a lot of her schedule. No, no, no, no more trainings. I was on the phone last night with her. And guess what?

H: *She decided to take the training?*

E: She'll be at the April training in New York. That's what happens. Anybody who experiences Havening gets hooked. You're hooked because you get immediate results. And my own passion when I'm speaking to people about it comes across. They see my face light up.

H: *So your advice to somebody considering learning it is—'try it, you'll see'?*

E: Yes. It's going to enhance their career, their business. I recently did a presentation for social workers who are in their Master's program now or who have recently graduated. I told them you want learn tools that you can pass on to your clients that are going to help them heal and get out there to live the life that they deserve. I tell people who come into my office this all the time. I do not want to see you week after week, month after month, year after year. There are plenty of people out there hurting. Let's make room for them to come in. I want you out there living the life that you desire and you deserve. And we're going to help you get there in the most efficacious manner, the most non re-traumatizing manner, quickly, effectively, and permanently.

H: *I love the way you put that—helping people live the life they desire and deserve. That's a wonderful way for us to bring our conversation to an end for now. It's always a delight to see you, to hear you, to collaborate with you. And thank you for shining your light so brightly and for sharing Havening with the world.*

CHAPTER 5

Dissolving the chains of addiction

Ross Hyslop

Ross Hyslop is director of Synaptein Coaching & Neurofeedback Services in Edinburgh, Scotland.

Harry: *Ross, how did you first discover Havening?*

Ross: I was aware of Dr. Ruden through reading his book, *The Craving Brain*, at least a decade previously. I then heard his name mentioned in connection to Havening and my ears perked up. When I made the connection with the book, this book I had read that was collecting dust on my shelf, I e-mailed him directly in New York and expressed my interest in his techniques, his findings, and their application. I also had a desire to train in the model.

I was actually a bit of a pioneer, because my e-mail with Dr. Ruden at the very early stages of this work ignited his interest in possibly coming to the UK. He realized that there was a group of people who would be interested in training. When there was a sufficient number, Dr. Ruden came over and worked with us. That was the first training in the UK and that's how I came into the world of Havening.

H: *So you were one of the people who helped inspire Dr. Ruden to share this in a broader sense in the first place.*

R: I believe so. I only became aware of that very recently in a recent conference call with Steven Ruden. He said, "You were the first person who e-mailed and said that you wanted to train in this."

H: *Wow. Your initiative has borne very rich fruitage so far. There are over 150 certified practitioners in 16 countries, 22 trainers, and many thousands and possibly hundreds of thousands of people who are benefitting from Havening. So, thank you for sending that email!*

Ross, I'd like to know more about your own practice. You are one of the people Dr. Steven Ruden recommended to me with great enthusiasm, specifically in the context of your work with addiction. Who are your typical clients?

R: First of all, I had an awakening to myself and my own behavior patterns over two decades ago. When I was fourteen years old I went out to a party. That party didn't stop until I was twenty. In 1993 I got sober. As I look back, although I didn't know it at the time, I was preparing myself for working with addiction as a result of somehow healing myself.

I went into therapy. I committed to a three year program and was in therapy from the age of twenty to the age of twenty-three. I then went to India for a year, studying Ayurvedic medicine and body psychotherapy, looking at different ways of releasing trauma.

Then in 2006 I went to university and got a post graduate certification in counseling and psychotherapy. I've also studied a number of additional modalities as a way of attempting to cure my own ills, and I've been sober 23 years now. My work and practice now is predominantly in the field of neurofeedback and brain-based biofeedback coaching and counseling.

I prefer the word coaching because it's much more solution oriented. My client base varies widely, from primary school children, where I am doing play and art therapy with minors age four to nine; to secondary school aged young people, to working with teenagers, to adults dealing with bereavement. However, the majority of my work is with substance misusers or drug and alcohol misusers.

From my perspective, drugs and alcohol are a way of self-soothing the trauma, another survival coping mechanism. So I choose not to label myself a drug and alcohol counselor, but I'm always working with trauma.

H: *I appreciate your commentary about the craving for drug/alcohol/whatever, simply being an attempt to medicate and deal with the trauma itself. Considering that perspective, how has Havening transformed your practice and the work you do with your clients?*

R: Havening speeds up the process. It's very difficult for someone who's in a trauma to take accountability and acknowledge that they're getting some unconscious needs met out of having that trauma. Through the use of Havening you're able to depotentiate the actual traumatic memories. This then makes it much more acceptable for the client to see how that trauma was affecting their day to day interactions.

Economically driven symptom reduction approaches to psychotherapy work with verbal techniques and check lists at a level that has little impact on the core feelings about the self. My experience with clients suggest that Havening is effective for a deeper level of the psyche, one I believe has neurological correlates in the midbrain.

Havening also allows us to go beyond the mind and cut through the cognition—the story—which is associated with the perceived trauma. As Einstein beautifully put it, "You will never solve a problem from the same level of mind that created it."

H: *What place does Havening occupy in the larger repertoire of tools that you might draw upon in a client interaction?*

R: Well the depotentiation that Havening brings, brings with it a freedom to move with more ease to a shift of perception. Then the client has the ability to look at the secondary gains that they were getting out of having that trauma dominate their mind.

When you are able to use the gift of Havening in a way that breaks down or resolves or changes the perception that the mind holds about the traumatic experience, which is a relative truth, then the client's much more able to talk about those secondary gains and coach their way into a better way of being and managing and navigating their world and their environment.

H: *Yes. So one result of the depotentiation is that it dissolves some degree of defensiveness that would get in way of owning the secondary gains. Once a person owns and acknowledges their secondary gains, they are liberated to live more fully in the present instead of living in some projection of the past.*

R: Absolutely, very well put. Thank you for translating my answer.

H: *Thank you for this clarification because the perspective that you're holding around the place that Havening holds in the larger picture is very significant. It's not simply about depotentiating the trauma so you feel better. You're saying, "Let's depotentiate the trauma so you can see how to become more present and take responsibility for what this is gaining you."*

R: Exactly. Beautifully put.

H: *In my experience it's only that level of radical self responsibility, where we can actually be present to what is in front of us, that allows healing to occur. It peels away another layer of the multiple layers of projection that we tend to live inside of. What I love about what you're saying is that you're framing the entire process, including the tools of Havening, within this larger context of radical self-responsibility.*

I can see how particularly if you're working with someone who is in the throes of some kind of addiction, whether it's an addiction to drugs or smoking or food or sex or work or addiction to being a "good person", whatever the addiction is, that you're using the Havening process as a tool to unlock the defensive walls that keep us from owning our own lives.

R: Exactly. Those defending walls are keeping out the immigrants of acceptance because once you allow the immigrant of acceptance to infiltrate your country it then dissolves many walls within walls.

H: *That's particularly important right now in our conversation because we're speaking on November 13th, 2016, and your country just went through Brexit, here in the USA we just went through the* *election of Donald Trump, both which were actualized in part by communicating to the public the fear of the other—the 'immigrant'.*

R: Yes.

H: *And it's only when we resolve the inner fear of the other inside us that we can hope to resolve the outer fear of the other out there.*

R: Yes, exactly because it's the judgment that keeps the behavior perpetuating. The only thing 'demonic' forces ever want is to go back to the light. If we judge them, then we keep them suspended in some place of purgatory. Whereas, if we're able to look at them without any judgment, we then allow that behavior to go back to a place where it wants to be.

That's why everybody wants to get caught. A schoolchild stealing a chocolate bar in a shop is being driven by a deep sense of wanting to be seen, recognized, accepted and caught. The behavior wants to be caught, but then when we catch the behavior we reprimand the behavior and throw it and incarcerate it into jail, which then only imbeds the trauma deeper into the psyche.

How many people come out of prison and reoffend? They reoffend immediately because they believe the trauma that put them there in the first place is somehow going to release them from the compulsion. If we were to look at it from the perception which you've offered to us here about Brexit and Trump, then if we saw it with no judgment, then we're looking at it through the eyes of innocence and there's no room for guilt or shame or indeed any other neural imbalance to hang upon.

H: *I find that remarkable and relevant to working with clients. What I notice is that as I've done my own inner work around clearing my* *own traumatic encoding, it allows me to be in front of the person in front of me with more freedom of judgment. And, the less judgment that I hold about the person in front of me and their past and their experiences, it seems the easier the process of healing becomes.*

R: Of course.

H: *You said it so beautifully: my judgments keep the shadow from ever going to the light because my judgments are locking it in place. If I can release the hold of my judgments then that energy needed to transform them is released.*

This also brings me back to my interpretation of your use of Havening. As I see it, you're using the tool of Havening to depotentiate the locks that we place within ourselves when we have some kind of traumatic experience. You're using the tool of Havening to help us bring more light ,more ease and more acceptance to these shadows, these pains, these traumas.

R: And of course the shadow is neurochemical! My experience and my work over the last twenty-three years has brought me to this belief system. This is not from reading or research, this is from my experience.

The judgment that we're speaking about is a three way process as I understand it. You know in the UK when we're sitting for a driving test it's a three way process: mirror, signal, maneuver. You look in the mirror, you make sure there's nothing coming up your blind side, you put on your signal to make sure the road users know where you're going and you make the movement.

That's exactly the same as in judgment, because anywhere there's judgment, there's attack. Anywhere there's judgment, there's attack on the other which fundamentally leads back to the fractured mirror which points back at us.

And unless you're a sociopath, anywhere there's attack, there's guilt. The judgment equals attack. Attack equals guilt. Guilt keeps us perpetuating the behavior which we describe with a word which I wish could be taken away, and that's the word addiction. I would absolve it completely because it's outdated nonsense. It's the guilt of the behavior that actually perpetuates the addiction.

In my experience of working with alcoholics and repeat offenders, rapists and a large spectrum of people, the same answer comes up continually for me. Someone's been sober for twenty years, they go out and they have a drink with an old colleague, they wake up in the old colleague's floor the next morning. What's the very first thing they feel? Guilt. What's the very first thing they do? Have another drink because the mind believes that the issue that put the guilt there in the first place will somehow release them from the compulsion. But what it actually does is further embeds the trauma and guilt. That cycle is prevalent in all behavior."

You know in the book of Genesis chapter four, "God took man and from his rib created woman. And the snake tricked her into eating from the fruit from the forbidden tree, telling her 'you will not die, you will be like God." She ate the fruit from the forbidden tree because the serpent told her that her eyes would be opened. Then she allowed her husband to eat some of that fruit from the forbidden tree. What was the very first thing she noticed? What was the very first thing she did? She realized she was naked and she covered her nakedness because she felt an emotion which was the birth of what? The birth of shame and guilt.

And it's that shame and guilt that keep us perpetuating and validating an experience of existence that we believe is real. These feelings are based on running old scripts and schemas that keep us stuck in that loop of thinking, perpetuating shame and guilt.

Havening allows us to be momentarily free of all of that and look at it from an objective perspective, thereby changing that subjective experience of reality that's been set up based on old scripts and schemas. That is my opinion, but I don't know.

H: *So what you're doing with Havening is cleansing the doors of perception. So that the person can see with greater awareness and freedom the entire gestalt of feelings, perceptions, beliefs that continue to perpetuate whatever the so-called problem is.*

What I love about this conversation and about what I understand of your work is that it's profoundly integrative. There's the neurobiological, psychological, spiritual, metaphysical. All of these aspects reflecting this fundamental idea that it is our sense of guilt, shame and disconnection from the fullness of our experience that is at the core of our suffering.

R: Of course.

H: *And that we can bring light. Light which could look like awareness. Light which could look like depotentiating the trauma. Light which could look like recognizing the mirror aspect of our projections. Light which could look like disconnecting from the egoic nature of our perceptions. When we bring light to the so-called dark, then the so-called dark then becomes the light.*

R: Of course.

H: *And what I'm loving about the brilliance of your synthesis of all this is the role of traumatic depotentiation and the role of a tool like Havening to again cleanse the doors of perception so the person can be more self-responsible, more self-aware, more self-accepting. And self-responsibility, self-awareness, self-acceptance are the beginning, in my experience, of true healing.*

I'm touched by your presence and your work on three levels: your head, your brilliance and synthesis of so many perspectives, models, domains; your heart, your compassion; and your hands, your commitment to doing the work.

What I sense in you just from this conversation, is your own ownership of both suffering and sobriety; all that you are. This is also my experience in my own world and my own work. Everything that I have experienced in my life, the suffering and the joy, the light and the shadow, all of it comes into play in each moment, as I am open to that.

Again, one of the greatest insights I'm gaining from our conversation around Havening specifically is the place that Havening plays in this larger understanding that you are helping your clients come to. What I'm hearing is that at the core, at the essence, you are assisting, facilitating, supporting the people who you work with to break trance, to wake up.

Waking up to the present moment. Waking up to their capacity to be. Waking up to their agency, their capacity to act, to create, to choose in every unfolding moment who they will be and how they will be.

And you use the tool of Havening and I'm sure other tools as well, to serve this process of waking up. In other words, when you use Havening it's not just about clearing this trauma, or feeling better, or changing this memory. You are using Havening in a much larger context to help the person wake up to the role that guilt and shame and projection and perception have had in their life, so that they can access a deeper dimension of freedom.

For me, talking with you is inspiring because the place you're coming from is this very comprehensive, multidimensional place whose goal is very simple. It is to support the full and unconditional freedom of those who you serve. Am I interpreting it correctly?

R: Yes. I certainly believe that it can be valuable to question everything about your reality. Is this real? Am I perceiving this the way it actually is or am I perceiving this experience the way I need it to be to validate a process that is much older than I could consciously understand; to keep me trapped within a perception of a world that's keeping me small, keeping me stuck, keeping me traumatized, keeping me angry, keeping me addicted?

A decade ago I worked in a women's refuge with women who had been battered by men. To be a man in that environment and feel the projections that were placed upon me by women was a real privilege. You get to know those women at a very intimate level.

Often I would see that a woman had set up with an abusive, violent partner and had to move to the other side of the country and change her name and change her address and change everything about herself in order to feel that they escaped the perpetrator. And she would continually go into more experiences with other perpetrators. She's playing a DVD in her mind that she perceives as being real or valid.

Now if one of the those women I had spoken with had met a man who cooked them dinner, who ran them a bath when they came in from work and put lavender oil in it and rubbed her feet during a movie, it was actually more scary for them to be with that sort of man then it was to be with an unpredictable predator who might attack them at any point.

H: *Yes.*

R: Just watch your brain. It wants to pull up that old DVD, like the old IBM computer. It wants to run that program so that you couldn't feel this good all the time. But the only thing that's stopping you from accessing this feeling all the time is you. Because you want to believe in a construct of separation rather than a construct of togetherness, oneness, wholeness, and freedom. Make sense?

H: *Yes. I continue to reflect as you speak on the role of a tool like Havening in this larger process. I work with clients not only on depotentiating trauma but also building the resilience of their landscape and reducing their overall stress. And when you build the resilience of the landscape, you increase access to positive emotion, and joy and gratitude and appreciation. You are helping or assisting this process of expanding the perceptual realm beyond the fight, flight, freeze of the reptile.*

R: Yes.

H: *I talked to Carol Robertson the other day, who's another one of our brilliant colleagues. She said she thinks in terms of helping the client sculpt their neurology. She used the term sculpture because on the physical level you're literally doing that, when you release that trauma.*

I'm a performing musician. I used to have stage fright that was very difficult to deal with. That became an opportunity for me to learn how to use my own mind more constructively. One of the things I learned was to use mental rehearsal a great deal, wherein you imagine yourself as the person you want to be.

Later I realized that that process of imagining yourself as the person you want to be, especially in terms of a physical act like playing the piano, or playing tennis, or playing basketball, actually builds those new brain circuits, and is literally sculpting the brain.

So when I work with clients on building resilience, the focus is on resculpting their neurology in such a way that they can more easily access what I would define or describe as their true self.

This is the self that is available to watch and to act independent of these barriers, these perceptions, these so-called addictions, these traumatic encodings. As I talk to you I'm having more of a sense of a place that Havening plays in the larger context of healing.

I keep thinking of Aldous Huxley's phrase "to cleanse the doors of perception." So often Havening allows a client to glimpse this state, even if it's just at the end of a session. I worked with somebody just yesterday who had an abusive situation with a stepparent and they were tortured, not physically, but tortured emotionally for forty, fifty years. After forty-five minutes of Havening they sat in astonishment that the old emotional pain was simply no longer there.

Because of the nature and the timing of the session I did explore with this client what I'm learning from you, which is to look at what you've gained from holding onto this pain for so long and look at...

R: What did you get out of it?

H: *Yes. What do you want to create next from a place of freedom from this? So, what I'm appreciating about our conversation is the multiple layers and the place that you are coming from which again is focused not on the the trees but the forest.*

Clearly, learning Havening along with the neurobiology behind it has impacted the work that you do. How do you see Havening im-

pacting the care, both mental and emotional and psychological and spiritual of people into the future?

R: Well, spiritual is such a loaded word. We place so much meaning on that. We say spiritual to someone and they think of the Vatican and Christianity and things that often don't carry any positive connotations at all.

But for me, spiritual is pretty simple. It's having a friend, and that friend is yourself. Spiritual to me is being able to tend to my own garden and no longer requiring someone else to take care of my garden for me. Of course, you could never take care of my garden the way that I need it taken care of, and then weeks or months down the line I'm only going to blame you for not being able to tend to my garden in the way that it needs tended to.

Havening is a tool that therapists can use that allows clients to access more readily a sense of self, which is a psychological use of language to explain something that's profoundly spiritual.

I believe that all healing modalities in the future will have to have a spiritual component. The issue is how we dress that spiritual component up to be accepted by the masses that already have spiritual phobia because of what happened to them in their churches or beyond. And, bringing a spiritual aspect into our work is absolutely crucial. I genuinely hold the intention that therapeutic interventions in the future will bring that forth.

People even misunderstand AA, Alcoholics Anonymous. They don't say hand it over to God. They say hand it over to your understanding of God and whatever that may mean. It's your understanding of spirituality rather than what we put onto it.

Havening allows you even to talk about rape after you've worked with a rape survivor. It allows the stimuli from the word rape not to curl up the precognitive memory that's stored and traumatically encoded in the brain that would otherwise ignite the memory within that individual. So then the system of the client is no longer triggered by its perceived environment around the word rape. That in itself is spiritual.

The beautiful thing about Havening for me is this. I'm very much grounded in Freudian perspectives. My first three years of personal therapy was in Jungian psychoanalysis. I then went on to study Freudian psychoanalysis and I genuinely believe that in order to understand Jung or Ernst Rossi or Wilhelm Reich or any other complex models you have to understand Freud. I know he gets bad press but I really like him.

And Havening works across a wide spectrum from psychoanalysis through to rebirthing or hypnosis and systemic work. You can work with any model; certainly any model that I've trained in. It fluidly adapts and molds itself to the moment and just seems to bring with it a sense of peace. That's the word I've been looking for. It brings peace.

I think it was in the book of John: "What is our work? Our work is to take love where love is not." And Havening in a way allows you, through the depotentiation of the trauma, to then create space. When the trauma is gone and there is a space available there, how do you fill that space? You fill that space with love and with compassion.

That's the work we do, to take love where love is not. And to assist the client in taking love to a place where there is not.

H: *It makes sense. I'm reminded of a quote—I think this comes from A Course in Miracles: our only job is to remove the blocks to love's presence.*

R: Of course.

H: *Love is our nature and our work. We try to manipulate in so many ways and we try to fix and repair but the essence of our work is to remove that which blocks us from experiencing the pre-existing eternal flow of love.*

And what I'm gaining most from our beautiful conversation, Ross, is that depotentiating traumatically encoded memories allows us to do this. Every we release an old trigger, an old hook, an old traumatically encoded memory, we open more space in our awareness for the presence of love to enter.

R: Of course. You know it's such a paradox that the nature of the universe, the language of God, speaks in complete paradox. Our natural state is to be present, yet the survival instinct of the brain pushes us off to not be present. Our natural state is love! But through the evolution of our survival, it's not helpful for our survival for us to feel loved, to be present.

So our natural state on one hand is presence but the paradox of the nature of separation, or division or fall, the original fall is this: we're made to be present and within this existence we have to survive.

So how can you both be present and survive? Well, it's to take that leap of faith and know that love will conquer all. I don't know many people who have that level of faith.

H: *At the same time it seems that the world, if you look at the external world and what's happening, is calling us, individually and collectively to that degree of faith.*

R: Of course.

H: *So what we're doing with Havening is that, as we release the trauma, we are Havening our way to the heaven within.*

R: Of course, because it's the traumas that are the doors that are stopping us from entering the kingdom of heaven, which you could go to whenever you want to go in. You know that place is not out there. That place is internal. What's stopping us from entering this inner heaven has been the traumas we've created throughout this lifetime and also in utero (which are completely non conscious), because we came into a world which our mother was already neurologically experiencing which keeps this (really boring) trauma story going.

I also agree with you completely in that both collectively and individually we're being called to move towards a place of greater freedom, where we can exist in our natural state. I love to speak of this.

H: *I'm also thinking about one of the places you started which was the Genesis story about Eve consuming the apple given to her by the snake. From a symbolic perspective I'm seeing the apple itself as representing the process of traumatic encoding.*

R: Of course! That was it.

H: *The serpent then represents the reptilian brain or the amygdala and its propensity for protectiveness. So as we heal ourselves in some way transcending time and space, perhaps we can help Eve and Adam heal as well.*

R: Of course, because that's the only way that healing can occur.

H: *Thank you. Ross, if you were someone who was considering training in Havening or you were talking to somebody who was considering getting involved in learning this tool, what advice would you give them?*

R: You've really got to do it. And why? A quote came into my mind from one of my early teachers and the question we put out there was "If you knew of something that could help another individual and you didn't use it would that be seen as unethical or indeed malpractice?"

So, we have a technique here that does work. With my limited understanding of neurobiological models I don't know whether or not Dr. Ruden's understandings of the mechanisms of action are completely accurate. But I know that it does work. My advice would be, as with anything, use Havening to help you do your own work. Do that and then you'll be hooked into wanting to do it with others.

It's not something I use every session. I've got a very eclectic approach to therapy and I may bring it into my second session. I may bring it in the fourth session. I may bring it into the very last session. But I integrate it with absolutely everything.

And I believe that if I'm able to do that with my limited understanding in the world, all therapists that are seeking another way of working with clients could certainly benefit from using it. It cuts to the chase.

H: *Thank you so much Ross. This conversation has inspired me. I look forward to sharing your observations and perceptions with many who will become part of the Havening family and community.*

CHAPTER 6

Animating the process

Tam Johnston

Tam Johnston is director at Fresh Insight coaching, based in London, UK

Harry: *Tam, how did you first discover Havening?*

Tam: I heard about it via the Web, from a few UK practitioners. Then I went to a conference and saw a presentation, but I was still a bit skeptical. I have a medical background, so I'm generally skeptical about things until I know enough about them and see some evidence. But I was interested enough to look into it a little bit more. Then I tried it on a client of mine, and had remarkable results, and that's what absolutely made me take a step back and realize I really need to go and learn this thoroughly.

H: *So, the experience with the client, this was after just reading the book or going to the conference?*

T: Both. So, I'd heard enough about it and I'd done a lot of my own research. There wasn't very much available at the time, and I think that's a good thing, because practitioners shouldn't necessarily just be doing it off their own bat without training. But I had enough where I'd looked into it and heard enough at the conference and been taught how to do it in a very basic way.

And actually, the client who came in was having a huge abreaction. He knew he was going to work with me and explore some really deep issues that he'd never told anyone about. He came in with a full-blown panic attack that, even with my nursing experience and my experience with every other modality that I've learned, I would have struggled to help him resolve.

So I just started Havening him, and within about 20 minutes, he was able to sit there for the first time in his life and tell me about some exceptionally traumatic things that had happened to him. But he's sitting there in a very objective, healthily detached way, because he'd come in already, as I now understand, completely and utterly activated. So, the Havening did its work within 20 minutes of us meeting each other. I just kind of took a step back and went, wow!

H: *There's something here.*

T: Absolutely, yes. Something that, you know, even with all the other kind of tools that I've got in my kit, and even with my medical background, he was having such a severe reaction and nothing else was working.

H: *Absolutely. Who are your typical clients, currently?*

T: They tend to be struggling with anxiety, self-esteem, trauma. Self-confidence, anger issues.

H: *How has Havening transformed your practice?*

T: In a lot of ways. Phenomenally. Even if I'm not using the technique, that kind of archeological digging, as we call it, of tracking back and finding those seed events really helps. Then working on that, where it then has a domino effect on everything else.

I'm trained in hypnotherapy, as well, although I don't do it in the traditional sense; I do it more conversationally. A lot of my clients seek me out because they don't want hypnotherapy. They may have issues around control. And Havening is phenomenal, I have found, to help the client access a beautiful, hypnotic, freely-associating state, the difference being that the client feels—and are—completely and utterly in control. So, it's phenomenal for that with clients, that you can do the work, but they're finding their own way with it, as you do Havening with them.

H: *Yes. I've really enjoyed that, as well. A Havening session, sometimes to the outsider, can simply look like you're stroking somebody's arms and palms and having a conversation, because once you access that particular state, that altered state that gets activated by the touch, if you understand the science and you understand how to navigate the distractions and transpirations and so forth, then it does begin to feel like a very natural, lovely conversation. And during the conversation, healing happens.*

T: Absolutely. I'm very committed to not imposing content onto clients unless necessary. I'd much rather they come up with what they need and where their mind naturally takes them, and that's what I find useful with Havening.

H: *That brings up a very interesting point. I once studied with a woman who is really an innovator in energy healing approaches. And she asks the client this question: "If your problem was a place in time and space, what would it be?" And that instantly evokes an imaginal scenario for the client. It might present as an arid desert, or a dark cave. And then, as you do the work, whatever process you are working with to help the client shift, that landscape transforms spontaneously. So, the problem gets expressed as this metaphorical representation, and as the metaphor changes, the problem goes away.*

T: That's what I found, and it's beautiful. In my work, I incorporate clean language. It's purposely ambiguous language and questions for your client where you're not using any content imposition or installation (as much as humanly possible). The concept of clean language comes from psychotherapist David Grove, who was very much against imposing content onto the client's experience.

He realized that when you work with what the client is giving out, in terms of their metaphors and symbolism, and allow them to explore that territory, the symbolism changes as the healing process takes place, and that's very much what I try and do with my clients, as well.

If their mind is throwing up symbolism and metaphors or analogies, then I absolutely reckon that's so much more powerful than doing it consciously. You know you've got the full package there with whatever they're bringing up in that moment, and it changes as you're doing work with Havening.

H: *Yes, exactly. So, speaking about metaphors brings me to the next question for you. Something that I believe is one of your enduring contributions to the Havening community is a YouTube video that you created within the last year which uses the metaphor of cultivat-*

ing a garden to describe and explain the neurobiological process by which Havening works.

Would you tell me a little bit more about how that idea came to you and what it was like creating that video, which I think now has been viewed by many thousands of people and has become a go-to? I send it to every Havening client, everyone who's interested in Havening, everyone who is in the orbit of my Havening work in general, and they universally appreciate it.

T: Wow. I have a very educational approach to what I do, and I think the more clients understand what's going on for them and where things come from, the more they feel back in control and actually can start working solutions out for themselves. I also like to give my clients stuff in between sessions to work with. And I tend to work with people who are very often in their head and quite analytical, so I think they really appreciate having that scientific understanding.

I started the project solely with the intention of creating a video that would help them understand what Havening is all about, and I got a bit carried away with it. [Laughs] It started off quite simply, and as I was going along, it became more and more detailed.

H: *Yes. Now, did you do the animation, all of it yourself, or did you have a team help you with that?*

T: I worked with a software program. I had to do an awful lot of work finding images to convey what I thought was going on, in terms of the neuroscience aspect of it. I had to track down the images and put all of that together as I went.

H: *What feedback have you gotten about the video thus far, from your clients as well as from the larger community?*

T: It really seems to help them understand, and they say they love it. The feedback has been brilliant and humbling. The Havening community has been wonderful about it. They really seem to have loved it, which I'm so pleased about.

H: *Wonderful. As I mentioned, I believe it'll be a truly enduring contribution to the world of Havening and the whole global movement that is emerging. Ten or twenty years from now, when everybody is using and understanding these tools, your video will have played a major role in getting this message out. So, thank you for that.*

T: Pleasure.

H: *Do you have any client stories that you'd be comfortable sharing about interesting experiences you've had as you've used Havening with your clients?*

T: The feedback from clients never ceases to amaze me. You only get the slightest bit of an inkling of what their experience is when you're doing Havening. It's a very personal experience, and although you're in it with them, obviously you don't fully know where their brain is going with it, or how deep they are going.

I've used it an awful lot to help clients with anger. I have one client that went back to her husband afterwards and said, "I feel like I've just had an exorcism." All of the anger simply let her; she just felt like a completely different person afterwards.

I've used it often with people who have experienced abuse and had remarkable experiences with that in a very short space of time. One client who I saw felt, after abuse in her past, felt utterly disconnected to her sexuality. She literally felt disconnected from the lower half of her body. We worked with the event itself first, and then deepened the work using metaphor and symbol, and a bit of parts work, as well, to reconnect her. The result was remarkable. She suddenly felt feelings again. She felt temperature and felt this was absolutely part of her, and genuinely, she could not actually feel it before, and afterwards she did. It was a beautiful, beautiful piece of work with her.

I've had a young lady that had a very rare condition; I won't say the medical name of it because it's very long and tedious, but she was having extreme pain, and she had been seeing doctors for years, was on all sorts of medication, and the last-ditch attempt was that she was going to go and have surgery. I saw her for one session with Havening and worked a little bit with her anticipatory anxiety, as well. The pain completely went away. I couldn't believe it, after all of that time and seeing goodness knows how many specialist doctors. So, I seem to be angling a little bit more towards the medical stuff as I work with Havening more and more, I think just naturally, because I've got that background.

H: *Of course. And it's truly remarkable to reflect on how this simple synthesis of touch, attention, and imagination could actually have such a significant impact on our physiology, that chronic pain that's sometimes been held for decades can dissolve in minutes or hours without medication, without you as the therapist having to know the story.*

T: Yes.

H: *How do you see Havening impacting the future of therapy, coaching, medicine, mental health practice, and so forth, ten, twenty years down the road?*

T: Well, I genuinely and sincerely hope that it has a significant impact. Having come from a medical background, I know how solid the skepticism can be, in terms of needing an evidence base and so on. Obviously within the community of Havening, people are doing a remarkable job of getting the evidence base together.

I would hope that it becomes commonplace to address issues of chronic pain and physical manifestations that don't have any particular mechanical cause for them. I think what needs to go hand-in-hand with this is more of an education within the medical world that connects mind and body.

If you can't find anything mechanically, then absolutely think what is going on in the mind and make sure that that is covered, that you're referring the patient to someone who can help them in this area.

You have chest pain or stomach pain or knee problems or back pain that an orthopedic surgeon can't do anything with. And these doctors at the moment and nurses—all medical professionals—are not educated to be thinking, okay, the mind and the body are as one. It's a system. So, who's looking after the mind? Who's exploring that? You know, they're brilliant at the backtracking of physical symptoms and taking a history in that respect, but they are not taking a history in terms of experiences, events, traumas, and things that go with it. So, that's what I would like to see, that that is more commonplace, that it's just the automatic way of thinking. So many clients who I've seen have got all this physical pain, and it's often gone within one session of Havening.

H: *Yes. I think it's also really significant that more and more people, like you, who have both a medical background as well as a skill in the psychological therapeutic coaching arena, embrace tools like Havening because I believe it's the synthesis of backgrounds that allows for the new possibilities to really emerge and take root.*

T: Yes.

H: *One more question. What advice would you give somebody who might be looking into the possibility of adding Havening techniques to their toolkit?*

T: Do it.

H: *Why? Why should they do it, Tam?*

T: Because I think a lot of practitioners think, as I did, that although I've been curious with other stuff, I'm doing a really good job. I've got enough in my toolkit. And then Havening came along, and now I think , "Wow, what on earth did I do without it?"

And it's not that I wasn't doing a good job before; it's just that this makes it so much easier, safer, gentler, and really develops the skills of the practitioner at the same time. Also learning how to do the archeology, kind of digging with intake and history.

So, it develops those skills phenomenally and is the most flexible process. It can be used with anything. I don't want to diminish it by calling it a tool, but just for the sake of explaining what I'm trying to explain here, which is it's the perfect bolt-on tool to supplement every modality that's out there. It celebrates everything else.

H: *Yes, I agree with that as well. I was talking with Tony Burgess and he really clarified something for me. He said Havening's a tool, not a therapy. The idea is the neurobiology underlying Havening and the synthesis of touch, attention, and imagination can radically transform the effectiveness of any modality on the planet.*

T: Exactly.

H: *It doesn't matter whether it's primarily linguistic or medical or imaginative or whatever. The understanding of the neurobiology and the synthesis of these components can impact it all.*

T: I agree, and I think having this knowledge changed my practice phenomenally, really understanding what's going on. It was the thing that I think I needed, and therefore I would suggest that other practitioners could benefit from as well.

For a lot of the modalities that I'd studied, there wasn't an evidence base, and there wasn't really a scientific explanation. And I'm quite the science geek, so I love to have that, and I think there's an awful lot of people out there that are looking for that credibility and that understanding, and that's what Havening provides.

It can also alter the relationship between the client and the therapist in a really positive way. It creates a rapport and a sense of trust that, in my experience, helps the client heal in a very different way than conversation or other modalities.

H: *Thank you so much.*

PART II

Releasing The Pain
Of The Past

CHAPTER 7

A tool, not a therapy

Tony Burgess

Tony Burgess is Head of UK and Europe for Havening.

Harry: *Tony, how did you first discover Havening?*

Tony: I remember it very well. It was back in 2012. I was in a networking meeting with someone who had seen Paul McKenna do a Havening demonstration. They knew that I worked with people who experienced trauma. The person said, "What do you think of Havening Techniques®? It seems very good!"

I had not heard of Havening, so I asked some questions. Where have you experienced this? What did you see? How does it work? And she recommended Dr. Ron Ruden's book, *When the Past is Always Present*.

That was my first time delving into Havening, through the book. At the time I can remember searching online for any trainings or any people who are offering Havening, and there was nothing available in 2012.

So, I went from the book. I had clients who gave me their permission to work with them, with the textbook version of

Havening. It was not until 2013, a year later, that there was any training available.

H: *It's remarkable how far things have come in the four years since you first read the book and the three years since the trainings have occurred.*

T: Yes, it feels like forever.

H: *At the same time, I think we're standing at the threshold of a significant expansion both of our understanding of how Havening works and of the number of people who are embracing this tool.*

Tony, sometimes Havening looks and seems to be too good to be true. Many people are skeptical when they first hear about it. Were you skeptical at first? And if so, what changed your mind?

T: I'm open minded, but I'm skeptical. So, I'm willing to try new things and test new things. But I like to experience something first hand. If someone had just told me "Oh, you stroke someone's face and you stroke their arm and it gets rid of their life long trauma," I wouldn't buy it. I'd need to see it with my own eyes and test it with my own hands.

Reading the book was my first dip in. When I read the book, I understood straight away that this guy knows his neuroscience. He put a lot of work into explaining it from a scientific perspective, and that spoke to me in terms of credibility.

Then, once I got permission from clients to try it out, once I tested it and had seen it with my own eyes, I was absolutely, immediately convinced that this was a powerful tool and I needed to learn and know more about it. My skepticism disappeared pretty quickly.

H: *Do you recall any of those early clients that you tested it with and the results that you experienced?*

T: Yes I do. They came in with really significant, heavy duty, traumas. I didn't start with someone who had a minor issue with confidence. I knew I was a competent therapist and I knew I had the tools in the toolkit to help people. So, I wasn't afraid of taking on those tougher clients. And the results were remarkable. Havening proved itself convincingly.

For example, one client comes in having had experienced personal attacks that they couldn't even talk about without being overcome by floods of tears at the very beginning of the session. Within a single Havening session, they're able to talk about these experiences, knowing that it all happened, but completely free from all of the emotional upheaval that went along with it. It really felt like they were again stepping back into freedom.

H: *Who are your typical clients?*

T: Julie, my partner who runs the business with me, and I both love to work with a variety of clients. We've got personal coaching clients who are working with confidence issues. We've got executive coaching clients where the focus is more about maximizing resilience and performance. We've got therapeutic clients who are coming with more heavy duty issues.

We also work with teams and managers and leaders in business as well. A wide, wide range of clients. I've found that Havening can have a part to play with all of those different clients and the work we do with them.

H: *That's interesting. Since you work with people throughout this wide range, from those who are severely traumatized to those who are essentially healthy but want to get an edge in their performance., I would suppose you have a comprehensive sense of the various applications of Havening.*

I know that you have a solid grasp of many tools for facilitating positive change. You're an NLP practitioner, a coach, and a therapist. You had lots and lots of effective tools in your toolkit before encountering Havening.

T: Yes.

H: *Given that you were coming into Havening, already working with a wide range of clients, already having a solid container of tools to use, why did you choose to use and integrate Havening and then to move in the direction not only of becoming a practitioner but becoming the head of training in the UK and Europe?*

What was it specifically about Havening that inspired somebody like you, who was already successful, already possessing plenty of effective tools and techniques, to embrace it so fully?

T: I wasn't looking for anything, but I'm open to what's out there and I guess I get curious when I hear there's something new I'm not aware of. That's what grabbed me with Havening in the first place. I picked up the book. It spoke to me. And it was those first experiences of using it that were so convincing.

Something that really surprised me was how rapid, complete and lasting it was. The skeptic in me was thinking, "Is this problem really gone for good?" Obviously, I've been able to follow up with those people now. Here we are in 2016, four years later and the problems are still gone. There's the proof.

Havening is also clear cut. My client who was in tears and unable to communicate about something because of the trauma was able to talk about it freely and easily afterwards. That's a big transformation in a very short period of time.

My NLP toolkit can get quick results. But with Havening, from the very first time I take the tool out of the toolkit, and the first client I use it with, we get such compelling results. And then the same thing happens with the next one, and the next one. This is remarkable.

And when I began using Havening, I was careful to strip it down to its bare bones and use only the basic Havening protocols. I wasn't weaving it into my other tools and techniques at the time. I was testing it in its essence. And I saw—I knew—that this stuff just works. I love stuff that just works.

H: *I'm assuming that Havening has transformed your own practice in a sense. Is it one of the first tools that you now use regardless of the issue?*

T: It is with many of my clients, certainly my one to one clients. Whenever I'm working with a one to one client, I'm aware that Havening can help serve this person one way or another, whatever the starting point.

Now when we're training trainers and corporate teams, that's a different side of the business, where I'm not as likely to introduce Havening—at least initially. But in my one to one work, it's become my tool of choice. It's right at the top of the toolkit.

H: *What does Havening do that other tools and modalities cannot do, or do as easily or readily?*

T: From my perspective, it's how it directly gets to the part of the brain that we need to access. When you start to learn the science of amygdala de-potentiation, what's happening is that we're literally stripping receptors off of the surface of neurons in the amygdala. That's clear and direct. We're not persuading someone. We're not giving them some clever suggestion. We're directly getting to where the memory's been encoded and we're making biological changes in there that free people. To me, this is remarkable.

I'm sure that all the other methods in the toolkit in some way are influencing brain chemistry, even in the way that the mind reframes things; there's a biological equivalent to that. But there's something nice and clear cut about what occurs in Havening. We use the protocol, neurons lose receptors and it changes everything.

H: *Yes. Brain surgery in the palm of your hands, in a way.*

T: Yes!

H: *That's exciting. What was most difficult for you as you integrated Havening into your current work and your current practice. Were there any challenges?*

T: Well I suppose some people are skeptical, so there's a bit of a sales job in a way.

H: *Sure.*

T: Because I get it. I'm seeing it with my own eyes. You tell someone again that you're going to stroke their face or arms and it's going to do so much for them. It can seem a little un-believable.

I tend to explain a bit about the neuroscience, and tell them stories of people who I've worked with, without naming names, simply telling those success stories. But the skepticism can be a little bit of a challenge because it does often seem too good to be true.

I remember Ron Ruden at the first London training I went to in May 2013. He said to the group, "You know, you'll get success after success after success, rapid, amazing almost miraculous change happening right in front of you, session after session. And you could start to think that you can just do that with ab-solutely everyone, no matter what they bring, and you could get a little bit cocky if you're not careful. And then something will blindside you and you'll come across one that will seem on the surface like it will be so simple, but it will just stump you. It will not go according to plan." I suppose a positive challenge for me is that there are those cases where you've got to have that detective hat on and you've got to keep really alert and curious and quizzical to really get to the bottom of the issue so that your client can heal.

You have to look more deeply at what's going on for this per-son. Where's the real origin to this issue?

Now we've got the tools to clear it, but where are the origins, where are the layers and how do we get to the absolute core of this? So it's a positive challenge. I didn't see it as a problem; I found integrating Havening into the toolkit a very easy thing.

H: *And it is deceptively simple. The one thing that becomes clear as you explore the neurobiology of what's happening and you study Dr. Ruden's work, you see that the apparent simplicity belies significant complexity in terms of process and understanding. It took a lot of* *research and a lot of real work to first understand this process of depotentiation and then to make it so simple.*

How about the issue of touch? It hasn't been standard practice to use touch in this way in a therapeutic context with clients. How do you discuss this and how do your clients respond?

T: For me, it's about making sure there's no surprises. My clients know and are fully informed that Havening involves touch. It's a permission-based, respectful, client-centered approach.

We also know that we can do Havening without needing to touch our clients. They can do all of the touch for themselves if that's ever an issue. In fact, some practitioners run their practices entirely without ever touching their clients, using Havening. So that is also an option.

For me, it's about making sure that they know what's coming. That I've described the process clearly. I've positioned my hands around the areas that will be touched and shown them exactly what to expect.

"This process will involve me stroking around this area, around this area, is that okay? Is it okay for me to sit here?"

It's all permission based, very respectful, making sure that they're the one who's making choices and in charge. And if touch is okay with them, brilliant. We can go for it. If it's not, then we can just guide them through the touch for themselves.

H: *Yes. And most of your clients respond positively?*

T: Yes they do. In a way, I've been surprised just how infrequently someone has a problem being touched, particularly considering the issues people come with. Sometimes touch has been part of the trauma. And so I was a little surprised that they were okay with it, with someone they trusted and felt safe with and had rapport with. But immediately once the process begins, it's very soothing and naturally reassuring, and I think that helps.

H: *Yes. Also, Tony, I've observed you work and you have a very powerful, yet soothing and comforting therapeutic presence. I would imagine that such a degree of therapeutic presence and rapport would also create a tremendous degree of safety and ease for your clients.*

T: Thank you.

H: *You're welcome. What is the range of conditions that you've been able to successfully address with Havening?*

T: The main areas for me are clearing traumatic events, stress, and confidence. As far as other Havening practitioners are concerned, there are people who specialize in treating addictions, or sexual disorders, or OCD, or whatever. Quite a variety of things.

My therapeutic work is more focused on clearing event trauma, and for my coaching clients, removing anxieties and negative stress. Sometimes someone can come and they wouldn't even describe themselves as having trauma, but they're effectively almost at a breaking point. Their tank is so full of frustrations, stresses, strains and pressures from the day-to-day grind that may not be being expressed or released in any way.

When that tank's so full, they might as well have had a major trauma because they're functioning at a much lower level. They're just not coping well, small things are setting them off and they're only half living, really.

With these clients, I help them deal with their stress and anxiety issues. For example, someone's not happy about making sales calls. Or, someone's not happy about standing up and speaking in public. Or, they are hesitant or anxious about going and asking the boss for a raise or have other issues around their lack of confidence.

From the therapy standpoint, I'm using Havening to remove phobias, to help people who are having nightmares and flashbacks, to help people who have had physical conditions where there's been a stress or trauma origin to those physical conditions, to help people deal with pain. There are so many applications. Sometimes I'm doing content-free work, so I really don't know what the issue is that I'm working with, and the clients report great benefit afterwards.

H: *You mentioned content-free work. Would you elaborate?*

T: What I mean is that sometimes people avoid coming to therapy because they can't face disclosing what happened to them. They just don't want to talk it through. They may suspect that could be beneficial, but they just can't face it. And so what I tell them is "Look, if you feel you want to disclose what it is and you want to get into content that's fine. But if you actually want to keep to yourself what it is that's going on and you just want to clear it without so much going into the content then we can do that."

As long as they can access it in their own minds and experience feelings around it, then we can work with it, without me needing to know what they're accessing.

H: *So you find that working content-free on those cases is just as effective if they had articulated and shared the content?*

T: Yes. Obviously there will be times when maybe it wouldn't work so well if someone comes with a lot of complex issues that are interwoven. We need that detective hat on. But, when people are coming and they say, "I know what this is about. I just really want you to help me get rid of it. I don't want to go over it. I don't even want to tell you what it is," Havening clears it just the same. I think it keeps it clean for the practitioner as well, because I'm not going to start having opinions or judgements about or try and second guess what their experience was like. It's the most client-centered approach you can have.

H: *Certainly. You've shared a lot about the various kinds of conditions that you have successfully used Havening to address. Are there any specific stories that you would be comfortable sharing about client breakthroughs or transformations as a result of the application of Havening?*

T: Yes. There have been people who have come to me who have been severely abused for many years. As a result, their confidence and sense of self has been massively, negatively impacted by their experiences, which is completely understandable and natural. We have used Havening to help heal those multiple layers of trauma while also helping build a new sense of self that is more resourceful, more worthy, more resilient.

Obviously this is not a one session situation. There have been quite a number of clients where this has been their story. They've come out on the other side of the treatment completely free from the emotional pain of those years in the past, still knowing it happened but feeling like they've released their real self. In the process they have built a new self concept. That's been really rewarding.

And, I've found it equally rewarding when people have had very specific traumas, for example, a car crash. I've had people who have come to me who have been involved in car crashes and even where they have not had a physical injury, the shock of the experience is being replayed within them. They've not been able to get back into a day to day activity, like driving a car confidently to work or to wherever they need to be. It is incredibly rewarding to be able to help the client clear that kind of thing quickly and solidly and see that the very next day they are out and about driving and feeling normal again.

I recall one client who released a rather odd phobia. This person was terrified of buttons, and was responding to buttons as if there was a lion in the room and it was going to kill them. On one level, they knew this was ridiculous, but on another level, they just couldn't help having this fear. And after Havening, the fear is completely gone. It seems like a very small silly thing for anyone who doesn't have a fear of buttons! But you can imagine the number of contexts that this fear would show up in their life day by day.

H: *Of course.*

T: The impact of Havening just helps them get back into what they constitute as normal living.

H: *With that client's fear of buttons did you go back to a specific event that was the source?*

T: In that one we did not. We couldn't, because they didn't have a sense of its origins. So we ended up going with the most recent times where it terrified them, and also the earliest one that they could remember. Between those two categories, we managed to tap into the neural pathway, and it cleared. We don't always need to find the originating event. It's great if we can. But there are enough ways into that pathway where the fear was encoded that it cleared anyway.

H: *It's clear to me, both in my own practice and in my conversations with you and others that having the neurobiological understanding of depotentiating the encoded traumatic memories in the amygdala powerfully informs how we work with people, how we see them, and how we see the transformation happening.*

T: Yes.

H: *How do you see Havening impacting mental health practices, particularly in terms of the treatment in trauma, say 10 to 20 years in the future? What do you imagine?*

T: Well, in a way, we're still in our infancy, aren't we? In terms of Havening being a discipline and being known and accepted, it really is in the early stages. We've already got streams of research starting to happen. Once the studies start coming to fruition and results begin to be seen, people will open their eyes and ears and take more notice of it.

I'm excited about the possibilities. I'm seeing so much great work being done globally and it feels like we're just approaching the starting block. I believe that in 20 years time it will be something that most people who are dealing with trauma will have at the top of their toolkit as an offering.

At the moment, the word is spreading through people who are directly experiencing the results going and telling other people who need those results. And there are some early adopters who are coming on, getting trained in it and doing great work in the world.

We also have organizations, like small veterans charities, where enough of their members have experienced the value of Havening that they're really on board. What we want in 20 years time, hopefully a lot sooner than that, is for Havening to be really mainstream.

By that time there will have been enough clinical trials that are accepted by, for example in the UK, the NHS, National Health Service, and also by the big military charities, such that it becomes a tool of choice, a key offering. Instead of turning to drug treatments as a tool for managing someone who's stressed out or someone who is struggling to sleep because they're having flashbacks, rather than just reaching into that medical tool-kit and that being the only offering, you would be able to use it in combination with Havening, or use Havening on its own as the amazing tool it is.

H: *Thank you so much. We've talked a lot about Havening in terms of trauma and releasing the pain of traumatic memories and so forth, and most of that work is appropriately in the domain of mental health professionals, counselors, psychologists, therapists and so forth.*

Can Havening be learned and used effectively by lay people, those who are not counselors, therapists, psychologists or even coaches and the like? And if so, how might a person use Havening for their own self care?

T: Yes! I think theres a massive place for Havening for self-care and self development. I think what we've got to be aware of here is if someone's got some really heavy duty stuff that they're carrying around with them, it would be better for them to work with a certified practitioner to help them on that journey.

At the same time, there's another level at which, we want to empower people to have these tools literally in their own hands. First of all, they can use self-havening to supplement any work that a practitioner's done with them.

So the practitioner might say, "Okay, we've done some clearing today. What I want you to do is go away and apply some Affirmational Havening," for example. This is because if we are clearing we also want to be building in some good alternatives to begin to move towards. This is one way they can begin to build resilience.

Havening can also be used for state management. There are people who work in schools for example, with kids who have got exams coming up and they can teach the basics of Havening for state management, to get rid of those exam nerves. Or, if you're going into an interview, and you are feeling a bit of anxiety, how about using a bit of Havening to calm yourself down and get yourself in the best possible state before you get out of the car and go into the office.

So you can focus on dealing with things live as they're happening, as well as building in some positive resilience.

When she was 10, I taught my daughter Havening because she was having a bit of trouble at school with a few friends and it was starting to upset her. It was small stuff to me but you know how this kind of social stress can affect people, especially young people. So she was taking this tool to school and she could just nip off to the bathroom, make a few strokes on the face, say a few positive things to herself and she would leave feeling a little bit more grounded, a little bit more calm, having things in better perspective and more ready to get on with her day.

Families can use this beautifully. I've seen couples use positive touch as a way of communicating with each other, to be part of the solution rather than to be part of the problem. It's wonderful to see these tools in the hands of families.

H: *Thank you. Would you speak a little bit to the distinction of using Havening as mental health professional therapist and using Havening as an executive coach? You happen to be both, which is a wonderful combination. What are some of the distinctions of appropriate use in those different contexts?*

T: When people are coming for coaching they've obviously got very different expectations than if they are coming for therapy, even though they may have some of the same needs.

But we frame things in different ways in a coaching session versus a therapy session. When someone comes for coaching, I'm teaching them tools that they can apply to increase their capacity to perform and their capacity to think, plan, lead and manage more clearly.

Usually the business is paying for the coaching, so the conversation is framed in terms of work-related performance. We ask, what's going to help you function more effectively in your work role?

And although there can be massive personal benefits to that as well, this is how it tends to get framed. In the therapeutic room usually the client is paying and is open to whatever it is you are able to offer to them to get the job done.

H: *Yes. And of course in terms of scope of practice it would be appropriate for someone who was a mental health professional to work with someone to clear their trauma. It wouldn't necessarily be appropriate for a coach.*

T: Correct.

H: *Havening is a tool, not a therapy, as we discussed before. And so, how that tool is applied very much depends on the scope of practice of the person who is using it.*

T: Absolutely. Lots of different people are coming to learn Havening. We are constantly saying to people you know what your expertise is, you know your experience, you know what you've trained in. You know you can do wonderful work with Havening within that range of competency and legal scope of practice. There are plenty of people you can refer to if you need to help someone who is outside of that range. That's absolutely right.

H: *Thank you. What excites you the most about Havening? Of everything we've discussed, what excites you the most about having this tool available to you and more and more to the world?*

T: Wow. I just think about those early, first times that I used Havening and the wow factor. That has stayed with me. Every time I'm working with a client I still experience that wow factor. But the first time I saw it, I thought, "my goodness, what a difference this can make to individuals and in the hands of many therapists, coaches, supporters, carers of one sort or another." The reach of possibilities with Havening are unlimited, especially when we can work via Skype, where there are no geographical boundaries.

We have people going to war torn areas, helping individuals who are fleeing for their lives from their own countries. They're offering Havening to people whose lives are in tatters and it's helping to get them back onto an even keel. It's so powerful and so easy to teach people, and in the right hands easy to do very deep and life-changing work on the therapeutic side of things. I'm just excited about how far this could reach.

Every time we've done a training, different kinds of professionals show up. I think, "Gosh, there's another area I hadn't even thought of where Havening's going to be doing some great work in the right hands with the right specialist."

We were in Denmark recently and there were several teachers from a school that specializes in working with kids with autism. Of course in this context there will need to be some tweaks to the way in which it's delivered and the way in which they interact and introduce Havening, but already so many ideas are coming out about just what a great place Havening will have within that school as a core tool. Parents came to the training as well and it was exciting to see that there's so many possibilities. That's just one example.

H: *Are there specific situations and contexts where it's not advisable to use Havening?*

T: First of all, make sure you're the right person to be using Havening in the right context with the right purpose. Beyond that, don't put any limits on using it. I mean, you wouldn't want an inexperienced therapist to work with someone with complex PTSD, or schizophrenia. But that would be the same with any tool. You wouldn't want someone without sufficient experience and expertise to be working with really complex issues with any tool.

On the other hand, someone who's experienced and qualified to be working with people in many different areas will be able to see how Havening could fit in. They'll be the best expert to determine where it's going to be used. I wouldn't want to limit that.

The question to ask is this: are you the right person to be doing this work with this individual given your specific experience and expertise?

H: *Yes. Thank you so much. Tony, at this point you have trained, over the past couple of years, hundreds of people in Havening. You're the director for training in the UK and for Europe. You've trained in many countries throughout Europe. I met you in Los Angeles, so you've trained in the United States. There was recently a training in Australia. What are you observing as you travel around the world, training, and spreading the word about this tool? What are you seeing in terms of people's level of acceptance, excitement and enthusiasm?*

T: One thing I'm delighted by is that culture or language doesn't seem to matter, it's carrying well. So we've now done this in Sweden, Italy, Germany, France, Spain, Denmark, Norway, Australia. We've got activity in the US and Canada. So there's lots of great work. Ulf Sandstrom, one of our trainers, has done work in India as well.

H: *Yes. Ulf was just in Turkey last week, working with folks who unfortunately had been impacted by the crisis in Syria.*

T: Yes that's right! Havening is being taken on board in different cultures and different languages. The science and the technique is translating well. I've done some trainings where everything I've said is being translated as I go and I've been kind of a bit nervous about how this would carry. On the whole, they're getting it, they are excited, and they're reporting back about their positive results.

What also stimulates me is the range of people in the room. I've got my own areas of expertise, and I'm learning from the people in the room as much as they're learning from me.

I'm able to share about Havening, but their different niches, expertise, areas of application are fascinating to me. It's challenging as well, because I'll get some neuroscience questions that I've never been asked before. And that inspires me to get curious and to go back to Dr. Ruden and ask more questions. So this international activity and expansion is keeping me stimulated and on my toes.

H: *Wonderful! One last question, Tony. What advice would you give someone, mental health professional, coach, nurse, teacher, or lay person who is looking into the possibility of attending a training and adding the Havening Techniques to their toolkit?*

T: Well, you probably won't be surprised for me to say this, but just do it. Just do it because even if you're skeptical, which I can often be, the best way to prove it one way or the other is to find out for yourself, to actually get hands on.

That's the best way to prove it to yourself. Even if your current role will not allow you to use Havening yet. For example, here in the UK if a psychiatrist who is working for NHS or a psychologist working for NHS comes and trains, they wouldn't be allowed to use it in their NHS practice yet, but they're early adopters, they want to be ahead. They want to understand what's coming. They want to be the ones who have already been trained in it so that by the time the research studies appear, they will be ready to help lead the way in their scope of operating.

I strongly encourage you to be one of those early adopters. And beyond thinking about what you could do for others, there will be many benefits for yourself. Havening is not going away. This movement is growing globally, month by month. In the international Havening practitioner conference last year, for example, it was delightful to see that there were 14 countries represented.

And Havening has only been available to the general public since 2013. So, this is going places. Soon, everyone will know about Havening who is in any way involved with change work. To be on board in this stage is exciting.

There's also a great community you will be joining. And everyday we see on the Facebook page, where the doctors are taking part and answering questions and asking stimulating questions, we see people reporting success after success as well as asking for help with specific cases and situations. It's heartwarming to see how much good in the world it's already doing.

So to be part of that community, part of that journey, I think you'd look back in 20 years time and say, "Getting involved with the Havening movement was one of the best decisions I ever made." Certainly for me, given I wasn't looking for anything new, it's been one of the best decisions I've ever made to go to that training and integrate Havening into my day-to-day practice.

H: *Yes. I've found the community of practitioners and trainers to be invaluable. And one of the finest communities in terms of a good balance between head and heart. It's full of people who are intelligent and focused on expanding their knowledge and at the same time they express a tremendous degree of caring for other people. And as you mentioned, it's a truly international group. It's an honor to be part of truly a global movement that is helping to heal people in the most essential way. Thank you.*

CHAPTER 8

Sculpting your own neurology

Carol Robertson, PhD

Carol is the founder of Psychosensory Academy, based in Edinburgh, UK.

Harry: *Carol, how did you first discover Havening?*

Carol: I learnt about Havening when I attended a training given by Paul McKenna PhD and Richard Bandler PhD. Paul McKenna got everyone in the room using self-applied Havening Touch and the Event Havening technique. I was very intrigued at the results I experienced.

After that, I searched the web for more information and came up with a really clear article that Steven Ruden had written regarding his work with dental phobias. I used that template and my own experience with Havening to begin using it with clients immediately. Then Dr. Ronald Ruden began to offer training in the Havening Techniques. I had the right qualifications to go, so I attended the very first training in 2013.

H: *Who are your typical clients? I know you work with a wide range of different kinds of issues.*

C: It's a big range. I'm on the JustBeWell team which is a fantastic international team of NLP master practitioners, trained by Richard Bandler. Through being the Scottish representative for JustBeWell I get to help a broad range of clients. I see clients across the full range of ages from very small children to very elderly people, as well as people at the end of life sometimes. And the range of issues covers all sorts of things from straightforward fears, like dealing with a recent accident, or long-term fears from sexual abuse or bullying. Or sometimes people just want to achieve more with their lives. Other times people come because they're curious and they want to experience what a session is like.

I also do a lot of pro-bono work. I volunteer at the moment for a place called Chris's House which focuses on suicide prevention. Here we are using Havening to help people in crisis.

H: *So you work with people from every walk of life who have all sorts of different problems.*

C: Yes. I have also worked with people who are long-term handicapped and have severe learning disabilities. I can't discuss their case histories because their confidentiality is protected as they can't give permission. I've been working with them using Havening in combination with horses and I've seen some incredible things.

H: *Yes, later in the conversation I'd like to talk about Equine-assisted Havening which you've developed.*

You already had a high level of skill, particularly in terms of NLP and hypnosis, before you learned about Havening. How has learning and using Havening transformed how you work with clients?

C: It's been a massive transformation. When I'm working now I'm looking for very different things. I'm thinking sculpturally and I'm thinking about the science which is related to the Havening Techniques.

H: *Yes. So, what you've learned from Havening is not simply the technique of Havening but the scientific knowledge of the entire process now informs how you work with clients in general.*

C: Yes. When I say I'm thinking sculpturally, I mean I am thinking about the shape of their neurology. And I am thinking how the alterations that they make in their neurology will result in changes in the chemical response that they experience when they are triggered (for example, by a sunny day, a piece of music, a program on the TV, a thought about something, their own breathing, posture or movement). So I'm very careful and very aware. I think one of the other things I've learned is that this kind of biological change is very, very fast. And the history taking, getting them on board, helping them to understand what they're going to do (because it's their brain that's going to change) takes time. So I think of sculpting the neurology as having both fast and slow activities.

H: *Yes. Sometimes the history taking and the rapport building and the exploring and explaining take a lot more time than the actual depotentiation.*

C: Yes, because the depotentiation's fast. I also think of how you can use Havening to build. So when I say sculpture, I really mean that. The person is taking something away in order to liberate themselves. Other times they're adding something. And I see that as an ongoing, even daily process. Once people realize that they're building their own neurology, you know, it's both fast and slow.

H: *Exactly.*

C: It might not take you long, but you might just do a little bit every day, when you're in the shower or when you notice yourself being triggered. For example, I remember we were going over to pick up a car in the north of Scotland and we went over a bridge on the way up there. I thought to myself, 'That's gonna be horrible on the way back down in the snow, in the dark, in the strange car that we just bought. And then I thought, "That's really interesting, I wonder when was the first time I got scared of that bridge."

Then I remembered. It was when I was about six, in the back of my grandmother's car. She was in the front passenger seat wearing a big hat. We were having a Sunday out. The bridge was new and we drove over it. It's a dramatic bridge over a beautiful Scottish glen.

Granny had a panic attack and started screaming. I was trapped in the back. I felt very stuck. I couldn't get out. I couldn't understand why she was screaming. My parents love driving. They're calm drivers, so it seemed really odd. She must have given me a real fright and it must've been encoded in my amygdala. And all these years later, as we drove over the same bridge I was triggered. So I thought to myself "I must haven that either when I'm up there or when I get home," because I was a passenger and we were going to drive back. I did a little bit of havening touch on my arms as I was thinking about it, just as I'm talking about it now.

After we came back down in the dark, and we finally arrived at home, I said to Robert, "Did we actually go over that bridge? Did we come back over the same bridge?" "Yeah." "That's weird, I never noticed!" He said, "But it was pitch dark and snowing!" I said, "I know it because it makes a noise. It goes clunk clunk clunk clunk as you go over the concrete things."

So I'd just havened that, and the response was changed. I was completely calm. And I've been over the bridge a few times since. I love the view.

I want my clients to have Havening as a tool and to be able to use it and understand what they're doing on their own. That's a massive change in my practice. I can give my clients a really solid grasp of Havening. And my clients also have access to on-line support.

H: *I love the framing and the words that you used in terms of building your own neurology because for me, understanding the paradigm of Havening, the neurochemistry, the neuroscience, is so vital.*

I remember when I did my very first mentoring call with you and you said "Well, there's some things that you depotentiate and other things that you potentiate," that comment completely shifted my sense of what was possible with this tool. The idea of consciously taking control of your own neurology is so empowering and really puts the power in the hands of the client.

C: And can you imagine if we were teaching this in nursery school? It's so empowering to realize that we are building ourselves.

H: *Yes, with every thought, every relationship, every action, every interaction, every act of imagination. Every time we apply Havening touch we are literally sculpting our own brains. It's such an empowering, inspiring, and ennobling realization.*

What are some of the most remarkable and interesting things that you've personally observed in your application of Havening with your clients and with yourself?

C: I've seen all sorts of things. I've seen people experience changes in their attention span. They've moved from being in pain to feeling comfortable. Their mobility has changed. Their health has changed. Their ability to learn has changed. There's been removal of fear. They've been empowered.

People in sports competitions have gotten completely rid of their nervousness. I've seen very interesting cases where the sporting nerves didn't seem at all connected to the things that we havened yet the result was we got rid of the fear of doing certain things within their professional, competitive life and they've had huge success.

I've worked with people who have been told they would never achieve anything due to learning difficulties. That they would never have a relationship, that they would never have a job, or really be able to do anything or maybe go to college.

With one person, in three minutes of Havening that all changed. A three minute Havening, because that's about all their attention span could take. And now that person gets in touch with me frequently and says things like, "Well, my boyfriend said, "Would you marry me?' and I said no". And, "I'd like to do math at university" and, "I'm competing in horse riding competitions." Just phenomenal changes that really amazed me.

H: *It's interesting because we do see these amazing changes and they're quick and lasting. Many people are skeptical when they first hear about Havening because it seems too good to be true. Were you skeptical at first at all, and if you were, what changed your mind?*

C: I was totally skeptical. I think I was fearful about the humming and the singing, about how it looked or something like that. So I wasn't just skeptical, I was actually a bit afraid of doing it. I thought, "I'm not going to be working with these criminals in Scotland and getting them to sing Happy Birthday. No way, Jose!" I get a lot of clients sent to me by judges and they arrive saying, "Oh you're my last chance."

I realized this fear was connected to a past memory, so I used Havening to change my own beliefs. It was hilarious because my perspective completely changed. I was using that event as a major story. It was building a major belief system.

I havened for 10 minutes. And almost immediately I could see that I had some responsibility in what had happened. I could see that I had built this big story. I actually started giggling. It's been life changing.

H: *I had a similar experience about a week after I got Dr. Ruden's book! I was going through a personal challenge related to my belief system about what was possible for me. I decided to try Havening with it. And it took about 10—15 minutes to completely dissolve this old belief that I thought was intractable. I had previously tried NLP and hypnosis and tapping and all these other modalities, but this one wouldn't crack. And in 15 minutes with Havening, everything changed.*

You've explored so many tools. What does Havening do that other modalities either can't do or don't do as easily or readily as Havening?

C: I understand what I'm doing now, so I can do it more deliberately. When I'm working with Havening, since I'm thinking sculpturally, I'm thinking about what's going on with their neurology, their biochemistry, their electrochemistry. What's happening now? What would happen if this or that changes? And I might use an NLP process and combine it with Havening process. Or I might use the fast phobia pattern along with Havening Touch. Or I might use Havening Touch so they know how to get chilled out, calm down and then maybe do a bit of trancework. I use it amongst the other things.

H: *I love the metaphor of sculpting and building neurology. What do you notice as you mentor and train people in the Havening Techniques?*

C: When I'm mentoring people who are training with me, I notice that Havening Techniques® are incredibly robust. People come to the trainings, amazing, brilliant people from different skill bases and backgrounds. There are doctors and psychiatrists, skilled NLPers and hypnotists, TFT and EFT practitioners, school counselors. So many different types of knowledge and so many specialities. They're all learning Havening Touch and the various Havening processes.

They're learning a lot of science, they're learning a lot of techniques and they're doing a lot of practice in the first stages. Then they send in case studies, some on video. Sometimes I'm watching and notice that they are obviously combining something that they knew before, going in a certain direction that maybe would be different from how I would do it. Then, it still works! The process is so robust.

It's also really easy for people to learn. So easy that sometimes people think they can learn Havening on their own.

They're very skilled. They think they can learn by copying what they see in the videos. They might watch me in a video or Ron or Steve or Paul McKenna and think, 'I can do that'. That's how I got started. However, there's much more to it than that.

Being part of the Havening community brings a lot more value, particularly in how you think about the science. I've seen people attempt to do Havening and not understand the science.

H: *Yes, as have I. I did a demo the other day. The person was able to resolve the issue very powerfully. As the demo completed I had people ask questions. It was very clear to me that the external appearance of simplicity concealed a tremendous amount of refinement, sensory acuity and skill. As I was unpacking it for them they began to see "oh this is a lot more than simply activate, distract, and test".*

The process is so deceptively simple on the surface that someone might think, "Oh, I can do this!" but then they really can't. They really need the training. They really need the certification. They really need the scientific knowledge. They really need to understand it.

C: Yes, and when they have that they'll find they can do so much more.

H: *Exactly. Thats what I enjoy about the online forum; there are so many brilliant people. Somebody posts a question, and you have 20 different people responding as to how they would approach it. And each approach can work!*

C: Yes, and they're all different and that's what I love. It's really, really robust.

H: *What was most difficult for you, if anything, as you integrated Havening into your work?*

C: The thing that I found most difficult was how it effective it was.

H: *What do you mean?*

C: Before I went to the Havening course, I was already quite confident using it, getting quite good results. I had read Ron's book, so I had a pretty good idea of the science—I thought.

Here's an example: This woman came to see me and she was talking a lot. She was in her sixties, and her whole life was a total disaster, all blamed on a family member. Normally we have a cup of tea at first but she was really raging when she came in.

So, we did a really quick Event Havening and then I said when was the first time you realized you were afraid of this person and she went straight there—right to the memory. You could see she was accessing everything she saw, everything she heard, everything she felt, all of the sensory information. So I got her Havening and she completely transformed. She looked like a completely different person.

So then I said, 'you have a seat and relax and I'll go and make some tea'. I was stunned. I asked her, 'what do you think when you think about that person now?'. And she said 'I'm fine.' Her perspective had completely changed.

When I went back through the room with a cup of tea, there was nothing else to be done. I had the two hour session booked and there was nothing to be done. It actually made me panic. I knew I really needed to go to the Havening course! After that I started doing Havening at the end of my sessions. Anything I missed I would get with Havening.

H: *Otherwise all your clients would be done in ten minutes!*

C: I just didn't know what to do with them at first. But now I start helping them build new possibilities, not just get rid of the old stuff. It was the strangest thing with her, because I felt I hadn't even started!

H: *Right. And the work was all done.*

C: It was all done. So that's what I found most difficult.

H: *That's a good problem to have!*

C: Yes. I thought originally that the touch and the humming and so forth would be difficult. But actually people really love it.

H: *Here in the US, in many of the therapeutic communities touch is frowned upon. You don't touch patients, you don't touch clients. I don't know what the legislation is in Scotland, but how did you discuss this, how do you clients respond, and what have you experienced as you introduce the issue of touch?*

C: I really want my clients to be self sufficient. I tend to explain it in a scientific way and I tend to show Havening Touch on myself.

I have clients self haven. I want them to self haven because I want them at the end of the session to be really used to doing it. I want them to be going home and feeling really confident about doing it, like it's a normal thing. We talk about how in a few years time everybody will be doing it.

Children often have fallen out with their families and they don't want anybody touching them. I see a lot of kids who have been diagnosed on the autistic spectrum. Working as well with a lot of mute people and disabled people, or people who are really distressed, quite often they don't want to be touched. So I have a bunch of ways of working with it.

The way I'm thinking about it is you're generating the delta waves and the chemical changes through the activation of the palms and the face and the outer arm. I don't really mind how we get that.

So when somebody's self-havening I want oxytocin as well. So I'll get them to think about somebody they really love, or it could even be a fairytale character or a celebrity or even somebody who's not with them anymore.

When they close their eyes and start doing the Havening touch they're imagining it being somebody else. I might show them a few different touches. I might say this is how so and so does Havening touch and then give them a range of touch, expanding their idea of what that touch might be like.

I also use the dog and the horses. So, I've had clients, disabled clients, and clients with learning disabilities stroking horses with their palms and putting their face on the horses shoulder, standing up. That works really really well. Holding maybe the front of the horse. These horses are trained for that kind of work. So that works really well, and we're getting the delta wave activation there.

The dogs are also really great. I have dogs that do this kind of work and allow themselves to be stroked and their faces rubbed on.

Recently I've developed a great teaching tool that has been a huge hit. People who have been really really traumatized and found it quite difficult to express themselves have used it and had good success.

It is a toy monkey. A big puppet monkey with long vibrating arms, so you can wrap him around you. His whole body vibrates. He's big. And his whole face vibrates. I have people hold him and they put their face into his face and he's got a lovely big smiley face. So when they look up they just see this face and people love him.

H: *So the embrace of the monkey becomes the same as Havening touch.*

C: Yeah. At first I was getting them to use their palms on the monkey but now the monkey's got such big arms you can wrap him right around their arms and shoulders and they can hold him on the front of them and they put their face in his face. He provides a kind of privacy for them and reminds some people of childhood pleasures.

H: *How beautiful. And through all of these different things, the horses, the dogs, the monkeys, the self-havening, what they're doing is they're increasing the delta wave production, the serotonin, the GABA, the oxytocin.*

C: Yes.

H: *Which speaks to the point that you made earlier: once you really understand the science, then you can access your own creativity and find so many different ways of accomplishing these core aims of potentiating, depotentiating and sculpting the neurology.*

C: Yes. I've also used riding the horse and have developed a very unique method, not a normal way of riding at all. I learned a lot from an amazing guy called James Shaw who's a Tai Chi master and author of the book Ride from Within. I've combined a lot of what I've learned from James.

James taught me a lot about how when you move the pelvis it changes what's going on in the skull through what moves up the spine. So I created a combination of what I knew myself, what I learned from James, and what I learned from the Rudens.

I also do a more straightforward Havening with the horse but I also do other things that are slightly different but connected in terms of understanding the science. And I use dance as well and music.

H: *This was one of the things as well that I admired so much about you when I first got involved in the Havening community. I also love to synthesize and synergize and integrate and you demonstrate that so beautifully. You're again taking the structure, the knowledge, the basic principles that Dr. Ruden articulated, but you're also integrating principles from Tai Chi and principles from NLP and principles from all of these other areas that you have studied.*

I was talking to Ulf Sandstrom in Sweden about this as well. I asked him what he loved most about Havening. His response? The structure. As we talked about it more he explained. "I love the understanding of what's happening neurobiologically, how that helps me integrate other kinds of tools in service of the client".

Paradoxically, Dr. Ruden's greatest contribution to the treatment of trauma as well as the activation of potential, may have more to do with the science behind Havening than the Havening touch itself.

C: And the beautiful thing about Havening touch is that you have it with you all the time. You don't have monkey there or horse there or whatever, but you do have your palms and you face and your arms.

It's so mobile and it's free! It's completely free and natural. And, it gives us an understanding of how we learn and how we unlearn.

I'm also fascinated how we can use it in education. One of the trickiest things that I've come across as an educator is how if I'm teaching an eight year old Havening, they'll get it just like that.

When you're teaching somebody who knows a lot, they can find it really hard and it's like something is blocking the new learning. So I've been finding that doing Havening before beginning to teach about it makes it easier to learn. Easier to teach as well I think.

H: *Yes, I do that as well. That brings me to another great point. There's are two schools of thought around tools like Havening. On the one hand, if you think about EMDR and how EMDR was introduced, it was introduced only to psychologists and trained mental health professionals. On the other hand, many of the energy psychology tools, such as tapping and EFT were introduced to everyone. Two schools of thought around how to introduce a tool and a modality like this. What's your perspective on who can use Havening and how they can use it in different contexts?*

C: I've had an interesting previous experience which might relate. I think I'll tell a little story because I find it a fascinating experience.

Before I was doing Havening I got involved in changing printmaking, which is an art form. It was developed 600 years ago as a certain way of doing things. The people who developed it were looking for materials to use, but in their time, the materials they used never really worked very well. 600 years later, along came me as a young teenager. I was learning NLP at the same time.

I noticed that the process of printmaking wasn't working well, and I noticed that everybody pretended it was. Basically they were in a kind of trance. So I thought—this is very interesting, everybody's hypnotized, so how can I de-hypnotize them and make them see that this doesn't work?

So I found a way of doing it. I ended up actually working out the principles, almost a bit like Dr. Ruden did with Havening. I worked out the principles of how these things work, I got involved with a top polymer scientist and we answered those questions from 600 years ago with modern science. We created materials that worked.

However, they were different colors, you put them on in a different way, and you washed them off with water. They were completely safe. The other ones gave people cancer and central nervous system depression and all sorts of dreadful things. They were also explosive and flammable.

So this was a super change. I was very excited. I wanted to go out into the world, give everybody this great gift and share these toys. What I found was that I could teach people who were completely new to it, people coming into the art world for the first time, for two days, and in those two days they could work to a professional standard. They knew what they were doing and they were making something that looked professional.

I could take that work, show it to the top professionals in the world, and ask them, 'What do you make of this—can you assess this for me?' They would say to me "Oh, this is so unfair! How'd you get all the best people coming to your studio? Where do you find them? We can't even find them at the best colleges in the world! Where are you finding these people?"

So I'd tell them: "This girl's sixteen, this guy's a plumber, this guy's eighty-two." The professionals were outraged.

In contrast every weekend professionals would come all from all over the world to learn and it was so difficult to teach them.

H: *Yes.*

C: Sometimes what would happen is I wouldn't have a space available in a professionals course so I would put them into a newcomers course. Literally the newcomers would look at the professionals who are going, "Wow look at that!" and they'd think they were mad.

The newcomers actually thought the 'professionals' were mad. The newcomers were just using the materials and getting results and it was safe. They weren't going to be poisoned or anything else. The professionals were going in and saying "Well yes but that's blue and you're using water with it. How could that possibly work?"

I see a parallel in that now because I believe that you can teach Havening to anyone so that the person can use it safely. I think that's true. And I think sometimes what happens with some professionals is the power of Havening makes them want to build a fence around it and say only a professional like me can use this.

H: *Yes. I've seen that in my various conversations with people around not only the use of this tool but other tools. It's almost as though the more knowledge that you have about something and the more fixed your paradigm of what is true, the less open you can be to new ways of thinking.*

C: Yes. Now you're touching on something that you asked early on, a question about what I had seen that was extraordinary. Here it is.

The way that the Victorians went out and categorized flowers and trees was this: they named some after whoever discovered it, others after Greek gods, others based on appearance or shape. They got all their names that way. Then quite recently geneticists analyzed the DNA of flowers. Lo and behold, they discovered that cabbages which are of the genus brassica, and roses, were actually part of the same family, with similar DNA.

H: *Of course.*

C: And this idea is important for the medical community, because it makes it much easier to see what the families are if you're looking for a drug or something. So they talked to the botanists and the botanists said 'no, let's keep the old Victorian names'. Even though the names were only labels that didn't express the deeper relationships.

What I'm noticing a lot is that we look at behaviors, we humans, and we label them. So if somebody's got some problem with food we look at them and say they're anorexic or they're bulimic, or they're overweight. If they've got some problems with some social phobia, or they are very sensitive to certain noises or color or some things like that, then we start saying they're on the autistic spectrum.

So there are all these labels and I'm seeing them through these labels. And that's fair enough, because that's a way for professionals to assess if somebody's doing this behavior and somebody's doing that behavior.

However, when you start really understanding the science of it and you start seeing what's up above those labels then you realize that these behaviors are simply the result of amygdala activation, the physical traumatization in the brain. So when you apply Havening and they depotentiate the AMPA receptors related to traumatic experiences so that the neural pathway is no longer there, the behaviors stop, and somebody analyzing that person could not label them in that way anymore.

H: *Exactly. And isn't it fascinating that all these so called different pathologies could be seen as basically various expressions of potentiated traumatically encoded memories.*

C: Yes.

H: *I mean what if that was the key underlying all of these different labels that people have spent billions of dollars and thousands of hours and hundreds of thousands of Ph.D.'s labeling?*

C: But sometimes finding that trauma linkage can be the tricky thing. So I've seen these labels come off. I've seen people no longer doing their anorexia. You couldn't put an OCD label on them, because they're not doing it anymore.

H: *Yes.*

C: And that fascinates me. Obviously I've seen things like that in NLP and hypnosis as well, but just being able to look at this through a neuroscientific lens has changed that for me.

H: *This is beautiful, Carol. I have just one more question to explore with you for now. Suppose you're speaking with a person who's looking into the possibility of adding Havening Techniques® to their tool kit. This person might be a counselor, therapist, mental health professional, coach, perhaps even a parent or teacher. What advice would you give somebody who's thinking, "maybe I want to take that training"? What would you say to them?*

C: Do it as soon as possible! Just do it. Really do it. Get the knowledge and get the hands-on training and become part of the community so you can ask the Rudens questions and you can ask the trainers questions. We're there and we're amazingly available. It's a very generous community.

H: *I can say this is the most generous, brilliant and giving professional community I've ever been part of. It's remarkable. What I love about the community is that it's filled with people who have really brilliant minds, loving hearts, plus, they are doers who get things done. For me this combination of head, heart, and hands is really very powerful. Thank you Carol.*

CHAPTER 9

Touching the future of
health care

Kimberly Ann Davis

Kimberly Ann Davis is a registered nurse, Medical Device Sales Manager, and founder and CEO, Endless Evolution LLC.

Harry: *Kimberly, how did you discover Havening?*

Kimberly: I was first introduced to Havening through a NLP class I attended. One of my fellow students had become interested in Havening because he was working in the criminal justice system, dealing with some highly emotional cases involving children's issues as well as child pornography. He'd made inroads with some of the criminal justice people regarding applications of Havening and after I spoke with him he introduced me to Dr. Ruden's book, *When The Past Is Always Present*.

The book intrigued me so much that I immediately sought out the training and purchased a ticket to attend. I felt that this was a tool that many nurses didn't know about; a tool that could be highly valuable to patients in their treatment regimen.

I found that because of my work in nursing that there was a high level of interest.

H: *Yes, that immediacy is familiar to me. You heard about it from your friend in criminal justice; you got the book; you signed up for the training almost immediately. That's what happened to me.*
Tell me about your nursing background and your current work.

K: I have worked as a nurse in the hospital, in the ER and in trauma care. I currently work in sales with a medical device that people can use at home for self-treatment. Much of my day-to-day routine involves interacting with doctors, nurses, and patients. My work focuses on education to increase patients' level of wellness and outcomes.

H: *In your daily work environment, who are the people who you interact with that you use Havening to help or who you teach Havening to as a self-care tool?*

K: I have close contact with patients. My speciality is nephrology. A lot of patients that I come into contact with are people who no longer have sustaining kidney function and are now reliant on a machine to keep them alive. Often they've had a lot of underlying trauma.

H: *So they're in dialysis?*

K: Correct. When patients go through this experience the nurses did not always understand that this patient has undergone this underlying trauma.
From what we've learned in Havening, a lot of people have a vulnerable neurochemical landscape which is impacted by the

person's history. Their history now includes going through this very traumatic medical experience, next transitioning from a hospital environment where they've learned that their kidneys have failed, and finally, transitioning into their new lifestyle, which includes their chronic need for treatment.

It's an interesting process because many people who undergo a lot of hospital experiences are traumatized by the news they're given, by their medical condition, and by the way they're feeling.

Part of the challenge is also in the way they personalize it and react. We know that some of the underlying trauma they've had in their earlier stages in life impacts whether or not they are able to follow a healthy life plan.

We also want to enable the patient to become empowered to pursue other methods of treatment which are better for their quality of life and help them live longer.

So I've worked with the nurses to help them understand why someone may be resistant to self-care. Also I've worked to help them understand more about this process and how far back in the patient's history this traumatization may have occurred.

I've also worked with nurses to help them understand their own history and landscape so that they can see how they may not be effective with patients because of their own underlying unaddressed issues. And that's where I found a high level of interest, working with the nurses, because they were taking care of the patients, but I identified early on that they weren't necessarily taking care of themselves.

H: *So you're comprehensively educating both the nurses and the patient about their role of traumatization in their symptoms and their well-being.*

K: Yes.

H: *That's beautiful. This educational aspect allows people to become more aware of the possible causative factors. How do you go from educating the nurses and patients to actually doing the Havening? Do you Haven them? Do you teach them how to use basic Havening processes? How specifically do you integrate Havening, beyond education, into your work?*

K: Because I have the nursing license, it allows me to be able to touch someone. So we have the ability to talk about Havening and demonstrate its impact.

In some instances I've demonstrated some of the techniques with the healthcare provider staff. We've had fun during a time when I've been in the clinic. Once they've experienced Havening, I've commented: 'since this is impactful for you, now do you want to do this with one of your patients?'

I have a patient who works with me who requested, after she learned that I had been through the Havening training, that I haven her. Now she shares her story with the nurses and doctors that I work with. She tells them how impactful the trauma of this physical experience was, shares the experience she had with me with Havening, and demonstrates how it's possible to do more for people without so much medication.

You know, in the medical community, because it's very research-based, sometimes there is some skepticism with physicians and nurses. They wonder if this is something that can really be impactful. So with them I've responded, 'well if you don't believe it, that it will work with a patient, I think the best way to try it is on you'. So the rapport I've built with some of my customers in the sales environment has allowed me access to working directly with the nurses.

H: *So you're leveraging the position you have and the trust you have with your clients and customers to bring this innovation into an environment that otherwise might not be as open to it. This brings me to my next question.*

Many people, for good reason, are skeptical when they first hear about Havening. The possibilities seem to be too good to be true plus it seems so simple. Were you skeptical at first? If so, what changed your mind?

K: I wasn't skeptical. I was intrigued by the technique and I volunteered for the demonstration for a specific reason. I wanted to feel the experience for myself. It was a perfect opportunity.

Havening intrigued me and I wanted to go through the physical experience myself. You know, you can understand the science behind it, but actually feeling it is a completely different experience. And during the volunteer experience that I had, I wasn't sure what would happen before I went in, but I was completely open to experiencing it. It intrigued me that something so simple could have a significant impact.

I have also found these tools very valuable with my children.

H: *How so? How many kids do you have?*

K: I have two. My children are 11 and 14. One of my children, the 11 year old, is very receptive to things that I learn. Around the time I learned Havening she would from time to time have periods of insomnia. She was very receptive to Havening and immediately grabbed onto it. She allowed me to Haven her and within 5 minutes she was completely asleep.

My older child has a diagnosis of Aspergers, and has had difficulty with self-expression. He was not so receptive at first. My daughter would rave about it and say, "You should try this." He was a little more cautious.

However, over time, we slowly started integrating it and from what I saw, he was actually able to start expressing himself more. Havening touch is actually very similar to a brushing technique that is used with children with Aspergers and autism.

H: *That's remarkable.*

K: His anxiety about expressing himself went down to the point where he is now receptive to more of the technique. This has made a profound impact on his life. We did Havening prior to him parasailing over the summer. He had a tremendous fear of heights. A half hour before he went parasailing we havened him. I noticed a tremendous decrease in his fear and anxiety level. I saw more relaxation and I saw his success. We have the whole thing on HD video! Amazing.

H: *I imagine it gives you a sense of pride and delight as a mother to be able to share that gift with your own children.*

K: It does. It's a learning experience for them and I can give this to them even at their ages of 11 and 14. We learned during the Havening training about the impact of early trauma. My son was born with a cord around his neck. And he had a sensitivity, although he didn't have a diagnosed medical condition, where his body postures himself to protect his neck. The Havening Techniques, along with that insight, allowed me to go all the way back to his infancy and help him address this.

H: *That reminds me of a client I worked with whose son was exhibiting lots and lots of unprovoked anger and rage directed towards* *his mom. And what we discovered is that when he was born he had a particular medical condition that required separation from his mother. It also required various procedures that were very painful and his mother was there when these procedures were happening.*

And so as an infant, we're talking 2 or 3 days to a week old, he took on this traumatization and associated his mother with the others who were doing this procedure. Of course the baby was angry; he perceived that these supposed caregivers, including his mother, were causing his pain and suffering.

Once we havened that experience, the anger and rage against mom completely dissolved. And this wasn't anything he had been conscious of. His mom just told me, these were the conditions of his birth. Literally at age three or four days this memory had become traumatically encoded and then twenty-something years later that unconscious traumatically encoded memory was activating this rage, this anger response. And then after one session of Havening, this issue simply dissolved. I spoke with his mom a few days ago. It's been a year since we worked, and that anger/rage response is gone. It's remarkable.

K: It is remarkable. It's amazing how you can help people.

H: *Yes, and once you understand the science, the neurobiology behind it, then I find that the questions I ask the client are very different. The intake interview is very different. The things that I look for in a conversation are very different, because you're constantly scanning like Sherlock Holmes, not only for these individual traumatizations, but also for the larger patterns, the different occasions in the persons life where traumatic encoding might have occurred.*

I'm fascinated with how you have implemented what I would call 360 degree application. You've used Havening for your own healing, you're using it with your kids, you're helping your friends, you're us-

ing Havening within the work context to help the nurses, the doctors, your colleagues and patients.

Do you have any other stories that you'd be willing to share about some of your experiences using Havening to help others?

K: The one story that really stands out to me was the opportunity to be with someone who was on a ventilator. And what happened with her and her response from the intervention which utilized the techniques, was so amazing because you were looking at someone who couldn't talk.

H: *What exactly did you do with this person?*

K: She was on the ventilator, receiving a dialysis treatment at the same time. That's how I gained access to her. The ventilator was alarming frequently. They were saying that she was agitated, they had mitts on her, saying that she was pulling at things. I asked, "Can I sit with her? I want to demonstrate something that could help." They said okay. And as I was working with her she started responding. Within a five minute period of time she relaxed, and the ventilator stopped alarming.

I used some other communication techniques with her, certain words, because you now have to speak for them because she can't speak since she has a ventilator. And she would respond through hand cueing. She'd start tapping my arm, when I'd hit the right button with her. There was an intuitive process that occurred along with the Havening.

You could see the relaxation and you could reinforce it. You could, through suggestion, find a path to relieve this patient of whatever she was going through at the time. I continued to work with her, and I said, "You know what? I'm not going to leave this woman until she's better". "Are you okay with me continuing to sit with her?" I kept asking the staff because they saw her continuing to relax.

I could see her respond. I didn't want to leave her because I knew I was getting through to her. So after working with her for about forty-five minutes, she fell asleep. Everyone in the room said, "We have never seen her sleep before."

During that time I was explaining the Havening process, including the neurobiology of the technique. For some nurses, who had a 'you need to show me to believe it' attitude, it was so significant for the patient to be cueing me in on certain things.

We actually did the humming; she couldn't speak but she could hum. I was looking for certain things that she could hum and I said have you gone to church? Do you dance? And there were certain things with her that just cued in, she said yes. And when she tapped 'yes' to church, I said, "Amazing Grace, is this something you like?" and she kept tapping and tapping and tapping. And that's what we did.

This was a person who was physically restrained. She not only has had this traumatic experience, which now required a breathing tube beyond her control, but also the nurses were misunderstanding why she was moving around and possibly at risk for dislodging this device. And they thought she was pulling at everything. I'm saying, 'no, she's trying to communicate with you'.

For the nurses who were there, I spent time with them showing them when she's on treatment how to reinforce what I did with her. And I came back and did the technique again. The administrator for the nursing home was there and said you need to teach all of my staff how to do this. There were fifty patients on ventilators in the unit. So I was able to train the respiratory therapist how to do this first because he had the most context.

H: *Now what exactly did you train them? Did you teach them Event Havening or basic Havening touch?*

K: Just Havening touch. And he'd call me on a weekly basis and say "I can't believe how amazing this is!" It's something so simple with such a profound effect.

H: *The fact that you could do this and this impact could happen with someone who is in such a significant degree of physical restraint where communication is blocked, where they're experiencing these physical challenges is beautiful.. As well as the fact that this simple tool, plus your skill in communicating, your sensory acuity, your attentiveness, your compassion and your love could open up a gateway of healing that had been previously closed.*

K: It's been so much fun to get out there with the Havening because it actually opens pathways and possibilities for people that you never thought would have existed.

H: *What's your vision for how Havening could impact healthcare practices in general in the next decade or so? What do you see happening in terms of how Havening could impact how we take care of ourselves, how doctors and nurses and hospitals and healthcare professionals care for their patients?*

K: There's several different components. Nurses have the ability to apply the physical touch; it's part of their care. We've used massage and things like that for a significant period of time, but if they moved forward with learning some of the Havening Techniques with patients, they could have many different applications depending on the specialty they work in. Depending on the goal.

Many times there's a big disconnect between what healthcare providers think and what patients feel they need. Patients have a very different perspective. They want more care from healthcare providers. They want more attention. They don't have a desire to particularly go in the direction of medication, of pharmaceuticals anymore.

In certain groups and support groups that I worked in, they're very receptive to learning about simple ways that they could help or heal themselves. Havening provides an avenue to help in many different ways, whether it's for pain relief, anxiety relief, drug and alcohol addiction, post traumatic stress disorder. It's somewhat overwhelming at first because you realize you can help everyone!

H: *When I was on my way back from New York, after my first Havening workshop, I was sitting in the airport, looking around at people. Everybody I put my eyes on, I'm thinking, "I can help you. I can help you. I can help you."*

K: It does become like that. You just want to be able to apply your hands to people and help them. I can tell you even in some of the environments I'm in, it may not be a frequent contact but it might be someone I see from time to time, and just a few seconds of some Havening touch has an impact on that person.

I don't think it always needs to be 15 to 30 to 45 minutes. Of course, there are different techniques that you could apply. But when you do the same technique on everyone in a short period of time, you leave the residual benefits behind. That's what I love about Havening.

In a sales environment it's been profound. You know you're having a positive impact on their brain chemistry because you can see them relax.

H: *I have this image of you. It's like the Disney cartoons with the fairy godmother who has a magic wand and when she waves her wand you see all this sparkling fairy dust! And it changes people. I'm imagining your hands are like her magic wand. You're going all over the place and everywhere you go this light comes out of your hands and then people are transformed!*

K: It's my goal and my passion now. Now that I've learned this technique from Dr. Ruden, I think that there's so much opportunity to educate healthcare providers. I think nurses are very receptive, as well as nurse practitioners because they spend so much more time with people in an office environment; they have more time to do this. And it's particularly important now because there's concern in the healthcare environment about patient re-hospitalization. About our need to re-treat and re-treat and re-treat. This all needs to change because it just seems like they're not using something that is so valuable—human touch.

H: *Yes, and as you also mentioned, nurses are licensed to touch, which is a huge advantage.*

K: Yes. Use your hands!

H: *Suppose you were talking to somebody who's a nurse or a nurse practitioner or a nurses aide or somebody in this healthcare field who was considering taking the Havening training and adding Havening to their toolkit, what would you tell them?*

K: In my career, I've used all of the nursing tools that I've learned over the last 22 years, but when I learned Havening it was the tool that I wish I had from the beginning.

For the nurses, it helps you as much as the patient, because when you're utilizing the touch technique you're also shifting your own neurobiology. So there's a mutual benefit.

Nursing can be very stressful. In the nursing environment there have been documented cases of nurses who have stolen narcotics to cope with their own stress. I worked with a nurse who did this. Sometimes nurses have substance abuse issues themselves. If you employed this technique all day long you would be self medicating in a natural way. What could be a better opportunity? It's a win for you, it's a win for the patient. So, you both could be doing this all day long.

H: *I was speaking to another Havening practitioner, a psychologist who works with chronic complex PTSD patients, and one of the things that she said is the most powerful for clinicians who would be interested in Havening is that fact that when you haven all day you don't take on any of the client's stress.*

Very often nurses or counselors or social workers feel exhausted at the end of the day because they've dealt with people who are in such intense physical or emotional pain. And when you're Havening all day, you don't take it on. So you can have a day of working with people who are suffering greatly and having difficult times and when you walk out the door at the end of the day you still feel better than you did that morning. And you've helped all those people! This self-protective aspect of Havening is one of the most remarkable side benefits.

K: It is. Before I worked in nephrology, I worked in emergency room and trauma nursing. When I was working in trauma nursing we would be riding on the helicopter, going to a scene of whatever trauma had occurred and you're going in there to save someone's life. Very similar to what an Army or a Navy combat medic might do.

That's why I know people can use some of the Havening Techniques® with policemen and also ambulance personnel and others in similar situations because what you see is quite shocking.

I think Havening should be part of the curriculum in nursing schools and emergency responder training, because you need to be able to self-heal or not take on that kind of work. It really impacts you to be in that environment every single day. It impacts you to deal with people who are dying. It impacts you to be with people who feel hopeless. You're constantly exposed to suffering. In these traumatic situations, there's no tool available to manage that vicarious trauma, and most people in that situation simply disconnect. How do you maintain a healthy sense of self without absorbing everything that you are exposed to? This is where Havening comes in.

H: *It's as though the Havening process inoculates you against the impact of the vicarious trauma that you're witnessing.*

K: It can. Sometimes when I'm exposed to something negative, I'll just use a little Havening while I'm driving the car and rubbing my fingertips together. Within five minutes it's gone. The negative experience doesn't exist anymore. It's no longer part of my realm.

H: *Remarkable.*

K: It is remarkable. I love it. It is like your fairy godmother metaphor. I do use Havening everywhere—if the person is receptive to it, we'll just spend five minutes, outside of what I'm doing within my work. I want to make you feel good. I want to keep you healthy in your environment. I care about you as a person. And it becomes a simple gift that I can give you.

H: *Kimberly, since you attended this workshop in March 2016, which was eight months ago, how many people have you touched literally or figuratively with Havening? Do you have an estimate of the number?*

K: 329! I have a ticker sheet.

H: *Wow! You've probably set a record there in terms of the greatest number of people reached within a few months of the training. That is beautiful.*

K: 329. I have the actual hashmarks. It was a distraction to my work as well because I asked myself, "What could be fun in this environment?" and then I started putting hashmarks on my calendar. And then I started thinking, 'I'm going to four places, can I haven five or six people today'? And it was a fun activity to do along with everything else. I just get absolutely giddy about Havening.

H: *Do you have a goal for reaching a specific number by the end of the year? 400, 500?*

K: I didn't really set a goal to the end of the year. I just wanted to continue the momentum and consider that I could be touching five, six, seven, eight people a day.

H: *Fabulous. I think we need to inspire everybody in the Havening community to do that. Imagine all of those hands touching all those other people all over the world. I'm just imagining the fairy dust spreading all over the planet.*

K: If you have the rapport, you can touch anyone.

H: *That's true. And you can touch them in many ways. You're touching them with your hands, but you're also touching them with your heart. And I think that's also one of the beautiful things about Havening; it combines the head—intellectual knowledge, the heart—love and caring, and the hands—touch—all together. Any final comments you'd like to share for those who will be reading what we've shared today?*

K: I would say to other people that hopefully my experience and what I've shared here leads you to take a look at Havening. I think that we are on the brink of something amazing for many people and all over the world. And I would highly encourage people to do it because of my experience. I know how much it's changed my life and how I can be of service to other people in my mission. So I would highly recommend Havening. Learning and using it can be a life-changing experience.

H: *Thank you.*

CHAPTER 10

Phantom limbs, chronic pain, and PTSD

Chris Meaden

Chris Meaden is a NLP Master Practitioner, clinical hypnotherapist and performance coach with clinics in Harley Street London and Tunbridge Wells, UK.

Harry: *Chris, how did you discover Havening in the first place?*

Chris: I discovered Havening through my mentor and friend, Steve Crabb, back in 2012. Steve works closely with Paul McKenna, who has been a champion for Havening techniques since the beginning. We saw Paul using it at one of his seminars, and I started practicing in 2012 using the techniques and getting good results. Then I attended the first official training in May 2013, when Ron Ruden came over to London.

H: *Who are your typical clients?*

C: The vast majority of my clients come to me for relief from panic attacks, anxiety and PTSD. I'm also a sports performance coach, and I've used Havening in that context with fantastic results. I found that the greatest results achieved using Havening happen at the more extreme ends of trauma, like PTSD. I find it's incredible how fast we can effect change.

H: *How has Havening transformed your practice?*

C: I was already getting great results, but it amplified the results and made them happen in a shorter period of time.

H: *And now, you use Havening with the vast majority of your clients?*

C: Every client. I've used Havening with thousands of clients over the years. It's groundbreaking, particularly in terms of the speed. And many of my clients have spent a fortune with other modalities, doing CBT, doing EMDR, counselling, spending thousands of pounds without getting the result, and then they come to me and do one or a few two-hour sessions and they're done after spending years and a huge amount of money to try and fix themselves.

H: *What are some of the most remarkable things you've seen? Any stories you care to share?*

C: There's too many! A lady I worked with recently. She was giving birth to her daughter, and they had to rush her in to have an emergency C-section. She actually died for a few seconds, and she had an out-of-body experience. She floated up out of her body. She could see the operating theatre and her husband

and the doctors around her. They had to restart her heart, and then she went back into her body.

She developed PTSD from this incident. She would recall this event every single day. As a result, she attempted suicide three times. She spent a fortune on therapies to try and get herself fixed. By the time she came to me, she was a broken woman. She had destroyed her marriage, she had destroyed her relationship with her daughter, and she was ready to give up on life.We worked together twice, for a total of four hours, and her life transformed. In fact, she tells her story in a video on our website.

I find that the videos which I post on the website reassure people that they can make a change. You can see the difference in her, and that she can't quite comprehend how much has shifted. That was an amazing case, and I saw her only a few months ago, in September.

I had a guy who came to me for anxiety. He was in his forties, and he'd lost his arm from the top of his shoulder. When he was about 20, he was visiting the Greek Islands. He hired a moped, came around the corner, hit a lorry. Woke up three days later in Athens, realizing his arm had been removed, amputated to save him from bleeding to death. He had a lot of phantom limb pains. It was taken off right at the shoulder, so there's no limb whatsoever. Imagine it: this guy has come around the corner and gone into this lorry. The last thing that happened was this: he's grabbing hold of the handlebars as hard as he can to brace for the impact. He couldn't remember the moment of impact, but his phantom limb, the whole of his hand, his arm, always felt taut, tense, like he was clasping his hands together. So, I got him to recall the event as best he could, and then I Havened him.

Afterwards, he said his hand had opened up and all the muscles in his arm (which, of course wasn't there—he was experiencing the phantom limb) became loose. So, it's as though he just let go of the tight grip on the handlebars, because the encoding was in the brain, not in the limb. And Havening allowed his brain to release the gripping in the phantom limb. That was really cool.

I had another guy, Ryan. When he was first born, he had a heart operation, and he was in and out of the hospital for ten years or so, so he had a bit of a rough start in life. He went on holiday to Mexico and had a real problem with his stomach, and ended up unable to eat. He had a series of four or five operations, which went wrong because of medical blunders. He also had extreme pain and anger.

The only thing that helped was standing in the shower with scorching hot water just on his chest to take away the pain. He would literally do this for an hour or two at a time. And he said he either did that, or he had to smoke some weed to ease the pain. Those were the only two things which could actually allow the pain to go away.

So, as you might imagine, this guy was really, really angry with how he was treated by the medical community. He spent a whole year in constant pain, and they kept on suggesting that it was all in his head, that there wasn't really anything wrong with him.

And every time he travelled overseas, this pain fired off again, since the first event happened overseas in Mexico. His amygdala recognized every time he flew away overseas, the pain would return, and he couldn't function. He would end up just drinking milkshakes at McDonald's.

I used Havening, got him to recall the events, used a lot of Transpirational

Havening and completely removed the pain and the anger. This guy no longer has any pain at all in his chest. All the anger and rage which was inside him is gone, and he's now living a normal life. He also had spent a fortune on different techniques. He's on a video on the website, as well.

I think with Havening, it's about having an open mind, because we're still only really discovering; we're just at the tip of what Havening can do.

H: *Yes. Many people are skeptical when they first hear about Havening, because it sounds too good to be true. Were you skeptical at first, and if so, what changed your mind?*

C: I suppose I've always been quite open to different techniques anyway, but certainly, you know, there was a certain degree of scepticism when I attended the first training. But I saw tangible results achieved so quickly, often in minutes.

I think one of the things to address with Havening is that, whilst we can remove encoded trauma, another important part is the coaching. You are often changing the identity of a person by removing an extreme trauma, so they need to be coached.

Although the Havening element is fantastic for removing the initial encoding, I think you need to have good skills and techniques to coach the person, because you are facilitating a huge shift, and you've got to make sure that when you clear that trauma, that they can move forward in their lives. Often, it's scary for them when the trauma is removed, because suddenly they're no longer in that familiar space. It's a new feeling, and often they respond with more fear.

So skilful coaching is needed with Havening.

H: *Thank you. Speaking of the kind of skills you need to successfully use Havening, I'm curious to learn your thoughts on this issue. You can look at a YouTube video and you learn the basic steps to Havening. Why is it important that somebody actually get trained in Havening who's interested in using it? Why is important for somebody to train?*

C: Yes there are quite a few videos. Also, Ron's got two great books out there—*The Craving Brain* and *When The Past Is Always Present*. So, there's a level of detail in those books—both great reads. But books and videos are not enough.

It's the understanding of how the brain encodes trauma, what happens at a neurochemical level that really impacts your level of skill and competency.

Whilst you can learn the basics of Havening touch by looking at videos, it doesn't give you insight as to exactly how to depotentiate trauma. I see hundreds of clients every year for PTSD, anxiety, and panic attacks, and anyone who thinks that you can just pick it up and use it with these kinds of clients is misinformed.

There can be extreme reactions, and it's really important to understand what you're doing. And the process of training and certification is about really making sure that the end user can feel reassured that the person working with them is competent.

H: *What excites you the most about the possibilities of Havening?*

C: I think to be able to help people heal in this way is amazing. And we're using something as simple as human touch. You know, it's the most natural process that we can effect change. I just think it's just amazing that Ron has looked at all the various studies and concluded that this is what we can do. And I think as it evolves, we're going to help heal so many people in the world.

H: *What advice would you give somebody who's looking into the possibility of adding Havening to their toolkit? Maybe they're a coach, maybe they're a therapist or a counsellor. What would you say to them?*

C: I'd say go ahead. It's a no-brainer. The other techniques, they all have their plus points, but adding Havening amplifies the results in so many positive ways. The small charge which is being made for the training is worth every cent, it really is. You will get that money back so quickly. And it's not only about using this technique to apply to other people. It's the impact it has on you as a person as well. Every practitioner who I've worked with has realized, wow, I was carrying things around I never realized. Even though these practitioners were well-trained in other modalities, they still found that Havening helped them let go of a whole load of things. So, there's a real personal benefit to learning Havening, as well as applying it in your practice.

H: *Thank you so much.*

CHAPTER 11

The sky's the limit

Bill Solz

Bill Solz is a licensed clinical social worker and credentialed alcohol and substance abuse counselor in private practice in Long Island, New York.

Harry: *Bill, how did you first discover Havening?*

Bill: It's an interesting story. I've been part of a networking group, and I'm the only psychotherapist in the group. There was a guy in the group whose job was cleaning houses, and he knew that I specialized in trauma. He approaches me one day and he says, "Bill, you hear about the Havening?" And I said, "No, what are you talking about?" He says, "Come on, man. You've got to get on board with this stuff." I said, "Lou, I've never heard about it." And, he said, "This is like the latest thing going. It's really catching on big time in the UK! You've got to come on board!"

Now here I am. I'm really scratching my head saying, why is this something I don't know about, but here's a guy who cleans homes who knows about it? So this was very much a puzzle. As it turns out, Lou is none other than Lou Falco, who is a Vietnam War veteran, and he heads up a group called Operations Initiative, which addresses the PTSD needs of vets.

I hardly knew Lou at this point, and here he is telling me I need to learn this, I have to find out more about it. And I'm just as skeptical as skeptical could be. Finally I say, "Okay. Okay. How do I find out?" So, he says, "Bill, I'm going to introduce you to the twin brother of the guy who developed it," who was Steve Ruden.

As it turned out, this was in the summer of 2013, and Steve had gotten a few other interested people together, and we met him at his dental office. So this is only getting more and more curious. I was not so pleased about any of this, because it was a bit of a ride for me to get to Steve's office, and now I'm going to a dentist's office to teach me about a trauma protocol? I was hardly enthused.

And then, I met Steve. He asked me my background, and I told him I'm involved with EMDR and the Developmental Needs Meeting Strategy, and he was curious about them, and we got to talking a little bit about each of them. And then, when a couple of other people got there, he started to just talk in general about Havening—nothing really too dramatic, only to really advise us that they were having their first New York City workshop in October of 2013, and he wanted to invite me to attend, and with that, he was going to give me a modest scholarship.

I was interested, because, I have specialized in trauma. It's been the big bulk of my practice. As a matter of fact, EMDR put me on the map as a trauma professional. I became the primary referral source for the Long Island Railroad, for TWA and for American Airlines. When each of those agencies' employees or family members sustained tragedies, I was the go-to guy for them, and that was all courtesy of EMDR.

So, now, if there was an opportunity to learn more, I'm always interested in growing, and so I signed up for the October workshop, really not having a clue what I was getting into.

As the weekend unfolded I really came to understand the power of this tool. Havening was quicker and more user-friendly than EMDR. Also, a real plus of Havening is there didn't seem to be restrictions for individuals who were abusing alcohol or other drugs, and a big, big part of my practice has been working with individuals with alcohol and substance abuse issues, and my belief is that, for quite a great deal of that population, their use only emanates from an inability to effectively manage their emotions.

So, as a result, over the years, I've been doing lots of relapse prevention workshops where, indeed, I've utilized and focused on EMDR, Thought Field Therapy, and the Developmental Needs Meeting Strategy. And for EMDR in particular, you definitely needed the client to first get clean and sober before you could implement it, which I understood, but at the same time, it really wasn't addressing my needs in the sense that I believe if we could clear out the underlying upset first, then there would no longer be the need to use. And Havening certainly gave me that ability.

As a matter of fact, I remember as I went into that weekend, and I learned more about Havening, I had in mind this client of mine, who was a 17-year-old kid with rage issues. He was a heavy-duty marijuana smoker, and he'd been suspended from high school multiple times. I had just started working with him in July. His rage definitely emanated from the fact that his father abandoned him, took up with another woman, and subsequently had two kids with her.

So, my idea, and the agreement I contracted with him, was that we would do EMDR to address the underlying issue with him, provided that he become clean from any other drug use. And he actually embarked on that for two weeks, but I told him I would have to drug test him at the end of the month. And, sure enough, before the end of the month arrives, he tells me he used, and all bets were off.

So I end up being very excited that weekend when I'm hearing there was not that restriction with Havening, because I definitely had this 17-year-old kid in mind. Indeed, he was the first client that I used Havening with. And sure enough, we end up addressing the abandonment. And this was my first session, the Monday after the training. His level of rage was a ten and I got him down to a five, and that was the end of it.

I never saw that kid again, which certainly disappointed me, but the reality was, for this kid, he did not want to lose all that rage. And I certainly believe he was fearful of that, and that's why he didn't come back. But the net result was, because I followed him with his guidance counselor, this kid went on incident-free. When I say incident-free, he never got suspended again for the rest of the year. This is going from the beginning of October through June. He graduated, went to college, and then I lost track of him. But this certainly spoke to the efficacy of Havening.

But even more so, I have to say, with each of the treatment approaches that I've learned, and I've already shared three of them with you, I find myself being the biggest skeptic going into it, and I feel like I come from Missouri, the Show-Me State. You know, show me.

Here's the difference Havening made for me, personally. In May of 2013, just a few months before the training, I ended up separating from my wife of 34 years. In general, I'm a very grounded, stable individual. However, going through this separation and divorce—which, mind you, still isn't even completely done —I ended up encountering tremendous emotional upset, more under the heading of anger, which is an emotion that has been foreign to me for most of my life.

In any event, what happened is I left the marriage at the end of May, and you are required to write a statement of personal net worth. Now, that, in and of itself, was very challenging for me, because she managed all the bills and I didn't. So it was a very big learning curve. But, every time I sat down to do it, I couldn't do it. The lawyers were asking me for it. And here was the weekend of the training, and I was actually considering blowing off the training just to sit down and get that statement done. But the reality was, I haven't done it for three months. What makes me think I'm going to do it that weekend? So I said, let me go to the training.

It turned out that Saturday night, we end up taking part in role-playing, therapist-client, and vice versa. So, the person who ended up Havening me was this gal, and I ended up working on my divorce, my separation. It was one of these 80-, 85-degree days in Manhattan, and I'm wearing just this cotton shirt.

At that time, I had just met a woman who became my girlfriend. We had plans that night after the training ended. I would meet her at a show in Manhattan and she would introduce me to her sister.

And now, I go through this Havening thing. Harry, I swear to God, my cotton shirt that I was wearing just became full of perspiration. I sweated through this whole damn shirt, and now here I am. I had to hop a cab to meet her on time, and I literally got over to her as a total wreck, my shirt all full of perspiration, and she looks at me and she says, "Bill, what happened to you?" I said, "Don't even ask. Don't even ask." And she said, "Bill, this is my sister," and that's how I met her family. In my sweat-soaked cotton shirt.

But, that night, let me tell you what ends up happening. We see the show, I take her home, then I return to my apartment. No sooner do I return than I sit down at the table and knock off that statement of personal net worth.

I saw right then and there the power of Havening as, indeed, my anger had blocked me from being able to proceed. And so, right then and there, obviously I was sold. And I haven't looked back since.

H: *Great story. Thank you. It's been three years since you took the workshop. Is Havening the primary tool you use with clients now?*

B: It has become that, and indeed, I no longer really use EMDR or TFT. I use some great protocols from EMDR that help reduce one's level of urge to use. But, in terms of actually addressing trauma, I definitely do not use EMDR for that.

H: *What do you find to be the most significant advantages of Havening versus EMDR? Because what I've noticed is, as I've spoken to about a half dozen people thus far, who, like you, were primarily focused on EMDR as their go-to tool for addressing trauma, and every single one of them who's become involved in Havening eventually replaces EMDR with Havening.*

B: Yeah. Havening is faster. So, let's say for EMDR, and I've been certified in EMDR since '96, it would probably take at least three sessions for me to set up things before I can even begin to address trauma with utilizing EMDR, whereas Havening, if I really want to be aggressive, as I tend to be, I can use

Havening in the first session. As far as I'm concerned, there's nothing more quick-acting than Havening.

What I found is that the clients who come to me come to me with a presenting problem. "I can't sleep," "I'm angry"—whatever their issue is. And what my practice has boiled down to is this: I'll do an intake with them, session number one, I do a full psychosocial history, alcohol and drug history, and a brief trauma history with them, all in the first session. And then, invariably, the second session, I'll do Havening. So, the net result has been after two sessions, my clients are feeling much, much better, their presenting problem has been ameliorated, and really, in truth, what has happened for me is my clients have been very grateful and they've gone along their merry way.

With EMDR it's much longer, even from the setup phase. Clients experience far more abreactions. And mind you, there are many, many people who have been trained in EMDR who never even look to utilize it, only because they can't take the emotional end of things. That is not at all the case with Havening.

Just to give you an idea, one of the reasons the Long Island Railroad loved me, and they would refer to me all their employees who were engineers who had killed people crossing the tracks, is that I could help them get back to work. What would happen is they'd be so traumatized, they could no longer continue. For many of the engineers, that wasn't just their one-time situation. It could have been their third incident. And, indeed, the railroad had a vested interest in terms of getting them back to work.

Interestingly enough, each of the guys I treated were able to go back. On average, it would take me six sessions to resolve their trauma using EMDR. EMDR worked great, people felt better and they went back to work. Now with Havening, I could argue that I could easily do it in two sessions.

So when you ask me where I stand, as far as utilizing my various approaches, Havening has easily become number one. Number two is called the Developmental Needs Meeting Strategy, and it's something that I'm really very proud of, as I'm very much the only practitioner in the metropolitan area who knows it. It's all about the healing of inner child wounds. So, when I compare Havening to DNMS I look at Havening as almost like a laser, and the DNMS is really the most comprehensive treatment approach that I know.

So when people take on negative beliefs, such as "I'm not good enough", "I'll never amount to anything", they've taken on negative messages from significant others, whether they're the parents, spouses, colleagues, friends. It could come from, really, anywhere, but those negative messages have become Velcro'd onto them in such a way that they become disempowered, and they could never fully, meaningfully achieve anything, because they have this underlying belief. So, DNMS is incredibly supportive and very effective, certainly much quicker than just traditional CBT, or cognitive behavioral therapy, or what I would regard as talk therapy.

H: *Based on your extensive experience as a therapist and counselor, how do you see Havening impacting mental health practice into the future, the next ten, twenty years?*

B: I think it's going to blow wide open, and believe me, I'm very proud of the fact that I ended up literally becoming the 17th person in the world to be certified in Havening.

If there was a good research protocol that was done, I am convinced that Havening will easily supplant EMDR and really just shoot right up there as a recognizable treatment approach.

Francine Shapiro developed EMDR. And huge, huge credit goes to her, because she was extremely proactive, in terms of encouraging colleagues who were new to the field. It was developed in '87, and I was one of the newer practitioners. But when I first got started, EMDR wasn't recognized as evidence-based, and indeed, I would put my work out there against the other psychologists, who basically told me that what I was doing was a joke. But once the research proved its efficacy, EMDR was able to make a name for itself.

H: *Yes. Dr. Shapiro has been incredibly proactive in terms of generating solid research. EMDR might be one of the most well-researched interventions there is.*

Any more Havening stories, Bill?

B: I'm at a networking event. It turns out I meet this chiropractor. He's talking about the good work that he does with athletes. And he goes on to tell me his one frustration is that he can't get on TV, and he would love to really promote what he's doing. So, of course, I said, "Why not?" And he ends up telling me he's had a history of panic attacks for 23 years.

So, I said, "Have you ever looked to get help for that?" He said, "Are you kidding me? I've been in and out of counseling forever and nothing's helped." So, I said, "How about my introducing Havening to you?", which, of course, he'd never heard of. "How would you feel about that?" And he says, "I will be personally indebted to you for the rest of my life if you could ever do anything for me."

H: *Wow.*

B: So, I know he's a busy guy. He's in Manhattan. I say, "You know what? You tell me when I could come over to your office, and give me, 40 minutes of your time, and I'm sure I could make a difference." So, we set it up, and what ends up happening is I'm talking to him, and I asked him, when he first experienced panic attacks.

Sure enough, 23 years ago, he had just gone into the field of chiropractic and he had a very demanding supervisor who was dissatisfied with him, would give him tons of work to do. This young practitioner couldn't cope, and that's when he started having panic attacks. It turns out he also has to do a ten-minute talk the very next day in one of his networking groups that he was a member of. So, I said, "Okay. Let's address each of those."

When I asked him to think of that memory 23 years ago, he was at a nine or a ten, and then I also asked him to think of his anxiety pertaining to tomorrow's talk, which was an eight. So, anyway, I decided to proceed with Havening the initial upset 23 years ago. Pretty quickly, that goes down to a zero, and he says, "Bill, I have never, ever felt so good." Period. "So, what number at you at?" He said, "Bill, it doesn't bother me." He's at a zero. The next thing is I said, "What about your anxiety related to tomorrow's talk?" And, he was at a zero with that, too. So, my whole point is if you get at the root of things, you have the ability to clear everything out. That's why he was at a zero.

Now what happens is the next day, he gives his talk, and then my phone is going bonkers with text messages from him. "You are the man, you're the man, you've got to get the word out. I just knocked this out of the park. That was the best talk I ever did. I was complimented up the kazoo by this one and that one." He couldn't stop raving about me.

And then he came to me for a couple sessions related to some other stuff, and unfortunately, I've lost track of him. Anyway, I looked on his Facebook page just a few months ago, and how does he regard himself now? On his Facebook page, it's "Mr. So-and-So: Public speaker, Chiropractor."

H: *What a transformation.*

B: Here's another story. Last one. I'm doing a presentation, a workshop at the Hicksville Chamber of Commerce. So, there are about 20, 25 people in the audience, and you know what? Quite often, it is hard to get a volunteer, but four people—obviously friends or colleagues of his—are urging this one guy to come up, and he does, reluctantly.

Mind you, I had only ten minutes left in my workshop, and I told the guy I wanted to do a demonstration at the end, and then all of a sudden he's telling me there's only ten minutes, so I wasn't too pleased with that. Anyway, I get this guy up. Again, I don't know what his issue is.

I ask him to think back to the memory. Zero to ten, he was at an eight. And we go through the Havening process, and I said, "Okay, where are you at now?" He says, "Bill, it doesn't bother me." And I said, "Just give me a number, you know." And he says, "Bill, you don't get it. It doesn't bother me." So, I said, "Are you telling me you're at a zero?" He said, "Yeah." He's at a zero.

And he was so excited, he ends up saying to me, "Do you mind if I share with the group what my issue is?" And I said, "Well, that's totally up to you." And, of course, I don't know what his issue is, so it's not a secret between us, you know. But he says, "No, I want to." So, I said, "Okay, knock yourself out."

What he went on to say gave me chills. "I happened to have been on the 78th floor of the World Trade Center in 1993 when they had to evacuate. And thank God I got out of there with my life. But I've had sleep irritability. I've had a whole host of symptoms related to that incident." And here he is, telling me he's at a zero.

That wasn't the end of it. This happens in April of 2014. So, I ran into this guy at a restaurant the following September, quite by accident, and I don't even know who this guy is, you know. It's not like he's a friend of mine. And I said, "By the way, how are you doing related to that memory?" He said, "Bill, I told you. It no longer bothers me." And I said, "Well, you know, obviously this is some time later." He said, "You don't get it. It doesn't bother me." He's at a zero. So, that's when, for sure, I saw how efficacious this was and that it can hold.

H: *What advice would you give somebody who's looking into adding Havening to their toolkit?*

B: What advice? Go do it!

H: *Period.*

B: Yeah. To me, it's a home run, if not a grand slam. Again, it really must become evidence-based. I have no doubt it'll just blow the roof off everything. And at this point, as you know, more and more people are getting trained in it, so slowly we'll have the ability to get more people the help they need. I mean, I would love, in truth, for Havening to become a household word as opposed to top secret material.

H: *I love the way you said that. It needs to be a household word, not top secret anymore. Well, thank you for your part in making that happen.*

B: You're very welcome. I've done about as good a job as I can in terms of getting the word out amongst my limited platform. But, again, I know once it's evidence-based, the sky's the limit.

PART III

Helping Those Who Help

CHAPTER 12

Rapid relief for survivors, soldiers, and first responders

Irene Hajisava

Irene Hajisava is a psychotherapist in private practice in Garden City, NY.

Harry: *Irene, How did you find out about Havening?*

Irene: Originally through Steve Ruden, who has been my friend and my dentist for the past 35 years.

A number of things were also happening in my life that ran parallel to the Ruden's development of Havening. I'm a level two EMDR therapist. I happen to be a 9/11 responder and did EMDR for over a thousand first responders and survivors of 9/11.

I also worked for a grant under the justice department doing recovery workshops for responders to the Pentagon 9/11 crisis. These first responders include EMS, fire, police, and the military.

I was also doing EMDR for first responder families, as well as those who had lost a police officer in the line of duty. So I really was getting around, doing this kind of work while Ron and Steve Ruden were developing and refining Havening.

Dr. Steve Ruden says to me one day, "My brother and I are developing this technique for healing encoded trauma. Would you like to learn it?." I said ,"sure". So I drove to his office every Tuesday night at 7 o clock when we were both done with our practices and we explored Havening with volunteer subjects.

H: *How long ago was that?*

I: It was before they started to present Havening to the public; seven, eight years ago.

I already had lots of experience with EMDR, which is a beautiful technique for addressing encoded trauma—and, it can be a painful process you have to put people through. So here we are trying this new thing. I became an absolute convert and believer when we worked with this one woman to haven the trauma of a divorce and her fibromyalgia went away.

She could barely walk for thirteen years. Then we did the Havening, processed the trauma. Afterwards, I kept calling Dr. Ruden and saying, "could you call your patient and see if her fibromyalgia came back?" And she never got it back. I've dealt with body parts, encoded trauma, people jumping from buildings, but I never cured fibromyalgia. That was how I got introduced to Havening.

H: *Did you immediately begin to integrate it into your own practice, with your own clients, or did it take awhile?*

I: It took awhile because of the touching. I'm a listened clinical social worker. There was another context, though, where I was starting to use it a lot. I do grief retreats for the families of police officers killed in the line of duty. At the retreat, different parts of the family are separated; the parents of the officer attend one retreat, the widows attend another. I worked at the children's camp. So these are the children, ages 6–14, of police officers killed in the line of duty, who attend along with the surviving parent for a week.

We had lots of counseling, but I taught the mothers how to haven their children. Of course all of the children immediately went to sleep. But these are children with lots of terrors because daddy was killed or shot or run over.

We had classes every day for the older children. I had two little boys, both on the autism spectrum, in my class. The reason they wanted to learn it is because they would go from a SUDS zero to a thousand and be absolutely out of control, their amygdala activity and reactivity being at such a high level.

So they would come everyday. We had a little class, and one morning, I get called over to the children's bunk. One of the boys who's about 11 years old is being restrained by two female police officers who are volunteers at the camp. Apparently he had gotten upset. So I went over to him. The thing that he and I used to do with the Havening is hum Twinkle, Twinkle Little Star. So, I said, 'you want to hum with me?' and he nodded his head. We hummed. I said, 'can I touch you?'. He agreed, and I started to touch his face. He immediately just dropped to the ground. Completely calm.

So the women, the police officers, say, 'What the heck is that? I want to do that'. That's how it got integrated in my work. I started to use it a lot as a technique that allowed people to manage trauma and anxiety and to self administer the technique.

H: *What place does Havening occupy in your full array of tools and interventions? You have so much experience working with people in* *these different, and profoundly stressful, contexts. What place does it now occupy in the whole repertoire of what you do?*

I: It wins the award as first place. Everybody in my practice is either havened or learns to self haven. Of course, now they no longer look at me like I walk on water, although that was very nice in the beginning.

H: *Always a nice thing.*

I: Because I did it with every client. There's no one I work with without some encoded trauma. There's no one without events that are interfering with their life. I'm a talk therapist. But the reason I got trained in EMDR was because of 9/11, because I knew I could talk to these people forever and there would be no impact. So Havening now takes a top place in my practice.

H: *Do you use EMDR anymore? Or has Havening basically replaced it?*

I: No, Havening has replaced it. Every year I work the police memorial in Washington and the cops who know us, the other trauma specialists and I, they line up people for us to see, cops and family members to help them with the trauma of death and shootings and the other not pretty things they have witnessed. Well, a couple of years ago they were so excited they invited me to train US marshals on Havening and tapping. In Oklahoma. So, it's getting integrated.

H: *Wonderful. How did the marshals respond to the training?*

I: I got a lot of ribbing from the marshals about both techniques, but they're using them, because they work.

And, of course, some people are skeptical, especially because of the touch component. When I first started to do EMDR people were challenging it and saying it's just a bunch of bells and whistles and psychobabble. So when they say the same thing now about Havening, it's not a big deal. Plus, we have the science to explain the process. And, of course, it works.

H: *You bring to mind a really interesting point. Most people are skeptical when they first hear about Havening, because the possibilities seem too good to be true. Were you skeptical when Steve introduced it to you? If so, what changed your mind?*

I: I was impressed by the fibromyalgia lady, but I was skeptical that this could possibly replace EMDR which was so specific and powerful to address encoded traumas. But, as it turns out, Havening is a gentle replacement and you get to add positive resources as well.

H: *Yes. It's interesting, every single practitioner who I've spoken to, who has at one point used EMDR, has essentially replaced it with Havening because of exactly what you're talking about. Because of the gentleness, the freedom from having to discharge the trauma in such a traumatic way, and the capacity to actually build resilience and positive growth beyond simply letting go of the pain. That's powerful.*

What was most difficult for you if anything as you integrated Havening into your work?

I: I had to make peace with the touching. My clients were already used to me doing EMDR; they knew I was running around the country. I had a lot of experience doing it for government and police and first responders. So I had a lot of credibility.

Now in my practice, I haven almost all the women, and probably 50% of the men. The other 50% of the men I let haven themselves. But I know some of my mental health colleagues won't ever touch the client.

H: *Please share some of the most interesting and powerful experiences you've had as you've used this tool with your clients.*

I: One woman had been sexually molested by her father. He worked as a clown, frequently wearing a clown outfit. He wore it to parties, not while he was molesting her. So whenever she would see a photo of a clown, a real clown, she would pass out, she would abreact, she would lose control of her bladder.

Her partner brings her to me and he sat in the room the whole time. She had never been able to actually get any help for it because the abreaction was so severe. So I told her that we were going to do this slowly.

I began havening her. All I said was the one word, 'clown'. As I was havening her, she's screaming, crying, kicking. I had the waste paper basket out, just in case. She's running out of the room, and then running back into the room. After about an hour of this, she could think of the word without a response. Then, sometime later, the two of them actually ran into a clown and nothing happened!

H: *Wow.*

I: I did Havening with one guy who had been in a shootout, a cop, and his colleague was killed. This was at a weekend retreat for police officers. He could not get the smell of the gunpowder out of his nose. So part of our distraction was I had him walk through a park and pick flowers. Then all he could do is smell roses because we were working on the olfactory area of the brain. So he lost the smell of the gunpowder and it got replaced by the roses in the park.

H: *Remarkable. How do you see Havening impacting mental health practice and the treatment of trauma ten, twenty years into the future?*

I: I think it's going to be the standard way of practicing. Talking will be an adjunct. But Havening will not replace all other forms of therapy. Let's say we helped somebody eliminate a lot of encoded traumas that were impairing their relationships. But suppose they've lived the last thirty years with impaired relationships? They still need support, through other forms of therapy to start to make corrections for life experiences they have not had.

H: *Yes.*

I: So, it's a duet.

H: *I like you describing it as a duet as well because the different therapeutic approaches can work well with Havening in an integrated fashion. What excites you most about Havening?*

I: It is so much easier to just resolve the thing the client is struggling with right then, in my office, and to know that I can also give them a tool that will impact their quality of life.

Eugenia Karahalias and I were in Greece over the summer, teaching Self-havening to unescorted Syrian refugee children.

That was a peak moment in my life. These were terrified children. I got to haven one little boy from Afghanistan. You could tell he was terrified by the look on his face. He was twelve, and in charge of his ten year old brother. The parents only had enough money to send the two boys. They wanted them to go to Germany, get jobs, and send money home. These were boys who still needed mommy to tell them wash your hair! We taught Self-havening to all the children, but I got to haven this boy.

The adults followed me around, appropriately so, when I was with him. I'm sitting in an isolated area with this child, and the Greek social worker from the house where the children live is right there. She reminds me not to bring up any of the horrible events. I agreed I wouldn't bring them up under any circumstances.

So I just told the little boy to pick a feeling. He picked 'worried' and we did Transpirational Havening with that. He repeated the word to himself. You could see how transformed he became. Then the Greek social worker looks at me. She says, "What is that? It's pretty nifty." I said, "I'll teach it to you later!" That's the power of Havening. It's a mighty powerful little tool.

H: *That's beautiful. Are there specific situations or contexts where it's not advisable to use Havening? Any guidelines?*

I: I have not had the experience with Havening that I had with EMDR where it can create a split off for people who had dissociative issues. I think if you have somebody that does have dissociative issues you should have a clinical background to work with them. Other than that, I don't see any restrictions.

H: *Tony Burgess helped me understand this. He told me, 'Havening is a tool, not a therapy'. What that means is that it can be adapted*

*and integrated to any particular therapeutic or non therapeutic mo-
dality but how you use it depends on your scope of practice, your level of skill and your ethical guidelines. You don't go where you don't
belong, but you also recognize that within your scope and within
your skill set it can be an incredibly powerful tool.*

*From your perspective, can Havening be learned and used effec-
tively by lay people, people who are not counselors, therapists, psychologists, coaches, etc.? And what are the guidelines for that?*

I: Absolutely it can. I have a couple hundred mothers and survivors that we've taught it to who are using Havening with their
family to mitigate abreaction and distress.

I'm not teaching them how to identify an encoded trauma
from your early childhood, or telling them that they should
go out and use Havening with their girlfriend who was sexually abused.

Rather, they are learning it just like these children and the
refugees, to decrease agitation and abreaction. Now, by default
what happens is that sometimes agitation and abreaction are
connected to a traumatically encoded memory.

A woman came to me one day. She was absolutely beside herself abreacting, because the guy who had molested her as a child
was trying to make contact with her. She could not even say his
name. I told her, "You don't have to do anything, you just have
to hum a song while I haven you. That's it, that's all we're doing here today." And that's what we did until she stopped abreacting. Whatever the unconscious material was got processed
in that session. I never mentioned the guys name. I never said
the word sex. I never said anything beyond guiding her through
the distractions. The following week she comes in. She says,
'You're not going to believe it! I can visualize his face and say
his name without throwing up."

We didn't do any therapy; we just worked directly with the abreaction. People can use the skill just for that. I would not want a lay person running around asking somebody if they were molested and offering to haven them. But once the abreaction is there, work with it.

H: *Thank you. When I do intros and demos I talk about five applications of Havening. Number one: reduce baseline stress, allostatic load, the stress stored in your body. Number two: build resilience and positivity. Increase your access to positive emotions. Number three: energize an outcome (as we do with Outcome or Affirmational Havening). The fourth: relieve present moment emotional distress, just like you did with the woman you described. And fifth, depotentiate encoded trauma. And number five is the application that is best handled by a professional.*

I: When I teach it at all of these retreats to these survivors, one on one, I'm going to address the encoded trauma. But I'm teaching them to do this so that they have a skill to manage the abreaction and disorganization that could get triggered completely without anything that they can identify!

H: *Exactly. Havening is such a great tool for navigating and relieving that distress in the moment, whatever the cause.*
Irene, what are you discovering as you're spreading the word about Havening within your professional community with these first responders, police, mothers, and others? How do people respond as you're sharing these tools with them?

I: Very positively. Eugenia and I did a class for adolescent boys with Doctors Without Borders. We spoke to a woman who spoke English and Greek, who then translated our comments to two men—one translated into Farsi and one translated into Arabic (that was the mix in the audience). And we're in a tent!

We are also presenting at the International Critical Incident Stress Foundation in Baltimore, to be held in May of 2017. We'll talk about our recent trip to Greece to help address the vicarious trauma of the Greek citizens who had a half a million refugees land there. We're introducing Havening as the technique that we used on the trip. The audience will be first responders and military from around the world.

H: *Thank you. What advice would you give to somebody who's looking into adding Havening to their toolkit?*

I: You're going to be very grateful you did this because it is a solid, on it's way to being fully researched, tool that is going to revolutionize the way that you work with people.

H: *Thank you!*

CHAPTER 13

Vigilance, veterans and "voodoo"

Malika Stephenson

Malika Stephenson is owner of Positive Change Work,
International Veteran's Coordinator for Havening Techniques®,
and developer of Colour Havening.

Harry: *Malika, how did you first discover Havening?*

Malika: I'd had chronic lyme disease. I was bed-bound for a number of months, and disabled for a number of years. I lost my hair. On a physical level I couldn't speak or talk. It was a horrendous time in my life and I had to find the resolve to find a way through it because the doctors in the UK were not able to help me.

Part of the journey to restore my health was to realize I needed to let go of a lot of things. As I came out of the chronic phase of the illness, I experienced my own variant of post traumatic stress, becoming hypervigilant about my health. I started to become preoccupied and worried that my lyme disease was coming back. I became extremely frightened and was in a state of lockdown terror.

I'd seen some Havening videos with Paul McKenna. So I havened myself. I hadn't been taught any specific protocol; I just copied what Paul McKenna did. The terror lifted.

This was a real defining moment for me. I wrote about it on Facebook and sent a friend request to Ron and Steve Ruden. And shortly afterwards I went to the training in 2013. That was my journey.

H: *Thank you. Tell me about your current work—who do you serve?*

M: I have three jobs. I have my private client work where I do incorporate Havening; I see veterans in that practice. With my private clients I work particularly with PTSD or PTSI. There's some controversy at the moment about the terminology for it, describing is as an injury, not as a disorder. Although symptomatically we're talking about pretty much the same thing.

Second, I'm a senior social worker, working directly with the military on base. I haven't introduced Havening in this context yet. I'm seeking permission, which takes some time. I'm also waiting for the next clinical research to be published in the UK, research involving 20 veterans I worked with who experienced Havening.

Third, I train people, not in Havening, but in other techniques that blend with Havening.

I'm also the Veteran's Coordinator for Havening and I've appointed two chairs, Donna Ryen in the USA and Louise Carmi in the UK.

H: *Why do you choose to use Havening Techniques? What specific benefits do they offer your clients?*

M: Havening is swift and I believe if you know what you're doing it's really an all-encompassing therapy that can really reach the heart of people's issues.

For some people it facilitates an instant shift; for others it takes awhile. I believe the process is so acute on various levels, creating biological, neurological, psychological, physiological changes that can take time to process and adjust to.

H: *What place does Havening occupy in your full array of tools and interventions in helping your clients heal?*

M: I would say Havening is one of the top three in my tool kit. I'm trained in so many different modalities and it's become my go to along with a couple of other things, depending on what we're working on at the time.

I tend to get very extreme cases of PTSD and trauma, for example, people who have been stalked for years.

I also tend to get professionals that work in the field, often who are dealing with very confidential and difficult issues, who know that I do and have developed a particular form of Havening myself using color. In working this way, we don't activate the traumatic memory in the standard manner, and I also don't actually need to know what the issue is. It's very confidential on many different levels.

Havening is one of my most essential tools these days.

H: *I think that's significant. With all of the modalities you've been trained in, Havening occupies a pretty major role in your work, especially with those patients who are experiencing high levels of stress and trauma.*

M: Absolutely. Havening allows people to process and build their own resilience and find their own solutions.

H: *Malika, most people are skeptical when they first hear about Havening because the possibilities seem too good to be true. They are skeptical that things can actually change so fast—and permanently, where the problem or issue does not not come back. Were you skeptical at first? If so, what changed your mind?*

M: No, I wasn't skeptical at all. I'm a bit of a believer that once you start seeking then things come to you and you find what you need. Once I used Havening for myself to release the fear associated with my illness, I knew there was something there.

I'm like most people. I like to see what a process is and what it does for myself before I try it on anyone else. And it was successful. If it was successful for me and I didn't really know what I was doing, then there must be something to it!

H: *And what a gift to the world that you discovered Havening. It helped you heal and now you're well and sharing and helping so many other people change their lives. That's beautiful.*

M: Thank you.

H: *What was most difficult for you as you integrated Havening into your work with your clients? Any challenges there?*

M: I had to get over being looked at in a very strange way when I'm starting to describe it! And even that kind of reaction became an aid to spreading the word, because the veterans that I work with, and please pardon the expression, they call Havening "voodoo sh*t". And that's how the word has gotten around, particularly in veterans circles.

We can talk about the science. We can talk about how it works. But they don't want to know. They just say to each other, 'this voodoo sh*t works, have a go'. Even some of the veterans got t-shirts printed with "Havening, it's voodoo sh*t." on them.

H: *How about the issue of touch? Here in the United States, psychiatrists, therapists, counselors, and social workers are not supposed to touch clients. How do you discuss this? Do you have them self haven? Do you facilitate the touch?*

M: I usually just facilitate self-havening because then you're giving them tools to do it anyway. I find that it's easier, because we're attempting to get people to suspend their disbelief on so many levels.

I've been a social worker for about 17 years now and I've worked in many different specialized fields. Some of the issues I've worked with have been around child protection. Here in the UK, we are now having once again huge investigations going on about child abuse, particularly from people in places of trust.

So I believe the way forward is facilitated self-havening. And it's less taxing on me, physically.

H: *Yes, and it works.*

M: It does.

H: *What are some of the most remarkable things you've seen and discovered in your application of Havening with your clients?*

M: There are many. Clients have freed themselves from chronic issues that have dogged them for years, things they just could not get rid of. Afterwards, it's wonderful to see the delight on people's faces when they check in on themselves and they're free from whatever it is. Whether it's fear, phobia, belief systems that prevented action, or pain, physical pain diminishing quite rapidly and swiftly, people are quite incredulous.

And you can see the lifting, visually, on the clients' faces; they're free of whatever it is that was their issue. It's giving people their lives back. I've also done demonstrations in front of people and observed the audience's shock at the swiftness of the shift.

H: *Yes. It's inspiring to observe that process when they release the pain, when they become more present, when their faces light up, when they look around with that quizzical look that this burden is actually gone. It may have been something that they held for 20 or 30 or 40 or 50 years.*

Any specific stories that you'd like to share?

M: Where to start? Many! I've been able to help veterans become free of their PTSD in a very swift amount of time, so that they are able to think clearly and with clarity, without fear. I see them becoming more calm and being able to then start to tackle other behaviors that are what I would describe as painkilling, like over drinking or over medicating. I've observed their pain diminishing, going away. That in itself gives people space to think and plan and move forward.

I've worked with some quite elderly members of the community who were dealing with chronic pain under the chronic pain clinic health service. I've seen their pain that they would describe as agonizing, rating it a thousand out of ten in agony on the scale, reducing significantly.

I've seen a patient with chronic rheumatoid arthritis actually un-stiffen within an hour after Havening. This is someone who had to use two walking sticks because they were unable to walk. Afterwards, they are pain free, not having to use the aid of the walking stick, with the nurses and doctors that treat them being absolutely incredulous.

There's so many. People who are suicidal starting to plan the future. People looking significantly younger, finally and completely released from their emotional burdens. People who have lost loved ones being able to recall their loved ones with love and clarity and smiling and laughter, not being in the overwhelm of grief. There are a thousand stories I could tell you, Harry. There have been so many.

H: *What advice would you give someone, it could be a counselor, therapist, a professional or a coach or parent or teacher, somebody who's looking into the possibility of adding Havening Techniques® to their own tools. What advice would you give them?*

M: I would say that I would research who the trainers are and find out and specifically if that trainer has a background that interests you. Research the training, have a look. And, have a go at Self-havening! See where you get.

H: *Thank you.*

CHAPTER 14

Healing the healers

Joanne Harvey

Joanne Harvey MSW, is a Pro EFT Master and Certified Havening practitioner in private practice in Northern California.

Harry: *Joanne, how did you first discover Havening?*

Joanne: You told me about it! We've been friends and colleagues for many years, and I trust you implicitly. Over the years, we've shared many wonderful EFT related techniques. When you told me about Havening I could feel your enthusiasm and naturally wanted to find out more.

H: *Yes. It was pretty mind blowing for me.*

J: And it was for me then too. As soon as I started using Havening, I knew that of all the tools that I had, this was the thing that was missing in my practice. Now I use it probably 95% of the time.

H: *Who are your typical clients?*

J: I am a social worker. I was a hospice social worker for almost eight years and I saw that the kind of work that I was mostly drawn to was energy work, working with energy tools.

My typical clients are people who experience some kind of life altering change in their life: a death, grief, divorce, a new diagnosis. I also oversee a hospital employing a little bit over 500 personnel where I respond to critical incidents. I work with the hospital employees. They see so much and have multiple stressors that impede their happiness, impede their satisfaction, impede their ability to live their lives fully. So I help the hospital personnel to address and manage their own traumatic stress. I also work with people who have ACES (adverse childhood experiences) multiple traumas, limiting beliefs and other lifetime challenges. My practice is very full.

H: *I met you originally because we were the first two people in the world to earn the Pro-EFT™ Master certification. Up until learning about Havening, your practice was primarily focused on EFT, correct?*

J: Right, it was.

H: *How has Havening transformed your practice?*

J: It's changed my practice in positive ways. I don't advertise. I have a website. I have a couple of postings on other people's websites, but mainly I deal with satisfied customers who pass me around like a party favor! They're satisfied, so they tell their friend or they tell their family member about what happened.

When I added Havening into my practice, my practice became so busy that I now schedule out three to four weeks in advance. I've always had happy customers; it's just that Havening transforms people's lives very rapidly. No matter what happens in a session, a client walks out, their stress is reduced, they're feeling more confident, they've got a little bounce in their step and a lot of the wrinkles on their face are gone.

H: *What are some of the most remarkable things you've seen and discovered in your application of Havening with your clients? Any stories you'd like to share?*

J: I've got lots of stories. When I first started Havening, I started working with this gal who's sixty years old. She couldn't drive because of a very traumatic accident thirty years ago. She'd been to a hypnotist and many others to attempt to heal the trauma, and she was frustrated because she had to have her husband drive her everywhere. We focused on some of the issues that were continually triggering her and in one hour she walked out of my office. Her husband was in the parking lot. She walked to the driver's side, had him scoot over, and she drove them home. It had been thirty years since she'd been behind the wheel.

We do live in the country (and I'm pretty sure she didn't have a driver's license that day) but she drove home. Since then, she's gotten her driver's license and I see her all over town just as happy as a lark.

Here's another story. There was a critical incident at the hospital, in the pediatric clinic. These little children had come in who had been abused and the staff were the ones who discovered this child abuse. So I was called to come in.

It was first thing in the morning. I thought there would be five people there, and fifteen people showed up. I had been trained to haven one person but since there were fifteen, I taught them all how to self haven.

When we started, all of them were triggered to a ten on the SUDS scale. I explained what they were going to do, and when we were done everyone had either completely resolved their triggers, or had gotten to the point where they were comfortable going back to work. Their SUDS now were either a zero or a one.

The process was also lots of fun. They both laughed and cried throughout the Havening, and after only an hour with fifteen people, everyone was willing to go back to work. The multiple traumas the staff were dealing with were softened or completely resolved and they were very excited about getting back to making a difference with all of their little patients' lives.

H: *Remarkable. As you know, many people are skeptical when they first hear about Havening. The possibilities just seem too good to be true. Were you skeptical at first?*

J: The way I was introduced to it, I was not skeptical.

H: *Because you trusted me?*

J: I trust you. And I thought, "Is this going to work better?" I already do weird work with people anyway. I had nothing to lose. Why not give it a try?

H: *How about the issue of touch? It hasn't been standard practice to use touch in this way with clients and patients. In some professions,* *it's frowned upon or not allowed. How do you discuss this with your clients and how do they respond?*

J: When I am first working with a client I send them an intake form and a consent form. The consent form goes over the fact that I could be asking to touch them but it doesn't have to happen and they will be asked permission.

And I ask permission every time. Even if I've worked with somebody four, five or six times, I always at the start ask, 'is it okay if I touch you?' If they don't feel comfortable, I can guide them through self-havening.

H: *Of course. Any other interesting cases that you'd like to share as you've introduced Havening to your clients?*

J: I've had big farmers come in. They've had an event that happened years and years ago. They come into my office, and it's a surprise because I wouldn't expect for them to be coming to me, but they come and they tell me at the very start this is not going to work. "I just want to let you know I'm just here really for my wife or for my family because they're tired of this." I say to them, "You know what? You're here, we have an hour and a half together. Let's just give it a try." Then they walk out and what's really remarkable is they become my best advocate. They start telling their friends.

And then there are the people who have remarkable recoveries. They come in coughing, feeling awful. When they leave their cough is gone.

Then there are the really notable things that happen with people who I'm not expecting. I'm expecting for them to come in and work on a traumatic experience from their childhood, maybe when they were seventeen years old they had a roll over accident and so we're working on that, but when we resolve the accident and they get up to leave, they notice that their hips don't hurt anymore. Then when they come back, they tell me again that they haven't had to take any medication at all, that their hip pain got resolved as they resolved the trauma that they experienced when they were seventeen. That's always a surprise to me. I never really know all the layers of what we're working on.

H: *Yes. It's remarkable that when you depotentiate a traumatic memory, so many implications that follow from that. There are physical implications, emotional implications, cognitive implications, spiritual implications. You never quite know all the ramifications of that healing.*

J: That's right. And the healing continues after people leave. It's not just in my office. And it's not about me. I'm the guide. I don't have a magic wand. People are doing this for themselves. It's their neurochemistry that's changing. It is so satisfying for a practitioner to see somebody walk into your office and their face is noticeably pinched and when they walk out they're smiling, relaxed and feeling confident in who they are. They don't feel dependent on me, they feel confident in who they are.

H: *How do you see Havening impacting the world of healing, emotional healing, psychological healing, physical healing, spiritual healing ten, twenty years down the road? What do you think the possibilities and implications are as these techniques becoming more widespread?*

J: I would like every practitioner to have Havening in their toolbox. I don't care what's going on with somebody, Havening can be very helpful. So I would hope that doctors, nurse practitioners, nurses, know Havening and are using it. I would love to know that all mental health practitioners know and are certified in Havening. I would hope that is the case. I'm already working on my little grandkids. They all know Havening now.

H: *How old are they?*

J: The youngest is three. So she can do self-havening and then the oldest ones are both six. The two six year olds haven each other. They're getting pretty good at it.

H: *That's sweet. What have you discovered as you're spreading the word about Havening within the professional community with doctors and nurses and the other people who you're working with? How are they responding?*

J: Once somebody's shown what it does, people are sold immediately. Then they become advocates for it. I've had a harder time really getting people interested who are professionals. It's more difficult for people who have traditional training to open up to it. It's almost like they're thinking, 'yeah yeah yeah, it can't be that easy.' But on the other hand, once I actually do a session with them they want to know everything they can.

H: *So it's really a matter of actually having people try it.*

J: Right.

H: *What advice would you give someone who's looking into the possibility of attending a training and adding Havening Techniques ® to their toolkit?*

J: This is the most fabulous tool to have in your toolkit that you can imagine. Every professional who works with people needs to know this, because even if you don't use it for your clients you need to use it for yourself.

We as healthcare providers, teachers, policemen, are experiencing multiple traumas, multiple stresses, every single day. Eventually it starts to show up in illness, in alcoholism, in drug abuse, in other ways. And with this simple tool, you can reduce that negative stress, you can take it away everyday, just by doing some self care. Everybody should learn it.

It doesn't hurt to try it and all you have to do is see it work. There's nothing magic about it. It absolutely works. And to see it work is the proof in the pudding.

I also want to say something about the training. I've been through a lot of workshops and classes to learn different techniques to use in my practice and I really appreciate the training to become certified as a Havening Practitioner. The training and mentoring support is very important. And then you also have the supportive Facebook group, full of people who are encouraged and enthusiastic about this possibility.

H: *Thank you.*

Part III

**Self-havening For
Self-Transformation**

CHAPTER 15

I became my own case study

Louise McKay

Louise McKay is the deputy head of UK and Europe for Havening.

Harry: *Louise, bow did you first discover Havening?*

Louise: I found a DVD in the back of one of Paul McKenna's books in early 2013. I didn't take much notice of it until I had quite a bit of anxiety and needed relief. I did the process which would've been what we call Event Havening. My anxiety disappeared. I didn't realize how amazing that was at the time.

A bit later, I was working with a client who had PTSD, looking for a state management tool that my client could use in between sessions. My mind went to this thing I'd seen called Havening, but I wanted to find out more about it rather than look at the DVD or tell him to watch it. And there wasn't much available at that time.

I trolled the internet and found a video on YouTube of Dr. Steven Ruden introducing Havening to a group at a biofeedback conference. The quality of the video was not great. But what I heard was about these receptors, neurons, and other scientific stuff.

Once I heard that and saw the demo, like a flash, it just clicked and I completely got it. I realized this is something I have to pursue. I had to find out more. And, I was lucky that within three weeks there was a training available in the UK. Next, I bought the book *When the Past is Always Present* and read it twice by the time I got to the training. At that point, it felt like my path had suddenly been shown to me. I haven't looked back since!

H: *There is something compelling about the combination of the science and the simplicity of the technique.*

L: Absolutely. And it was the science really that caught my attention. Interestingly, the amazing transformation I'd experienced earlier with Event Havening for my anxiety just didn't click. When I saw the science underlying Havening, everything made sense. It spoke to me instantly and I had to learn more.

I was already thinking of clients who would benefit from this potentially, but I needed to go do the training, learn how to do it properly, go through the process and become a practitioner before I went any further. I was really lucky timing-wise.

H: *When you see something as seemingly simple as Havening, it's so easy to attribute its impact to a placebo effect of some kind.*

L: I've heard people mention that before. It never occurred to me until people started bringing up that this might be happening. I can see how people might think that.

H: *And of course, once you do understand the science it does make sense.*

L: Yes, and it actually allows people to make sense of it. I find some people think that the science might be off putting, but on a whole, when I work with clients, I give a brief explanation and then go into it more deeply if they're interested. Because Havening has a scientific background, it makes it, in my view, much more accessible to people because they have something to grasp.

H: *That's been my experience as well.*

L: I had a client say to me, in a session just last week, that one of the things they really loved about Havening is that it has a scientific basis and that it had been clearly explained. And that made it make sense for them to understand that there's a process happening during their sessions. That makes it accessible.

H: *Yes. In one of my first Havening sessions I worked with a brilliant woman who is a healthcare practitioner. She had the experience of shifting what she wanted to shift very quickly and it was really powerful.*

But once we were done, she had this quizzical look on her face. She asks me, "Okay, exactly what happened?" As I explained the process to her, she responded, " Good. Now I can accept this change because I understand how it happened." The subjective change was significant but until she had a logical, cognitive explanation of it, it's as though she couldn't really settle into the reality of what happened.

L: Yes. It makes working with people so much easier and it makes it easier for them to get their head around what's occurred.

H: *You had a practice for years before you began using Havening. Who are your typical clients?*

L: Yes, I had a private practice within a doctor's office, and of course in the UK we have the national health service. So the doctors there were referring people to me for private work as a counselor. As a result, I had a very wide range of people with varying issues, from PTSD, relationship problems, panic attacks; anything and everything—whatever they come into the office with. Sometimes the doctor would refer to me and that's continued, but now it's for Havening, not counseling.

H: *How has learning about Havening transformed your practice?*

L: Hugely. I don't work in the doctors office anymore. I now have a private practice at home. However, I get a lot of referrals from the doctor.

Generally, when somebody comes in now they're coming in for Havening. I very rarely see anyone for pure counseling sessions anymore. But I use all my skills as a counselor.

I'm person-centered. I prioritize safety and trust and simply being a human being with another human being, and allowing that person to simply be themselves. I use the knowledge of how trauma gets encoded that we learn with Havening, and this makes it much, much easier for me to get to the core of the problem and truly resolve it.

So the work is no longer focused on talking about things, finding out what the problem is and then putting the lid back on, or maybe trying to help the client accept it, understand, and see where things are coming from. It doesn't stop there.

Now it's actually about making positive, permanent change, which makes all the difference to that person when they walk out the door.

On top of that, it's about being able to actually help that person learn how to help themselves going forward. And that, for me, is huge—to give someone access to a tool that they can use when and as they need it.

To give someone access to something that's fairly simple, something that they can apply at anytime when they feel distressed or stressed so they don't need to be with me to be able to help themselves.

That was a huge draw for me when I really understood the potential of Havening for my clients and for me.

H: *Yes. Not only can you use the tool in the session, but you can empower your client with things they can take away to work on their own.*

L: Absolutely! To help somebody help themselves long-term, so that 10 to 20 years from now they can still be using this tool to help themselves when life throws challenges at them. Because Havening doesn't stop life from happening.

I've used it when I'm in a public area, just using palm havening and distracting myself in my mind. It can be used anywhere, anytime. And it's very empowering for people. I love that about it.

H: *Yes, and of course as Dr. Ruden describes, every time you haven you're building the resilience of your neurochemical landscape. So you're building resilient capacity for the long-term every time you do the process.*

L: Yes.

H: *Louise, you have a wide array of different tools and techniques and practices, everything that you've learned over the years to help your clients heal and experience greater well-being. What place does Havening now occupy in that entire symphony of skills, in your whole toolkit?*

L: It is my primary tool. I can't emphasize enough how much my experience and development as a counselor helps me be a better Havening practitioner, clearly. But Havening is now my main tool.

Another important point is that being an effective practitioner is not just about the person you're working with, it's about looking after yourself. Self care is so important to me as a therapist and Havening is available 24/7 to me, anytime I need it.

As counselors, we hear some terrible things. We work with a lot of situations wherein sometimes you hear things you don't want to hear. With Havening, you can actually work on yourself so that when your client's in the room, it's about your client, not about your stuff. Your experiences don't get triggered and negatively affect the process. Havening is great for self care and I've used it a lot in order to be much more present for my client in the session.

H: *Thank you. Louise. When I met you last year in the October 2015 training Los Angeles, something that really struck me about you is you have an irrepressible joy that just seems to bubble up from within. To me, that is an indication that somebody has done their own work and is really taking care of themselves. Could you share a little bit more about how you have used Havening to build yourself up?*

L: This is one of my favorite questions! They call me the self-havening Queen. When I did my first training back in 2013, I decided right off the bat that I was going to throw everything Havening could offer at myself first. I would be my own case study. So I experimented with every type of Havening that I could do by myself.

Over the last three years I have consistently used self-havening, partly as an experiment and partly because the results have been so amazing. Every time I clear something I learn more and more about the process, and my conviction becomes more and more solid. Trust me, I know it works because I have used Havening so extensively for myself with so many different types of issues.

Whatever comes up, I deal with it. And that was all I needed to understand that this is an amazing process that can help my clients. I also tell my students that self-havening is one of the best ways to learn about the process because it helps you understand even more about how trauma gets encoded. You might not get to the core of something straight away, but as you continue to work step-by-step you eventually get to the bottom of it!

And every time I work on something with myself I'm learning more. Every time I work with a client I'm learning more. So, I can't advocate self-havening enough! Especially for people working within a therapeutic context because it's just a great way to learn about every aspect of the process.

It's been quite a journey. I've not only managed to clear a lot of my own stuff; I've also experienced the transition from my old self and the transformation into that person who is completely different from the person I was before I did the work.

I understand that it can be a bit strange when you get rid of something absolutely huge that you've had for very many years.

And then you have to get to know yourself again without that thing. And because I've been through that process, and understand it's perfectly natural, I can reassure my clients that they will get used to the new self.

I also teach them how to use tools to help with resilience, including Affirmational Havening, Outcome Havening and Hopeful Havening and the other variations that can help you develop as a person.

As I've let go more and more stuff, and experience more and more of my authentic self, I feel more and more like the me I came into the world to be with the benefit of the wisdom of life experience.

I now have 48 years of life experience but without a good deal of the old patterns based on things that have happened to me that have altered my behavior in negative ways. I see cognitively that something was not a good experience for me, but I'm no longer attached to it emotionally. Therefore I can make a decision in the present free from the negative influence of the past.

H: *It's wonderful to hear your enthusiasm. I share that because my life has also transformed exponentially through self-havening over the past 18 months. And in regards to authenticity, it's as though the real self and the most authentic true self can now express without being trapped behind the fog of the trauma or the past.*

L: Yes, absolutely.

H: *One of the things I'm sure you notice as well, as my resilience and my capacity to bounce back from things and my capacity not to be triggered by things increases, sometimes it astounds me. Something that a year or two would've just driven me off the rails and would've* *triggered upset for either an hour or a day or a week or whatever. It happens now, I haven, it's gone, I move on.*

L: Yes, and knowing that, when somebody comes in and they experience that kind of change, they realize more of their unlimited potential for change!

H: *Yes.*

L: About four months ago, I saw a video that upset me so greatly I honestly don't know what would've happened to me without Havening. Seeing it put me into a very bad place very, very quickly. But I havened myself out of it. And in the middle of every second of that distress that I experienced, which included an abreaction, I knew I was going to be okay, as horrible as it was. It took me 45 minutes and afterwards I was fine. Absolutely fine.

I became very distressed very quickly, and my distress came as a complete surprise. I saw something in this video that I find very difficult to deal with. And at no point at all during that whole time while I was so powerfully triggered, did I think, 'I'm never going to get over this. I knew I was just fine and I just needed to go through and trust the process, and I would come out the other side with no problem at all.

To have that in my life is an enormous gift. It's so powerful and to know that that's potentially available for my clients is amazing. I enjoyed working as a counselor but to be able to have this tool to work with my clients is so enjoyable. I feel very confident using it with myself and my clients.

H: *That brings to mind Dr. Ruden's idea that the sense of inescapability is one of the primary factors that contributes to traumatic encoding.*

So many people are walking around holding such burdens from the past or from current situations. They feel that they're trapped or that they'll never get out or that they can't get through it and this fear consumes them. And to have the experience that you're describing, of now using the tool so often and in so many different contexts that almost no matter what happens, you know there is something on the other side, is truly remarkable. You know there's peace on the other side. That's a priceless gift.

L: Yes. Peace on the other side is exactly how I see it. You know you can get to where you need to be in order to be okay. I haven everyday. I haven every single morning in the shower. I decided I would do Hopeful Havening every morning. I also do all sorts of affirmations.

If I don't feel in a great place when I wake up in the morning, which is very rarely, I will clear whatever it is that needs clearing or I will address it. And it happens literally in minutes. I'm not talking about long sessions, I'm talking minutes.

While I'm soaping my face in the shower, I'm thinking about something positive, maybe tapping into some resources or some gratitude. In a couple of minutes, I'm done.

I never miss a day. It's just part of my routine in the morning. I just tune into myself for a few minutes and I do my Havening and it's a brilliant start to the day. I recommend that people to do this for themselves. It's maintenance resilience and creates great brain chemistry first thing in the morning.

H: *Yes, and it also builds on the fact that neurons that fire together wire together. The more you do it, the more you practice, the more* *you haven, the more resilient you become, the better you feel. I don't think there's an upward limit to how good you can feel when you incorporate this as a practice.*

L: Yes.

H: *Louise, many people are skeptical when they first hear about Havening. The possibilities just seem too good to be true. Even the conversation we're having right now might evoke that response from people. Were you skeptical at first and if so, what changed your mind?*

L: Skepticism was never really an issue for me. I didn't acknowledge the power of Havening when I watched Paul's video. I didn't see it for what it was. I simply tried it because I was really anxious. As soon as I saw the video of Dr. Ruden speaking, it made perfect sense to me.

I do appreciate that when you're talking to people, and I do a lot of intros, that naturally people may be skeptical because when you see a demonstration it does look too good to be true. And, the scientific background, the neuroscience and the research behind it really does make a difference and helps people to give it a second look. It's almost like the intellectual understanding makes it okay for people. If somebody is just seeing a demonstration, I can understand thinking well that's a bit odd, you're just stroking someone's arm and they feel better, that looks very strange.

But when you explain the science it suddenly makes perfect sense, especially when people acknowledge in fact that we do haven ourselves and each other in small quantities all the time. I mean we all naturally do this.

When people are talking about their distress they might rub their face while they are telling you or we might naturally comfort somebody with a hand on their shoulder or a gentle rub of the arm. We do this all the time. Helping people connect that natural, intuitive act with the delta wave activity and the shifts in brain chemistry and the neurological changes, it all of a sudden seems to make it easier for people to take in and they click. It makes perfect sense. And they want to try it.

H: *What are some of the most remarkable things and shifts you've seen and discovered in your application of Havening with your clients?*

L: I think one that sticks out the most was a person who came to me after a very violent attack. And this person had been practically house bound for six weeks. Life had essentially stopped for them because they were so terrified.

Within two hours of Havening they had that quizzical 'what happened' look on their face. And I booked them a follow-up appointment and they came back and said, "I don't know why I'm here. The problem is gone'"

We needed to just check if there's anything more, and there was one more thing that needed addressing. After our initial session, their life opened back up for them. They were bouncing, absolutely bouncing. And I was thinking to myself "What else is available to help this person who'd had such a traumatic event that practically made them house bound?"

To this person, their life seemed and felt finished, and within two hours and a little bit of a follow up session everything has changed. How might they have ended up without access to Havening? What's most important is empowering them again to know that something as awful as that can happen and they can come out on the other side of it.

I've worked with clients who have experienced lots of horrendous situations. I sometimes wonder how people get out of bed and continue their lives considering what's happened to them in the past.

I've worked with all the amygdala based disorders. I've worked with panic attacks, pathological emotions, phobias, chronic pain, somatization. Everything that's on that list has found a way into my client base.

I also find that it's rare that on some level Havening cannot be beneficial to any client. A lot of the people who come in my office are people with long histories of trauma. The people who come across my threshold tend to be people who've not just got one event to address. Mostly it's people with years and years and years of horrible stuff that's happened involving many layers of trauma.

I explore three basic areas with my clients. We're looking for the history of trauma. We're looking to help with state management and we're looking for tools to help them with their personal development and their resilience. It's a formula that works with so many different issues.

In fact, another thing I love about it because as much as practitioners and trainers we absolutely need to know a huge amount about how trauma's encoded, what's happening in the brain and so on, as our clients start to understand those things it helps them in their healing journey. They learn how their mind works and how trauma affects them personally. They now have a tool and a fairly simple application to help them through difficult experiences.

H: *How about the issue of touch. It hasn't been standard practice, at least in the United States, to use touch in this way with clients and patients. How do you discuss this in the first place and how do your clients respond?*

L: It's interesting because as counselors, we are trained in the UK not to touch at all. A handshake is permissible only if the client offers you a hand first.

So for me, although I was really excited to use the process, it was a very odd transition for me to get over the fact that I'd be actually applying the touch.

Of course we know that we don't have to apply the touch but my experience with clients coming for Havening, is that they might be expecting the application of touch.

And, my experience has been that, once I explain it to the person everybody has elected this option. I had one person in all the people I've worked with that didn't want me to touch their face. Apart from that, everybody has been completely happy for me to apply the touch.

I always offer the option and tell the client you can apply the Havening yourself and I can guide you and we can do facilitated self-havening. The response I've had from most people is very, very positive. They feel nurtured. I feel that I'm looking after them.

H: *I wonder if there's something about it that's healing attachment issues. The whole theory of attachment is all about how we develop psychologically and emotionally based on our attachment or lack of attachment with our parents. Whether there's real safety in that connection. And that connection includes everything from visual eye contact to physical touch to the sense of nurturing. And it occurs to me that when someone is Havening another person it evokes healthy safe attachment.*

L: Yes. Absolutely. Yes. Because there's a sense of complete acceptance in that. And it's difficult to explain how precious it is actually and what a privilege it is to work with somebody during a Havening session. There's a sense of complete acceptance, belonging, just being present with the person. You are just being in that moment. It gives the person a sense of belonging.

H: *Yes, unconditional positive regard. And the caring presence of another.*

L: That is it exactly. It's just being in that moment with that other person. There's no expectation. There's no demands, no judgement. It's just you and that other person in a state of complete acceptance, total positive regard. It's quite remarkable.

H: *Speaking of this notion of connection, you and your partner, Ian, are both Havening practitioners. We talked last year when I met you about the use of Havening for couples. Would you speak to that a little bit?*

L: Yeah, as a couple we haven each other. And for the couples I have worked with, it has been the most wonderful thing to see them working with each other. I've not worked particularly with couples who are having issues with each other. But I've worked with couples who have maybe an issue around some event that's happening within their lives that they're both struggling with.

Personally for Ian and I, I've done a lot of my own work and he does a lot of his own work. Sometimes we request Havening from the other. Just to be able to say can you haven me I just need a little bit of Havening, connects you both in that special way we were just talking about. It's a wonderful way for couples to be able to really connect with each other.

H: *So I suppose they would build not only a sense of bonding with one another but also those positive neurochemicals, you know the serotonin and oxytocin and GABA, so that they become more resilient together and more connected together and more buoyant together.*

L: It's also wonderful to get that extra support from your partner in that moment where you need help. They understand how it can be helpful because they've been through the process themselves. Not only are they supporting their partner in that moment, they're getting some great shifts in brain chemistry for themselves.

H: *I have used Havening to help couples learn how to be unconditionally present with one another as well as to build that resilient brain chemistry. I had one couple that had gone through some fairly difficult times and they really needed to build their resilience individually and collectively. So they would haven one another silently sometimes or haven one another and affirm their love and appreciation for one another. Over time they began to create a conditioned response so that when one touched the other instead of remembering the bad things they started to remember more of the positive things.*

L: That's wonderful.

H: *How do you see Havening impacting mental health practice and counseling in general, particularly in terms of trauma, say 10 to 20 years down the road? What do you see as a possibility?*

L: I'd like to see Havening being done in schools in 20 years time as part of the curriculum so kids can learn it. In that way, they can have the confidence of knowing they have a tool that can help them help themselves. That would be the ideal—Havening is simply a part of everyone's education.

And from a health point of view in the UK it would be wonderful if it was available as part of our national health service, like EMDR and hypnotherapy. This would make Havening accessible to a really wide range of people.

I went to a trauma conference last year. A lot of top people were talking about new models of therapy and Havening was the first thing mentioned.

I recently attended another conference on trauma. As I was hearing the case studies and looking at some of the research I was thinking,"Wow. Havening would've been perfect for that one; Havening would've been perfect for this one." These classic cases would've benefited from Havening.

They discussed one case study from a man who was mugged. Seven years down the line he experienced several suicide attempts, became addicted to his medication, and eventually improved because one of the organizations described in the case study got him to a much better place. I'm thinking, "Wow. What if that guy had Havening right after he experienced the attack?" We'd potentially be looking at a completely different scenario seven years on.

So if our national health service can understand the impact of something as powerful and simple as this tool, that will be fantastic. Hopefully, one day that will happen.

H: *I think it's just a matter of time.*

L: Yes, it could take a few years, but if we keep plugging on and keep sharing this wonderful tool with the world it will get there eventually.

H: *One of the things I love about your being the Havening 'self care queen' as you mentioned is that you demonstrate and communicate the fact that Havening can be learned and used effectively by lay people. People who are not counselors, therapists, psychologists or mental health professionals. Everybody can benefit from using this tool to take care of themselves.*

Louise, you are the Havening Techniques Deputy Head of training for the UK. You go out and train all over the Europe and all over the world. What are you noticing and discovering as you're spreading the word about Havening within this now international professional community? How are people responding and what are you seeing as you go to these different countries and continue to train people?

L: A lot of amazement. I just did a training recently, in my own area, and by the end of the two days we have covered everything including many different types of Havening. Participants have seen and experienced demonstrations. They have gone through the process themselves with their own issues.

By the time they get to the end of the second day, they're completely blown away by the power of this tool. These are people, on the whole, who have many tools in their tool box and lots and lots of experience and knowledge around their own client base and the work they do. And they're still completely blown away by the end of the two days.

It's a magical feeling. They feel like they've got this amazing tool in their hands. They can now go and complete their case studies as they work towards practitioner certification.

For practically all the trainings I've been to the response has been very positive, with a lot of amazement and excitement and real desire to put their new Havening skills into practice for their own clients and so on.

H: *How many trainings have you participated in or led in these last three years?*

L: 18 or 19.

I've been very fortunate to have been part of a lot of those trainings, meeting a lot of people, and seeing consistently a very positive response from folks who've been on those trainings.

H: *Thank you. What advice would you give a person who who is considering the Havening training, looking into the possibility of adding Havening to their toolkit?*

L: The potential to make positive life changes and experience life without the burden of the past is just within your reach. I have a tagline, "The future of mental health is in our hands."

We are all capable with this model of therapy, of helping ourselves clear the past and start anew as we move into the future. We've got a tool to make positive permanent change biologically, and that's the difference. It's not just stirring the pot and putting the lid back on. This is about actually making positive permanent change biologically and being able to do that for yourself and help other people.

I urge people to get an experience of Havening, to work with a practitioner, to experience that transition from being emotionally linked to something and then delinked. To be able to do that for your clients and for yourself as and when necessary is empowering and amazing. I can't recommend it highly enough.

And if you only use Havening as a therapist, you have a great tool to help you be a better therapist and live life more fully. Carl Rogers talks about being a fully functioning person and that is what I feel Havening supports. It helps you to become a fully functioning person because I have something to help my-self as and when I need it.

Even though it may sound too good to be true, get out there and experience it! Have a Havening session. Pick something wherein you can tell the difference before and after so you can measure it.

Having that experience for myself blew me away. I can't recommend Havening highly enough. It's a win-win. It's gentle. It's like working with nature. We're helping ourselves with something that comes naturally. Human touch is such an amazing thing. You watch TV and you watch people and you see how much people communicate with touch and how we soothe each other with touch. It just makes perfect sense that this is the right way to go. So my recommendation is go for it!

H: *Thank you so much Louise McKay. It's always a delight to be in your presence. To me, you are a model of a fully functioning human being who's well on the way. I love your integrity in doing your own work and allowing that work to inform the wonderful work you do with your clients. So I can't thank you enough and I look forward to connecting and seeing you another time really soon.*

CHAPTER 16

No pain, no meds

Elizabeth White

Dr. Elizabeth White is an experienced therapist, speaker, trainer, coach and author with a private practice in Manchester, United Kingdom.

Harry: *Elizabeth, how did you first learn about Havening?*

Elizabeth: I was introduced to Havening by my old friend Paul McKenna, who is a well-known self-help guru. I trained with Paul and Richard Bandler in NLP more than a decade ago.

I saw that Paul was presenting the first workshop in London about Havening in early 2013. Unfortunately, I missed out on that one. I attended the second training they held which was later that same year. Many of the people who are now well-known in the Havening movement also attended that same training.

I was most interested to learn more, because like most people, I'm skeptical about new stuff. It sounded a bit too good to be true. Especially since it was addressing a lot of the same kinds of issues I was already helping my clients to address: post-traumatic stress, anxiety, phobias, and so on.

H: *Your description of how you found out about Havening reveals some common strands that I've noticed. A number of people, who as you mentioned, are predominant in the Havening community now, came out of an NLP background and/or came out of hypnosis and hypnotherapy. One thing I've noticed in the people I've known who have trained in those areas is that they possess what I would call open-minded skepticism. They have a willingness to try things, and if something works, they don't hesitate to adapt and use it. What matters is whether or not it works.*

Coming into Havening from this extensive background in therapy, in NLP, and in other modalities, what did you find most interesting about Havening?

E: I was very interested in working with specific traumatic events. When I first found out about Havening, the primary focus was Event Havening. And that was my area of interest. I work a lot with sexual abuse, with adults who were abused when they were younger. At the time, Havening was specifically focused on treating traumatic events, phobias, and other types of anxieties.

I thought, "If this is what I think it is, and it works like it says it does, this could transform what I do." Obviously, I was intrigued by the issue of touch, which in most other modalities, we don't use, even though touch has always been used as a way to comfort and support people. The other thing that shocked me about Havening was the speed and effectiveness.

H: *You're sharing some very common perceptions. The speed with which it occurs, the practically instantaneous change, the significant physiological change that you see in people. They look younger. They're more relaxed. They have this look that's become familiar to me. It's the what-just-happened-to-me look.*

E: Absolutely. It's almost shock, isn't it? They're looking around for the thing they've just lost, even though they don't want it back. That's the way I would describe it, when everything works well.

The most wonderful thing about it is we're talking sometimes about a 50-year-old problem being gone in just 20 minutes of actual Havening. The session might last an hour because you've got to do some history taking, and some digging to find out what's going on, but, on average the actual Havening session can be as little as 20 minutes. Then they sit there looking incredulous. They're looking up and down. They're looking under the chair that they're sitting on, wondering, where is it? What's happened? What's wrong?

Sitting there in amazement. Sometimes they're crying tears of joy. They're laughing and joking, and hugging you. The results you get can be incredible. And the amazing thing is so far it appears to be permanent, which was another thing that didn't happen before.

H: *Yes. It's interesting. What I've discovered is sometimes when someone really releases a core memory, experience, or emotional pattern that has become part of their identity, it can be a little bit disorienting. You really have to work with them to make sure that they can adjust and reintegrate, and that they've dealt with secondary gains, for example.*

E: Absolutely.

H: *Because it is so rapid, and so fast. It really represents a paradigm shift in how we think about and approach traumatic experiences.*

E: That's right. And you've got to follow through beyond that initial sense of relief, the sense of freedom. You can also get ab-reactions to this sort of treatment. The beauty of Havening is that you can bolt it on to almost any other therapy or modality very well. As long as it's in good hands, experienced hands, I think it can integrate very well with almost anything. Then it can be so effective, and so fast. And, you can maintain that prog-ress, keep building resilience, and teach them self-havening.

H: *Elizabeth, it sounds as though Havening has taken a pretty major role in your full array of tools and interventions. Do you use it with most of your clients now?*

E: I would say the majority of clients, yes, absolutely. Primarily in my therapy work. I don't do a huge amount of coaching, and I do use it with my coaching clients. I also use it personally. I've helped my family and friends with it.

It's evolved into being part of my everyday life. Yes, it has sneaked into almost everything I do in some way or other.

H: *That's wonderful. One of the distinctions that Tony Burgess helped me understand is that Havening is a tool, not a therapy.*

As a tool, it can be integrated into virtually any therapeutic approach, or even non-therapeutic approaches. A friend of mine is a havening practitioner in the US, and she has several grandchildren. The six-year-olds haven each other. One of the six-year-olds havens the three-year-old. .

E: Absolutely. Actually, if you think about what Havening is, most of us have been doing a bit of it all our lives. If you think about most greetings and how we comfort people, what do we use? We use touch, hugs, strokes. We use it anyway from when we're born, so what's not to like, or enjoy about it? It's so simple to blend that into your everyday life.

H: *And the full range of human experience, from positive to negative, is encapsulated in touch. Whether it's affection, whether it's sexuality, whether it's physical violence or abuse. It seems that all of the most direct means of impacting the human emotional system, for better or worse, involve touch.*

E: Quite right. That's what I realized. That we were using touch anyway, to some extent. Emotionally, many of the things that we care most about and how we address those situations and people, involve touch.

H: *Yes. My sense of the real innovation and genius of what Dr. Ruden has produced is the synthesis and integration of these three components: touch, focused attention, and imagination.*

All three components have been part of many modes of healing for a very long time. Whether it's massage, Reiki, yoga, meditation, creative imagination, hypnosis, NLP, guided imagery, attention, mindfulness, mental rehearsal. All three of those elements have been around for thousands of years, but they've never been combined in this unique way.

E: That's the thing. He has managed to consciously understand what they're doing and bring them all together.

And with the equipment that we have now and the ways that we can prove this, scientifically, there's no reason why it can't end up as part of the mainstream. Particularly in the UK, in the health service, because it's so much better, more effective, faster, and more efficient than what we presently have.

H: *I believe that we are on the threshold of an astonishing transformation. We have these powerful tools plus our emerging scientific, research-based understanding of the brain. We have tools and techniques like Havening, which is fairly new. We have tools and techniques like meditation and yoga, which are thousands of years old. And, we now have the capacity to look inside the brain and actually see and understand how these different interventions work on a neurobiological level. This has only been possible for the past few years.*

E: Yes. Even ten years ago, we weren't able to do some of this stuff. We didn't know or understand it properly. We had ideas of what we thought was going on. We guessed a lot. A lot of the time we were right about it. Also, we saw and understood the results. We just weren't sure what went on in the middle to get us to the results.

Now we understand, not totally, but we have a much better idea of what's really going on. And in our society, we've got to have evidence before people are willing to risk trying something out.

H: *One of my case studies, for my practitioner certification, involved my Havening a person who is very, very successful in the health field. It was a remarkable experience. We did the Havening, and the person released something that had troubled them for many years. Afterwards, they looked at me with this really quizzical face, which I'm sure you've seen many times. They said, "OK. What just happened and how?"*

So I took a few minutes to explain the science, traumatic encoding, the depotentiation process, the delta waves, the AMPA receptors, the calcineurin. They sighed a sigh of relief and said, "OK. I feel better now." It was the cognitive understanding of what happened that helped them feel safer with the whole process.

E: That's right. Because, again, it's evidence. They understand that. And it's wonderful afterwards, when you ask them to try and get their experience of that trauma back. You say, "Come on, really try. Try hard to get that back, that feeling back."

They're sometimes a bit frustrated, because they can't believe they can't get it back. I've been asked many times, "Are you sure this won't come back? Will it be back tomorrow?" They don't actually believe that it's permanent, and it's gone. It's too good to be true, almost. Although they're thrilled, they're a little bit nervous. They think, "Tomorrow morning, when I wake up, will it all come back again?"

In the past, they might have solved the problem, to some extent, or improved by disassociating themselves from the problem over time. Then, suddenly, something's triggered the feelings again, which we know often happens.

H: *Yes. Perhaps, that really is another aspect of the genius of what Dr. Ruden has discovered. Havening works on the synaptic level. When you have havened away the traumatic encoding of a memory, you are physically different. Your cells don't have those receptor sites. They're not going to grow back.*

E: Exactly. That's what we're changing. We're making epigenetic changes. This is something that, obviously, we can explore in the future. We are only just beginning to look at epigenetic changes. We are physically and genetically different after Havening. That's what's so exciting when you think about it on a deeper level.

The other thing about Havening is that we can use it for our own self-care, to maintain our health and equilibrium, build resilience and to look after ourselves and our loved ones. I've experimented with this quite a bit, personally, having had a few health issues in the last 18 months.

Here's a little story for you.

Last year, I went into the hospital, just for a day, for a small procedure. I had a blocked salivary gland, which is just under your tongue. They do something called a marsupialization. Basically, they open the duct up by stretching it open. This is done under general anesthetic because of the location—otherwise it would be rather uncomfortable.

It's a very quick procedure, about 20 minutes. They cauterize it as it goes, but, as you can imagine, if you're stretching and ripping something open slightly, and cauterizing, it's going to be sore afterwards.

The anesthesiologist comes to me in the recovery room, and asks about my pain level. I thought about it and it was pretty sore. He asked me if I would like some pain relief, some opiates. I said, "No, I don't want it." He said, "Why not?" "Because, I'm going to deal with it naturally, in my own way."

I decided to do some Havening for the pain. I thought, "What's to lose? Try it." I'm sitting in my recovery bed, with my blood pressure monitor on, and I start doing my Havening. Within 10 minutes of Havening my pain had gone completely. And I was actually just stroking anywhere I could find, since I was attached to all these monitors.

The relief lasted about 20, 25 minutes. Then it started stinging and burning again. I havened again and the pain was gone. I was blown away. I went home later that day. The only time it bothered me was when I was doing the statutory mouthwashes that you have to do for 48 hours afterwards. It stung as you would expect. Otherwise, no pain.

Here's another example. And for this one, I had two (previously skeptical) witnesses.

I had some dental work done in the area of my upper jaw. The whole of my face, from just below my eyes to my lower jaw was anesthetized. As that started to wear off, I started to get some serious pain.

I sat in my office, two or three hours later, as this is happening, just around the time where I'm thinking of making the evening meal, and my niece and my husband are with me. I say, "I don't think I can eat, this is hurting so much."

My husband says, "Why don't you take something?" Just as he said that, I decided to do some Havening. I did it in front of them on purpose. It was really painful. I've got quite a good pain threshold, I believe, but I would say the intensity was an eight or a nine. Again, I timed it. It took fourteen minutes to go to a zero and I had no more pain. I ate my evening meal. I went home. I went to bed. I took no pain medication.

Over the following couple of days, all that I had was tenderness on the upper gum, where all the injections had been, from the actual anesthetic for the treatment. My husband said if he hadn't have seen it for himself, he would not have believed what he saw. There's a perfect example of using Havening to address physical pain.

H: *Thank you for sharing your own personal example. I, too, have a number of stories of my own application of Havening for boosting resilience, lifting my mood, reducing pain, and more. I think many of us have been experimenting and discovering how, through the use of this tool, not only can we release what is in the past, we can empower ourselves to create a new future in a really beautiful way.*

E: Absolutely.

H: *Any considerations regarding when not to use Havening?*

E: Used appropriately, and in the right hands, it's very safe. I've heard a lot of people ask, "Is it dangerous?" And, "When shouldn't you use it?" Often, the worst that can happen is nothing. It doesn't work and there's a number of reasons for that.

I think the only time that you've got to be on your guard is, if somebody is under the influence of substances, chemical substances, or having a psychotic episode. And, even then, I have actually used Havening touch to help settle and calm things down.

H: *Thank you. How specifically do you see Havening and the research that's emerging from it, impacting both mental and physical healthcare into the future? 10, 20 years from now, what do you see and imagine?*

E: In the future, when we get more research and evidence, we'll be able to prove so much more, that it will become mainstream. It will completely replace the current beliefs and therapies that we're working with.

Here, we tend to work with CBT, Cognitive Behavioral Therapy. That's what normally would be prescribed, medication, CBT, and now mindfulness. I think the CBT and mindfulness are connected. They're quite closely-related. I think it will overtake those.

At some stage, we are going to be able to get this into mainstream medicine, across the world.

Also, to me, eventually, the obvious thing to do with it would be to get it into our education system in the long run just like they are trying to do with things like health, mental health, and nutrition. We're now building that into our curriculums in trying to educate people much sooner so that we intervene before the problems arise.

Imagine if we could do that with Havening. That would just be amazing. If we can get to children, if we can start this at a younger age, we can change lives right at the beginning. The sooner we can approach people, the sooner we can help them have a happier, healthier life. Things will be so different for those young people if they realize that they can use this as a resilience tool. It could also have a positive impact on any area where people are in a caring, helping, or teaching profession.

H: *Any limits to Havening's future, from your vantage point?*

E: I really don't think there are any boundaries within reason as I see it. It's evolved so much, already, in these three and a half years. I'm still discovering things on a sort of weekly, monthly, basis, that I'm helping or changing with it. We can continue to evolve it and apply it in so many different ways. You could adapt it to suit almost anything. When it's done appropriately you can really make fantastic headway into so many areas.

H: *Thank you. You are, in addition to being a Certified Havening Techniques® practitioner, also a trainer. What are you discovering as you spread the word about Havening within your professional community? How are people responding? How do you address their skepticism about something that's so new, representing such a paradigm shift?*

E: That, sometimes, is the hardest thing, because you're dealing with old attitudes a lot of the time.

At the moment we're promoting Havening primarily to health professionals, first responders, doctors, nurses, and other therapists. And there is a lot of skepticism around, in certain generations of the medical profession, particularly in mental health fields. Of course, that's where new and effective tools like Havening are most needed.

Often, they read up about it and think, "Sounds too good to be true. It probably is." Or they think to themselves, "It's so new. Let's wait until it's been around a while and they've ironed out all the glitches in it." I think the problem for a lot of health professionals is, unless they can see a white paper that explains it, they tend to be afraid of it. That's part of the problem. They're not prepared to take the risk, if you like.

That says a lot about the society we live and work in, doesn't it? From a business point of view as well, we've got to have proof.

I've discovered that the best way to shift those attitudes is to prove it, to show it in action so they can see it in action and experience it for themselves.

H: *As with many innovations, it may take another generation of young people, who are growing up with this understanding. As I interact with people around Havening and we discuss this, it becomes clear to me that tools like Havening are based on an emerging, fairly recent, understanding of the brain. Most therapies, including CBT and talk therapies, are, in many ways, based on an older model of the brain.*

E: That's the problem, absolutely, because they did their training 20, 30 years ago, and they're still stuck in this outmoded belief system.

H: *It reminds me of the debates that were happening hundreds of years ago when most human beings believed the Earth was flat, or before the discovery of telescopes, and people believed that the Sun revolved around the Earth. My sense is Havening, and these discov-*

eries connected to it, are an equally significant paradigm shift, and that's why many people don't get it—yet.

E: Absolutely.

H: *One more question. What advice would you give someone who's looking into the possibility of adding Havening to their toolkit? It could be a mental health professional, it could be a coach, it could be a parent, a teacher, somebody who works with young people, just a person who'd be interested in, possibly, looking at the training. What advice would you give them?*

E: There are so many people who should come and look at this. I would say, go for it, try it. What have you got to lose? It could be life-changing for a lot of people because they are going to be able to do their job so much more effectively and easily.

H: *Thank you so much, Elizabeth.*

CHAPTER 17

It was meant to be

Lynn Demers

Lynn Demers is a master sculptor, EFT practitioner and life transformation coach with offices in Vancouver and Salt Spring Island, British Columbia, Canada.

Harry: *Lynn, how did you first discover Havening?*

Lynn: It's a beautiful story that I think was meant to be. My son introduced me to a dear friend who had recently learned about and trained in Havening. From there my world opened up to Havening and before I knew it I found myself in LA taking the training. I intuitively knew that it was exactly what I was supposed to do. That was in October 2015.

H: *And in addition to being a professional sculptor, you also are a life coach and EFT practitioner. Who are your typical clients?*

L: My clients seem to come to me with all different kinds of challenges. However, most of the people who show up I would describe as highly sensitive. They hold a lot of stuff inside and they're not quite sure what to do with it. Or, they simply seem to feel more than the average person. I think maybe they are drawn to me because I can empathize with them.

H: *So you work with people who would be considered highly sensitive. Are these people who are artists or business people? What professions?*

L: All walks of life. Everything from nurses, first responders, day traders, school teachers. All ages as well.

H: *How has Havening transformed your practice?*

L: If I were to compare it to sculpting, its like I got a brand new tool—and this tool is magical! It allows me to help someone in a very gentle and loving and kind and intuitive way that I wasn't able to do before.

One of the really beautiful things about Havening is that it can be used content-free. For some people this is really helpful, because whatever they are struggling with, they hold so close to their heart that it's really challenging for them to share it. Over time they might, but the content-free work holds a space for them to get the help they need without having to expose themselves.

H: *Thank you. You have a number of tools as a coach and EFT practitioner that you already use to work with your clients. At this point what place does Havening occupy? How and where does Havening fit in with your overall repertoire of tools?*

L: I would say I use Havening 90–95% of the time. There are some sessions when I'm working longer-term with the client where we might go through quite a few Havening sessions to clear away specific events, particularly if someone has a history of childhood trauma. Then we'll get to a point where I'll use coaching with them to help take some steps forward. That way they can feel what its like to move forward having released some of those past painful experiences.

H: *What are some of the most remarkable and interesting things you've seen and discovered as you've applied Havening and used it with your clients as well as yourself?*

L: It's really interesting how someone might come to you, for instance, with something like a habit of biting their nails for thirty years and you just know that underneath that there's something else. Then with a few questions in your history taking, once you get the little nugget of information that you need, that nail biting habit of thirty years can be gone within a sixty minute session. That to me is a miracle because if you just try to stop biting your nails on your own, it's probably not going to happen.

H: *Yes. But when you're guiding the person through your history taking to really find the core traumatic encoding that's underneath the symptom then you can eliminate that really quickly.*

L: Absolutely, and it's not even something that they're aware of at the time.

H: *Many people are skeptical when they first hear about Havening, it just seems too good to be true,. were you skeptical at first?*

L: No. But I'm not a very skeptical person to begin with. I'm open to trying all sorts of different things because I know that even if something isn't all that it claims to be for one person, it might be for the next. And it's going to make a difference. It's not going to make the same difference for every single person. Although I have to say with Havening, in the year that I've been practicing it I have yet to come across a client who it hasn't worked for.

H: *Yes. It's basic neuroscience, that's what I say. It's like adding one plus one, you always get two. And if you make sure you set up the formula properly, you're going to get the result.*

What was most challenging for you as you integrated Havening into your practice? Any challenges you faced?

L: It resonated with me right from the very beginning. It was very exciting because, unlike the other modalities I use to work with my clients, I felt like I was sculpting, taking away every-thing that doesn't belong to get to the core of a person, to who they really are.

H: *It's so interesting that you say that. When I interviewed Carol Robertson, who you know is a really fine Havening practitioner and trainer in Scotland, she described the way she thinks about Haven-ing is that she's helping clients "sculpt their own neurology." It's beautiful that you both work with the same kind of metaphor.*

Any other specific stories that you would feel comfortable sharing as you've worked with Havening?

L: I can share my own personal story. When I went to LA for the training weekend, I had a specific challenge that I had had for thirty-two years at the time. I had gone to numerous coun-seling sessions including perhaps 20 EMDR sessions. This was a huge trauma and it was very challenging. In one thirty minute session Havening with Tony Burgess at the LA workshop it was completely cleared. When I think about it now, I remember the details but it has no emotional charge. Before Havening, it would always bring me to tears. So the experience really freed me up to living a lot more fully in the present.

H: *That's beautiful. I imagine you now see those kinds of transformations with your own clients.*

L: Absolutely.

H: *How do you see Havening impacting the world of psychological and emotional wellness, five, ten, twenty years into the future? What do you see on the horizon?*

L: I hope that it gets to the point where it's being taught in schools, and children and parents and teachers are taught to use it so that people aren't holding onto their trauma for so many years at a time. So things don't get so complex. There's really no need for us to suffer so much.

H: *Yes. You recently took the initiative to bring a Havening training to Vancouver, not far from your home base. What did you notice as you were sharing this tool with your colleagues, people you've known maybe from EFT or coaching? How did they respond to learning Havening?*

L: They are excited. It's opened up something new for them. They are able to go to a new place with their clients. Before they might have able to bring them some degree of release or help them move forward. Now, when they get to a certain place working with a client and they use Havening, they're seeing what they would call miracles.

H: *Can Havening be learned and used effectively by regular people? People who aren't counselors or therapists or coaches or psychologists or whatever?*

L: Absolutely. Self-havening can be used every single day. It can be used in families. It can be used in schools. It's a tool that can be learned and used by anyone.

H: *Thank you. What advice would you give somebody who's maybe thinking about attending a training, learning more about Havening, and adding it to their toolkit?*

L: I would encourage them to sign up for a complimentary session with someone. Many people are offering complimentary sessions in order to get their case studies for certification. I think to experience it personally is the best way to know that it works.

H: *Yes, thank you. Any other comments or reflections about how Havening has changed your life or how it's changed your clients? Or anything else about how learning Havening has made a difference for you?*

L: I'm just really grateful to the community for one. The Havening community is a beautiful, loving, supportive community. There's always someone who you can reach out to who is willing to answer questions or offer support.

H: *Thank you.*

CHAPTER 18

Me 2.0

David Chametzky

David Chametzky is a New York State certified peer advocate and certified life coach in North Massapequa, NY.

Harry: *David, how did you first discover Havening?*

David: I had gone through personal therapy, and the therapist, Bill Solz, tried it on me. We were doing EMDR and he said, "I think something else might work. Would you be willing to try?" I said, "Let's give it a shot." I was really in a state of distress and I wanted to try to feel better about things. And as the session started going, we're using a little Havening and a little this, little that, as well as talk therapy.

And it started working. Within one or two sessions, I saw changes in my mind, the way I was looking at things. And then I would talk to my wife, and you'd see a little spark in her eye open up, and I'd say, "What? What did I do now?" She says, "You would have never said that before you met Bill." And I said, "Oh, okay. Is that good or is it bad?" It was all positive stuff.

One thing started building on the next, and positive changes kept happening. Even friends of mine who I had known much longer than my wife would notice a difference. Things were changing, wholesale changes, and the people around me were noticing those changes. My stepdaughter says I was Dave 1.0, and now, with my improvements, I'm Dave 2.0.

H: *Wow. How long ago was that?*

D: About two and a half years ago.

H: *So, it was through working with Bill that you discovered Havening in the first place.*

D: Yes. Much like anybody else in today's society, I wanted quick results. Bill asked me to try Havening. And it interested me, the science behind it, and I kept on questioning it. But I agreed to try it.

I left Bill after about seven months because my issues were resolved. I was also able to do a lot of self-havening, which was really helpful. I admitted the errors of my ways and was able to see different perspectives much clearer.

In terms of my personal experience, here's how I look at it. When you watch a horror movie, you have the lights off and you get really scared. You think, "oh my God, what's going to happen? The guy's in my room. He's gonna kill me." And then afterwards, if you watch the same movie with the lights on, nobody's scared.

So, when you go through a trauma, part of the problem of the trauma is not only living through it; it's the inescapability of it. And you keep putting yourself into that place of inescapability. And you keep reliving that trauma. And certain triggers keep reminding you of it. It's like watching the movie in the dark—no escape in sight. Then after Havening, the lights are on in the house.

That's the difference it made for me.

I'm going through something right now with a family member that's been rough. And without Havening, there's no way I could have dealt with this. It's still not easy. It's not an easy situation. But I'm handling it much better, and that's been the trick for me. The lights are on in the room, and the monsters can't scare me anymore.

H: *That's powerful. How did you end up coming to the Havening workshop? I met you at a workshop in New York where you were assisting earlier this year.*

D: From the period of time when I was seeing Bill, I started picking up some other kind of tools to add to my toolbox. I became certified in NLP, I studied hypnosis, and most recently, I became a New York State licensed peer recovery advocate. This has all been in the last two and a half years.

Then the previous March, before we met, I took the workshop. They said, "If you want to be certified, you need 30 case studies." I got my certification for Havening within a couple of months, because we had an amazing practice group at the time. We would meet almost every week, practicing our craft, as well as talking about case studies that we had done.

At first I thought it would be daunting to even find 30 people who were willing to give me the opportunity to try this untested modality. Once I found one, I had friends that came out of the woodwork. They started talking amongst themselves. My goddaughter and I did some Skype sessions that blew her mind. And then some of her colleagues and friends started calling me.

H: *And how do you use Havening besides your self-havening? Who do you help? Do you have a private practice?*

D: I do have a private practice. I work full time, so my practice is part-time, and my clients come through word of mouth.

H: *You know, it sounds like you went through a transformation through your therapy, and then you began a new life, and now you're helping other people in the way you were helped.*

D: Yes. This is now my path. Everybody's on their own path and we're all on a path together. Ram Dass says we're walking each other home.

You definitely have that perspective once you've gone through something. And helping people is what I'm doing. I also do a lot of work with veterans, and a lot of that's pro bono.

H: *That's beautiful. So, what are some of the things that you've seen and discovered as you're working with other people? You have some stories to share?*

D: A lot of the stories are confidential. But there's one story that I can share with you. It's about my goddaughter.

She used to get panic attacks going on planes. All her friends were going to Israel with Birthright, which is a company that sponsors people who've never been to Israel before. If you are Jewish, you can go to Israel and learn more about your ancestry and heritage.

She says to me, "Uncle Dave, I want to go." And I say, "So, then go. What's the problem?" She says, "I can't. You know I can't get on a plane." I've known her all her life, and she's had

panic attacks with me on the plane. And I said, "You can do it."
"I'm going to walk you through it."

We had three Havening sessions total, and she not only
flew to Israel, lost her luggage—they lost her luggage for three
days—but she was able to handle herself beautifully and was
bat mitzvah'ed as a 21-year-old in Israel.

I get chills when I tell the story because it's so moving and
very personal for me. Now she's calling me all the time. "Uncle
Dave, where are we flying now? I want to fly with you. I want to
go on a trip with you."

H: *That's beautiful.*

D: The world literally opened up for her, and that's the incredible part. For her, originally it was just, okay, a car trip here, a car
trip there. Now, planes are an option. She flew halfway across
the world. So, not only isn't she scared about flying—even
though they lost her luggage—but now when you talk about it
with her you can feel the energy that got released because of
that trip.

H: *So, after three Havening sessions, her entire world opened up and
she let go of that panic forever.*

D: Yes, and the Havening went on the plane with her. We
walked her through getting on the plane in her imagination and
when she got on it, I said, "Just remember, one of the things
about Havening is you can rub your hands. You don't have to
rub your arms. But if you just close your eyes and say a couple
of the affirmations—'I can do this'— or anything positive like
that, you'll be fine.

Here's another story. An athlete I worked with just recently was an older gentlemen in a league. He didn't know what was wrong. He said he felt fine physically but he couldn't play anymore and he was thinking about retiring. He wasn't professional, but it's still personal, at least when you're playing as an older gentleman.

H: *Sure.*

D: So, I said, "Well, you were successful for a while. Can we just talk it out a little bit?" So, we talked and havened a little bit and I said, "This is what I'd like you to do. Can you try, in the first game you play, do the hand motions and things like that before the game, but only picture yourself hitting line drives." And we did that, and he came back. He called me that night from the bar. He goes, "I just gotta tell you: We need to set up another session." I said, "All right. Whenever you want." He says, "No." Tonight was one of the best nights of his life. It was everything he wanted to do. He says, "It was like being 20 again."

H: *Wow!*

D: And he says, "I got up there. And there was not a thought in my mind. I just let my body act." I respond, "That's all you need to do." Obviously, he did really well and all of his teammates were happy and made him feel better about things like that.

H: *Beautiful. That's the power of Havening. What I love about your story is you took something you learned in your own healing and now you're committed to serving others and sharing it with them.*

D: Definitely. That's what I love about it.

H: *Many people are skeptical when they first hear about Havening, because it sounds too good to be true. When Bill first introduced it to you, were you skeptical?*

D: Yes. I was completely skeptical. But, at that point, I was going through a lot of challenges with my marriage. I was willing to do anything to rebuild my life.

H: *So, you were willing to pretty much try whatever he recommended.*

D: Absolutely.

H: *What advice would you give somebody who was considering taking the Havening training and adding this to their toolkit?*

D: I definitely would go. Go in with an open mind and if you have the time and the funds, go do it and try to make sure that you see it through the eyes of somebody who wants to learn. And the practitioners and trainers are highly motivated people and, for the most part, accessible, and that, I think, is really important, the accessibility. There is follow up and support. I say to my wife, if I travel internationally, there are people who I could meet all over the world, that I feel that I know or I've met. So, it's nice to have those international connections.

H: *It's a wonderful network to tap into.*

D: It is.

H: *Thank you, David. Your story is inspiring and you're changing lives one person at a time.*

D: Thank you.

PART V

Becoming Your Best Self

CHAPTER 19

Optimal performance in poker, golf, and life

Dr. Stephen Simpson

Dr. Stephen Simpson is a mind coach, hypnotherapist, author and Fellow of the Royal Society of Medicine.

Harry: *Stephen, how did you first discover Havening?*

Stephen: I met Paul McKenna about nine years ago when I became interested in NLP. Since then I've done a lot of training with Paul and he's become a close friend. I respect his opinions on pretty much anything.

About four years ago, we were having a chat after one of his events and he said, "You've got to read this book". My ears perked up. The book was *When The Past is Always Present*, Dr. Ron Ruden's book. I read it. I thought it was a beautifully well-written book, but it didn't move me. But it certainly piqued my interest.

Then, out of the blue, about two and a half years ago, I got a message from Paul that he was launching Havening at a very high profile conference in London and he wanted me to be part of his training team for the event. Dr. Ron Ruden would be there.

That's when I realized what Havening was about, particularly during the two days of the conference when we were seeing transformational change happen over and over again in front of our eyes. I knew immediately that this was something that I had to learn a lot more about and to use with my clients.

H: *Who are your typical clients?*

S: The core of my practice is tour golfers and in the last two years in particular professional poker players. My clients in these areas have had some incredible successes, although I work with a wide variety of people who I would describe as aspirational, seeking to better themselves and their performance in various domains.

H: *And you've written books for those groups, correct?*

S: I have. The first book I wrote was called Play Magic Golf, which was for golfers. Recently I've written a book about luck because that's most definitely a subject that fascinates me. It's called Get Lucky Now. It's a study of successful people and the possible reasons that they are so successful, and luck certainly comes into it. I firmly believe that everybody can do something to attract at least a little more luck into their lives and that's what the book's about.

The latest book is called Poker Genius, actually published within the last few days. This book details my work with several of the world's top poker players, including the number one online player in the world. That's an incredible story that is almost hard to believe.

His name is Chris Moorman. He's won more money online than any other player living or dead in the history of poker. So he's an awesome player but even having said that, all of these poker players are fighting luck and statistics. It doesn't matter how good they are, there are times when they have long losing runs.

After a few weeks or a few months, it eats away at their self confidence and then the temptation is to start changing things and doing things differently. While sometimes that can be a good idea sometimes, particularly if you're already one of the top players in the world, very often it's best to go back to what you've always done, your tried and tested methods.

That's because generally speaking, this is what happens when players go into a losing run. They do start changing their approach and it doesn't help. It's often a good idea to get back to basics.

Chris Moorman is the world number one online poker player. When I met Chris he'd had a poor year by his exceptional standards. But the big problem was this. Even though he's such a good poker player, he had never won a live tournament. That was something that was missing from his legacy.

It was starting to get to him. Not particularly because of how he felt about it, but how other people felt about it. He got sick and tired of people saying, "Oh Chris, are you going to go down in history as the best player that never won a major or a live tournament?" That was getting to him.

And that's why he came to see me. It wasn't particularly his choice. He had a couple of friends who I'd worked with and they recommended me. His partner at that time, who's now his wife, said, "Come on Chris, what can you lose?"

So we met. He was definitely skeptical. but he was also open and prepared to try anything. We worked intensively for three days. He was the perfect student. He turned up on time. He did his homework.

So, when I left him, I said, "Look, Chris. I can't predict the future any more than you can. What I can say is your mind is in such a different place now, such a better place. It was in a good place before but it was even better now. All I know is that you've positioned yourself to make the best of whatever cards Lady Luck deals you."

Well, little did he know and little would I have guessed that about ten days later he did actually win his first major live event and a huge prize. Of course, that was just amazing and surprised both of us. Was that due to our Havening work? Was it due to other things? Who knows. In my mind, I think Havening had a big part to play in that.

H: *Of course. The work that you did with him allowed him to release whatever blocks were there.*

S: Yeah, exactly.

H: *That's exciting.*

S: Yes, that was pretty stunning. I should add, by the way, one of the things that I say, whenever my clients do really well, I don't take any credit for that. Chris was the guy who played the cards, it was the golfer who sank those putts. They did all that. I didn't give them anything that they had not had before. My role was as a facilitator, who used my tools, including Havening, to help free them to perform to the potential that they'd always had.

H: *Yes, it's all about unlocking the barriers to that inner freedom which is there already.*

S: Exactly. I use Havening with pretty much every client. One of the many magical things about Havening is that there really are no limits to how you can adapt it to your own practice; there are many creative tweaks that you can incorporate. I know from talking to Dr. Ruden and observing him, that he is also constantly refining his practice and changing little things.

H: *I was speaking with Tony Burgess about this very topic, and he said Havening is a tool not a therapy. What he means is that you can use the tool and adapt it infinitely to whatever therapeutic modality you are using.*

As more and more people use Havening and learn about the basic science, the principles and the protocols, my sense is that a thousand variations will blossom but each will be true to the core principles.

You mentioned using Havening with pretty much every client. What place does Havening now occupy in the full array of tools and techniques and interventions and practices and patterns that you use to help your clients?

S: It has a very prominent place. In my book I talk about my tool kit. I say the most powerful tools that I have are the three H's: Havening, hypnosis and HeartMath. I use all three of those with almost every client, working to create the perfect cocktail for that particular person, because everybody's different.

H: *Those three tools, a trifecta of transformation. I love that. What are some of the most interesting things you've seen and discovered as you've applied Havening with your clients and with yourself, in addition to your wonderful story about Chris?*

S: The thing that has stunned and surprised me the most is how effective Havening can be when used for post traumatic stress disorders.

We all carry traumas from the past. It's called life! Just being a human being. Some of these, if we are fortunate, are relatively trivial. But some of the things that happen to people are absolutely devastating and will be crippling physically and mentally, and they often tend to get worse with the passage of time. With these kinds of issues, the impact that Havening can have is enormous. You can literally see the changes happening in front of you. The client's body language changes, their face softens. It almost looks as if they've become ten years younger. These huge stresses and strains can be released.

Also, something that to you and I would appear to be trivial when we hear a client describe it, actually can have a profound effect on them.

When you are a child of seven or ten or something you might have experienced something as really acutely embarrassing or painful.

As an adult you will think it's something that you've moved on from. You will say to yourself, "That was when I was a child. I used to be frightened about things when I was a child that no longer frighten me."

But sometimes these little things that shouldn't have such a big effect, have obviously become encoded in the amygdala and they continue to exert their toxic effects many years later.

H: *Let's get back to poker and golf. How else does Havening serve your clients in those areas?*

S: As I mentioned, I use Havening with all of these clients one way or the other. For elite performers, one of the main challenges for them is how to get into the zone, how to find the flow state and stop worrying about being on camera.

They need to be able to stop worrying about the pressure of having to sink a four foot putt on the last green of the last hole of a major golf tournament and be able to control their nerves and their anxiety.

This performance pressure is caused by adrenaline and a variety of other neurochemicals. But often the side effects are that this over arousal causes people to freeze. There can also be physical effects, for example, their hands may start shaking.

When adrenaline is going through the system, there are three primary responses, and the two traditional ones that we've all heard about are fight or flight. That's what the adrenaline is there for. It's purpose is to help you get out of a dangerous situation and to release massive amounts of energy so that you can do that.

But when you're on a golf course or when you're playing poker at the final table and there's a million dollars in front of you, you're not facing any physical threat but the adrenaline is still coursing through your veins.

The third response to adrenaline is is to freeze. People tend to freeze, just like some animals, when they're being attacked will freeze or play dead. That is not helpful when we're playing sports like golf and poker!

H: *So you use Havening to help reduce that adrenaline response?*

S: I do. In the training that we would do before an event, once we're done cleaning up anything in the past we need to address, we would start looking at what it going to take for me to be a champion?

What do I need more of now that will help me to reach my highest potentials?

So for every person it will be different. I ask the client, "When you are under pressure, what is going through your mind, what are you thinking? Tell me. Describe it to me."

Of course there will be physical components to this as well. And then I get their desired outcome—"How would you like to be?"

In one word, if you could give me one word, how would you want to feel on that last green where the next thirty seconds are going to determine possibly the rest of your life? How do you want to be?

And they'll come up with fairly consistent words. A big one is calm. So I say okay, say it to me. And they will say, "I am calm. I am calm." Then we will do Outcome Havening to help them deepen the state.

Of course, I'm not going to be with them at that final table or the final green on the golf course. So that's when I teach them about self-havening. One can do self-havening quite discreetly and people really won't know what you're doing. It's such a natural thing to be rubbing your arm. While they're doing that, under their breath they'll be saying, 'I am calm, I am calm' or whatever their mantra is. I use Havening to reinforce that kind of thing.

H: *You're helping them orchestrate their own brain outside of the fight, flight, freeze response so they can bring that calm or confidence or whatever emotion or feeling is. Ultimately, they can bring it almost on demand.*

S: Yes, they can. It gives them an awful lot of confidence going into a tournament knowing they have this ability, this resource, that they can call upon. That takes away quite a lot of the fear on it's own because before they didn't have any tools. They would've had the usual advice. You have to stay positive. You have to stay relaxed, and so on. Those words, frankly, don't mean anything. In fact they can often do more harm than good. It's not as simple as that.

H: *So you are working on three levels: releasing the past trauma or fear, empowering the client in the present, and helping them to predict or map their desired future as well.*

S: Yes. I hadn't thought of it quite like that but I think that's a very elegant way to describe it.

H: *Many people are skeptical when they first hear about Havening because it just sounds too good to be true. Were you skeptical at first, if so how did that shift for you?*

S: I was skeptical. In the line of work that I do, I come across many different therapies. As soon as I hear something new I have to try it myself. So, when I first heard about Havening, I approached it in much the same way. And I knew I had to take Paul McKenna's recommendation very seriously. So skeptical, yes, and also open minded. As I mentioned earlier, once you see with your own eyes, it hits you like a sledge hammer. You know that something profound is going on. You don't know what it is but you can see how powerful it is and how much benefit it can be to people.

H: *Thank you. In addition to your work coaching elite performers, you're also a physician, who had a fully traditional medical education and practice. You've also evolved in your work to integrate new tools*

and approaches like the three H's that we talked about—Havening,
HeartMath and hypnosis. What impact do you see Havening having
on both the practice of medicine as well as mental health practice
over the next ten, twenty years?

S: I've thought about that quite a lot and that's a tough question. Here's what I would like to see. Doctors are trained in a
very conservative way. I would like to see a more open-minded
approach from the traditional medical community from which
I come. I would like to see more of an openness amongst the
medical community to at least consider things that are outside
their area of expertise. Of course many doctors do this. The
situation is improving all the time but I still perceive some en-
trenched views out there.

I suspect it will take time. I would like to think that process
could be accelerated. I think what would help if we can get
some very well conducted research on the table, written in a
language and style and precision that they would be familiar
with. I think that would help enormously.

Where are we going to be ten years from now? I think
Havening is going to have a much higher profile. Many more
people will be practicing it as therapists and that will include
members of the traditional medical community. I see a critical
mass building.

I also know that Dr. Ruden deliberately launched Havening
to the wider world only after he used it himself for many years,
and is doing this cautiously because he doesn't want to cause a
revolution. He doesn't want to alienate the medical community. He's going softly, slowly and step by step.

H: *And of course, as you mentioned, more research will help that*
critical mass build. The more we are able to present what's already

happening in Havening in our clinical experience in the language and the form and the style that it can be received.

One more question. What advice would you give somebody who is considering adding Havening to their tool kit? What would you tell them?

S: That's an easy question for me to answer because I've followed my own advice on this. If you're going to learn something new, particularly if it's going to be something really important to you, there is no substitute for being trained by the best people in the world. I've adopted that philosophy throughout my career. In the short term it might cost you more money or you might have to travel or whatever, but it will be worth it.

You don't get any better than Dr. Ron Ruden, so find out where he's doing his training. If you can't go to him, then go to his trainers because they are very carefully selected. There are many people who train others in Havening now. It doesn't matter which trainer you go to as long as you go to the best.

Havening sounds easy, but nothing as profound as Havening is really easy. There are things that you have to know about and be prepared to deal with. I don't think you can just come off the streets, go to a Havening course for a few days and set up your own private practice. It takes more than that.

H: *Thank you so much.*

CHAPTER 20

Transforming stress into serenity

Bonnie Park

Bonnie Park is an acupuncturist in private practice in Vancouver, Canada.

Harry: *Bonnie, how did you first discover Havening?*

Bonnie: I first discovered Havening through a good friend of mine. We learned EFT, emotional freedom techniques, together. She invited a few friends and colleagues of ours to attend the very first Havening training workshop to take place in Vancouver BC. The training was actually just in September, 2016.

H: *So you're fairly new to Havening?*

B: Yes.

H: *And you are an acupuncturist, correct?*

B: Yes.

H: *Who are your typical clients? Is it anybody who is dealing with a physical problem?*

B: It's a mix of people whose chief complaint is stress and also people who suffer from physical ailments like back pain, shoulder pain and neck pain.

H: *How are you currently integrating Havening into your practice?*

B: Thus far I've been using Havening for people who have come to me with a specific issue related to stress. With those clients I spend the first thirty minutes of our 90 minute session doing Havening. For the rest of the time I give them a nice relaxing acupuncture treatment according to what their body needs.

H: *So you actually start the session with Havening, and then once you've released whatever needs to be released on the emotional level, then you go to the actual acupuncture.*

B: I do.

H: *How's that working out so far?*

B: So far the clients that have been experiencing this combination are feeling very relaxed. They're able to fall asleep during the acupuncture session, which is so beneficial for amplifying the effects of acupuncture.

H: *So the Havening is actually making it easier for them to more fully receive the acupuncture treatment.*

B: I believe so, absolutely.

H: *What else do you like about Havening as you're learning to use it more and more?*

B: I love that it doesn't re-traumatize them and that they don't have to go into so much detail when they're talking about a traumatic event or a memory that they just can't get out of their heads. It's gentle and beautiful and it evokes a lot of creativity.

I really love that creative aspect of Havening. I like to give the client a lot of space to imagine what they like to see when we go into the distraction phases. There will be times where I just give them an open question, "What do you see?" They come up with the most beautiful scenery, the most beautiful images.

I like to work with them with their images, because what comes to them first can be really important. For example, someone could imagine a beautiful garden. I would then have them elaborate on the image by describing the colors of the flowers. If it's a ballroom we might explore the colors of the chandeliers or the rugs and just go from there. It's so much fun walking along with them in that creative way. They know what comes next and they know what makes them feel better.

H: *What I'm hearing you say is that you help the client tune into to the specific sensory details, the color, the shapes, and the smells so that they go more deeply into the experience.*

I love to use the client's imagery as well. I worked with a woman today in a demonstration and one of the questions I asked in my brief opening interview with her was about her favorite food, which happened to be macaroni and cheese. So during the distraction phase, I took her to her favorite restaurant for her very favorite macaroni and cheese. She picked up the fork, took a bite, described exactly what it tasted like. It's so wonderful when you use something that already appeals to the client's positive emotion. It can make the distraction phase much more elegant.

B: Yes. I think I'm learning a lot more as I work with more and more clients with this technique. Everyone is so different. It's so creative; there's no limit to where we can go with the distractions. I always start with going up the stairs. It's a good opening to get up into a creative realm. The kind of imagery that the clients come up with is fascinating. I'm even thinking about changing my intake form to include questions like favorite foods, favorite places, so that I can get to know them more. Then it becomes that much easier to find a safe and happy place for them to go to during the Havening process.

H: *Yes. I do something similar on my intake interview. I'll do a pretty comprehensive survey of the things that they enjoy. I learned this from Carol Robertson, a Havening trainer who was my mentor when I went through the certification process. She told me that two things are happening when you work with someone. You're depotentiating the traumatically encoded memory and you also are potentiating whatever other emotions or feelings you want to increase. So you're taking one thing away and you're adding another thing. So why not draw from what already makes a person feel good?*

B: Right. I think that's beautiful, and it works so well.

H: *You have experience with EFT and also have other tools to use when you're treating someone. What place does Havening occupy in the full array of tools and interventions that you use to help your clients heal?*

B: That's a very good question. I'm still experimenting with how I can make Havening a bigger part of the treatment protocol with patients that come in with pain, because I'm a firm believer that pain, especially chronic pain, is sometimes rooted in emotional issues and trauma from the past.

But to bring that up to someone who's just come to see me for something physical is a bit challenging at this point. They're not always ready for me to ask if they want to go back to the past and get to the root of the problem. So when patients come to me with a specific physical complaint I will only use acupuncture at those times. I currently explore Havening and EFT only with patients who are coming to see me with the complaint of stress.

H: *Since you've been using Havening what are some of the most interesting things you've seen or discovered with your clients? Any stories you care to share?*

B: I have to say honestly that every session has been interesting. This morning, I had a client who was just finishing up a five session package with me. Over the five sessions we were using Havening and acupuncture, focusing on her exam anxiety. In the beginning her exam anxiety was so severe that she felt like she was not in control.

Before the exams, she was so stressed her blood pressure went shooting through the roof. It was just too much for her to handle. Right now she is in the middle of finals. She came to me today after finishing six exams in the past two weeks and she told me not once did her blood pressure rise up again.

She told me that she had never felt this calm before an exam before and she actually used the words "I feel so much clearer" and "My mind was more clear". She had more confidence. She felt so much calmer. She was so happy. She said, "it made room in my brain. I was anxious, but I just didn't feel that it was a big deal anymore. I felt like I did my best to study and whatever happens will happen." She finally realized what it feels like to be free of this exam anxiety. To see that kind of result really humbles me and just makes me realize how powerful this is.

H: *I love that story. One of the things I enjoy about this kind of work is that it often feels as though we are breaking people out of jail and setting them free. They've been locked in an internal prison sometimes for thirty or forty or fifty years and then all of a sudden you give them a key. They turn the key, they open the door, they walk out and they never go back again.*

H: *Bonnie, many people are skeptical when they first hear about Havening. It just seems too good to be true. Were you skeptical at first? If you were, what changed that for you?*

B: I was skeptical. Will it really work as fast as it says it will? Will it really change the memory? Will it really help us move on and move forward?

I had a very big moment at the training conference. Dr. Steven Ruden chose me as a client in a small group activity. We worked on a very specific issue that I had already worked on with EFT for two years.

I thought I had gotten through it, but there was still a huge part that was unresolved. The issue involved my relationship with my mother. Dr. Ruden did a Havening session with me. It lasted 20 minutes. I cried a lot, I released a lot. It was gentle, beautiful, profound.

When we finished I was still skeptical. I thought after doing EFT for two years, I had worked on all of these issues. Dr. Ruden told me, "The way you look at your mother is going to change."

I didn't see my mom for about two weeks. When I did see her I forgot about having worked on our relationship with the Havening. A couple months passed and I didn't have any of the same emotions that I had before working with Dr. Ruden. That's when I knew this was phenomenal, because it worked on me. This had been such a complicated issue for me. And I felt so different.

H: *It is remarkable how powerfully, completely and quickly those perceptions can change. What happened when you had the Havening session is that it cleared not only a single memory but it cleared an entire network of memories, so that your experience of your mother was no longer the same.*

I've had that experience using Havening with clients around a specific relationship. and once the client does the clearing of their relationship with that person it's almost like the relationship becomes brand new again. I worked with somebody a few days ago who was struggling to heal some old hurts related to a relative, it might have been a mother or a father who had passed on. Afterwards, they said, "Now I remember the good things about them and the bad things no longer hold me as strongly."

H: *What advice would you give somebody—it could be a someone in traditional healthcare or an acupuncturist or a counselor or coach, somebody who is looking into the possibility of adding Havening Techniques to their toolkit?*

B: I don't think I'm in a place to say too much as of now because I am still in the experimental phase. And I am still in the process of becoming a certified practitioner of Havening. But my advice would be to try it. Don't be scared, because it won't hurt anyone. It's so simple—deceptively simple as Dr. Ruden says. That's where the beauty is. It's so easy for us to get traumatized but finally there's a simpler way for us to heal. My advice would be just be brave and go for it because it's worth it.

H: *Thank you. Yes, it is remarkable that these three simple components, touch, attention, and imagination, could be used to transform feelings, painful and difficult feelings that a person might have held for their entire life. It's a tribute to Dr. Ruden that he developed this elegant, simple tool through all of those years of research. It's like we have access to a miracle in our hands.*

B: Yes.

CHAPTER 21

From broken down to breaking through

Stephen Travers

Stephen Travers is a hypnotherapist and NLP practitioner based in Dublin, Ireland.

Harry: *Stephen, how did you first discover Havening?*

Stephen: I was reading an interview by Paul McKenna, where he is talking about this technique that he believes is going to change the face of therapy across the world. That got me very curious. In the interview, Havening was called Amygdala Depotentiation Technique.

Then I went online to research it more. I came across the book *When the Past is Always Present* by Dr. Ronald Ruden, the creator of Havening. I bought the book online, read it and was very impressed by the neuroscience behind the Havening Techniques® and the results that Dr. Ruden had been achieving with his own patients over nearly a decade. This was about three years ago—in 2013.

H: *Did you then attend one of Dr. Ruden's trainings?*

S: I'm based in Ireland, in Dublin, and I attended one of the first trainings in the United Kingdom. It was the second or third officially certified training.

H: *Regarding your practice, you are a hypnotherapist, is that correct?*

S: Yes, I have been in private practice for the past 15 years as a clinical hypnotherapist, psychotherapist and NLP practitioner.

H: *I would imagine you have a wide range of clients that come to you.*

S: Yes. I work with people on various issues. Anxiety, panic attacks, fears, phobias and other issues like IBS, irritable bowel syndrome. I work with people dealing with addictive or unwanted behaviors around weight loss, and emotional eating. I also help people quit smoking.

H: *So you already had a number of tools to work with to help your clients, particularly hypnotherapy and NLP. When you discovered Havening what changed? Did Havening have a significant impact on the work that you do with your clients?*

S: Yes. Havening has had a massive impact. First of all, what I found Havening did was it really educated me in the specific neurobiology of how trauma becomes encoded in the brain and body. When I'm working with people, especially with anxiety related issues, the information and the knowledge behind Havening has helped me to pinpoint what causes the specific trauma, how to find it within my client very quickly, and then the techniques themselves then allow me to remove or clear the trauma very rapidly and effectively.

H: *Do you use Havening with most of your clients now?*

S: I do. I use it with all my clients for anxiety based issues, almost all the time. I also use it with my weight loss clients. I find Havening is excellent for helping clients with emotional eating. I run a program called Think Yourself Thin and I do stand alone sessions within that program with Havening on emotional eating. I find that it's very effective. It gets to the root of why they're eating from the emotional aspect; then the Havening Techniques themselves help to clear the negative emotions or drivers that were causing the unwanted eating patterns.

H: *So Havening helps you get to the cause of the pattern.*

S: Yes, it helps me to identify what's driving the negative emotions with the client. What's behind this behavior. Once we can identify that, we then can shift and clear it with the Havening processes.

H: *Wonderful. Are there any particular client stories that represent the power of Havening that you'd like to share?*

S: Yes, a couple come to mind. I remember working with a gentleman, Ken, and he's actually given me permission to share his story.

He came to me with IBS, irritable bowel syndrome. He had been suffering with it for many years and it was really impacting his life every day. He was very anxious when it came to his social life and work because of the IBS. He'd seen many IBS specialists, and medical doctors about it. He was on a lot of medication, one of them being Imodium, but wasn't really getting great results. The IBS wasn't going away and his anxiety was getting worse. Combined with the IBS itself he was stuck in a vicious cycle. He came to me out of his desperation to find something that would help.

Within one session, the IBS completely cleared. It was gone. The anxiety completely shifted. The IBS itself completely stopped, the physical sensations he was carrying in his stomach, the pain, the cramps, disappeared. He had been taking 10 to 11 Imodium a week and his Imodium intake completely ceased after that one session. In the second session we did a little bit more work and by the time he came back for session three he was absolutely transformed. We did three sessions total. That was about two years ago and it never came back.

H: *That's remarkable. How long had he suffered with this before he came to you?*

S: About a decade.

H: *Wow. Any other client stories you'd like to share?*

S: Yes. I remember I was working with a lady who had a lot of problems at work, a lot of bullying was going on. She ended up having panic attacks. She was also feeling very stressed and depressed. She wasn't sleeping properly at night. When she first came to see me, I remember she seemed broken emotionally, very fragile, very vulnerable, very anxious.

Once again, as we pinpointed what was causing it, and we havened the events that were causing the anxiety, within one session the anxiety disappeared. She did two sessions total;

that's all she needed. Because of this experience, she ended up training in Havening and becoming a certified Havening practitioner. She left the job which she was working in. Now she lives in Spain and is a fully certified Havening Techniques practitioner with her own practice. It's been quite a remarkable turnaround for her. That one session completely changed her life direction. So I'm very happy about that. That one Havening experience completely transformed the arc of her life and where she ended up.

H: *It's beautiful to be able to help someone transform their life so profoundly even in a session or two. Many people are skeptical when they first hear about Havening. The possibilities just seem too good to be true. Were you skeptical at first, and if so what changed your mind?*

S: I was more curious than skeptical. I have a lot of respect for Paul McKenna as a therapist, so when I saw his testimonial about Havening, where he shared what he thought about it, I knew Havening must be something special. Then when I read Dr. Ruden's book, *When the Past is Always Present,* I was very impressed with the depth and breadth of the neuroscience behind the techniques and Dr. Ruden's understanding of how trauma gets encoded and why and how Havening clears this.

Then, the more I started to research and study it and then to use it with clients and see the miraculous results, that was proof in and of itself. I had both the neuroscience and the tangible results that I could see happening with my clients. That's all I needed.

I like getting results for people as quickly and as easily as I can. As I see it, my job as a therapist is to help my client as quickly, effectively, and easily as possible overcome their challenges and problems. Havening does all that and more.

H: *That's beautiful. How about the issue of touch? Here in the United States psychologists and other licensed mental health professionals are not allowed to touch their clients. How do you address this? Do you have people self haven? Do you facilitate it? How do your clients respond?*

S: I've trained and studied in various psychotherapeutic methods over the years. A lot of that approach is talk-based therapy where you don't use touch. With my clients, I explain first of all some of the neuroscience behind Havening and why the touch is so effective. I explain what's actually happening in the brain and the body when the touch is applied and how it actually helps heal the clients.

Then, I also explain to the client exactly what I'm going to do. I explain to them how we can actually test and measure the effectiveness of the treatment, even within the session. So for example, if you have a very distressful memory, I explain how we can then go back to that memory and the emotion after we do a treatment and test and measure how effective the treatment was.

The majority of my clients are very happy to do that. I think the fact that they can actually see and feel the results in real time within the session is a very positive aspect of the Havening Techniques, because people can really feel that something has happened or changed within that moment.

H: *Thank you. You began this conversation by quoting Paul McKenna speaking about how Havening could potentially change the face* *of therapy forever. How do you see Havening impacting therapy ten to twenty years into the future?*

S: It really depends on whether Havening is embraced by more and more clinicians. I think it will have a major impact in the field of psychology and the treatment of trauma. It helps therapists understand how trauma gets encoded and how they can more effectively and rapidly treat their clients.

There's so much potential for Havening to do so much good for people around the world. I think it could also potentially have a major impact globally, especially in countries that have gone through wars and some of the tragedies happening, for example in Syria. Havening could have a massive positive impact for the people in those places.

What I also find interesting is this. When I look at the field of psychology in contrast to the field of technology, in the field of technology, anything that's new and high tech that works better and faster is embraced very quickly. When a new iPhone comes out, or a new piece of technology or software, everyone seems to want it and everyone's using it very quickly because it works better and faster.

Unfortunately in my experience, I notice in the field of psychology a lot of people are caught up more in theories and dogma. They aren't necessarily very open to new ways of doing things. So I think if people open their minds up more, particularly the clinicians that are out there, that could make a big difference to the evolution of the field of trauma and how we successfully treat it.

H: *Thank you. What excites and inspires you most about Havening as a tool?*

S: It still inspires me even though it's now three years down the line after treating literally hundreds of people with Havening, and doing thousands of treatments. It's the speed and the effectiveness of what Havening can do in terms of creating results for people.

I'm most excited about the new applications that are emerging with Havening. We're understanding how Havening effects the brain, how we can help people change the way they think, how they feel, and how they behave as they move into the future.

We're understanding how we can apply Havening to speed up the process or produce more positive states and behaviors with our clients.

We're understanding how we can use it in conjunction to support the individual's personal development once we clear the trauma. I'm excited with that aspect of it.

We call that Growth Havening. We have the individual learn how to grow and develop or create and design their life to move forward and apply Havening to help them do that.

H: *Yes, that's very powerful. So we have two basic categories of application, one is removing the things that we don't want to hold on to, and the second is actually bringing into our awareness, into our brain and mind and habits the things that we desire. So it works in both ways.*

Stephen, you are one of the most prominent trainers in Europe. You do a number of trainings in Ireland and all over Europe and you're very active in training people who are new to Havening. The client you mentioned before became a certified practitioner. I'm sure others that you train do that as well.

What are you noticing and discovering as you're spreading the word about Havening within your geographical region? How do people respond?

S: I do a lot of introductory talks on Havening. For example, every year I speak at the Mind, Body, Spirit Fest in Dublin and there's lots of therapists and coaches attending. I find that when people actually see a live demonstration of Havening they're incredibly impressed, if not slightly skeptical, simply because of the speed and the amazing results the treatment can produce.

I find that once people realize how effective the treatment is they tend to be very excited to get involved in it, to learn it and to embrace it. I think all the neuroscience behind it is a great asset for the treatment to have. We can explain actually how we get the results and actually describe what's going on in the brain, what's going on in the limbic system and what's actually happening when we clear the trauma in the brain and the limbic system and the amygdala.

So I find generally therapists who really focus on getting results for clients embrace the treatment. More and more people are now seeking out Havening as a treatment because they can be free of trauma or various problems quickly and quite easily.

H: *Thank you. What advice would you give somebody, for example, a counselor or a therapist or a coach, maybe a parent or a teacher, somebody interested in looking into the possibility of going to the training and adding Havening to their toolkit? What would you say to them?*

S: I would say first of all, do your research. There's some great resources out there like the official website, havening.org., and my website stravershypnosis.com. There's a wealth of neuroscientific information as well as videos of live Havening demonstrations and client testimonials. I'd also say to speak to a certified practitioner or trainer in your area or country. Have a chat with them over the phone, send them an e-mail. If you have a problem, go and have a session and experience this for yourself.

H: *Yes. There's nothing like experience. I've noticed that once a person, no matter how skeptical, actually experiences Havening for themselves and they feel and see and know that the change has happened, then everything shifts and so much becomes possible.*

S: Yes, because they get a real personal experience of how effective it is then and that's what is quite interesting. Sometimes I have clients come in and even when we shift a major trauma they're surprised that it went so quickly. Sometimes people are a little bit skeptical; they come back a week later and they say, "I can't get that bad feeling back anymore, it's completely gone."

H: *Very often somebody will say to me, "Is it really gone?, or "How long will this last?" or, "Is it going to come back?." I tell them, "No. It's not coming back—it really is gone." Then a week or two or three or four later they realize it's not going to come back.*

S: Some people go off and they test this to try and get it back and can't get the bad feeling back which is great, because it proves to them that they're completely, permanently free.

H: *Yes, and what a wonderful thing to help people not only just cover up a symptom but to really clear it at the root so that it never comes back.*

S: Yes. One of the main distinctions of Havening is this: a lot of times clinicians are trying to manage the problem or mask it or help you cope with it. But what Havening does is it helps to pinpoint what's causing the problem and then to completely and permanently remove it so it's gone for good. I think that's the big difference.

H: *Yes, what a huge difference that could make in our world if Havening was available widely and universally so that people could truly let go of their problems for good.*

S: It would save a lot of people a lot of time, that's for sure.

H: *Yes. Wonderful. Thank you so much Stephen for your reflections and your stories and your answers and your fine work spreading the good news about Havening in Ireland and all over the world.*

CHAPTER 22

Seeing miracles every day

Donna Ryen

Donna Ryen is Veterans-Havening chair for the United States and maintains a private coaching practice in Ann Arbor, Michigan.

Harry: *Donna, how did you discover Havening in the first place?*

Donna: A colleague in the UK, who is a therapist and coach was familiar with Dr. Ruden's work.

H: *Who are your typical clients?*

D: My clients vary. I have worked for about 25 years as a corporate coach and life coach. I have an office here in Ann Arbor, working with various and quite diverse individuals and professional groups that are interested in Havening. So clients span from individuals seeking personal change to mental health professionals who are open to learning new techniques and business executives working with their teams.

H: *Since you've learned about Havening, how has it shifted or transformed the work that you do?*

D: As a coach, I've used, and still use, many different models for facilitating change in the people who come to work with me but Havening has become the core of my practice now. I've trained in TFT, EFT, NLP, and other modalities but, in my opinion, there hasn't been anything as elegant as Havening for transforming the unconscious often negative, emotional drivers people are struggling with. We can work on metaphorical, behavioral, psychological, practical levels, but there's always that emotional piece that can remain as a strong, unconscious driver for the individual.

So once the emotional/neurochemical responses shift through Havening, clients can experience a real change, make new choices and attract those things they've been wanting in their lives more effectively. This, in turn influences the client's fundamental ability to act from a more authentic sense of self and move toward a more productive future.

H: *Yes. That's really interesting. Adam Vane, one of our colleagues who's an executive coach, talks about the distinction between outside-in and inside-out coaching, and how so many of the models are based on an outside-in approach. And Havening is one of these tools that allows you to really change things from the inside-out.*

D: Yes. Adam is wonderful. That's always been my approach as well, I call it 'Leadership from the Core.' However, when you interview a lot of business leaders, their focus is how to change employee behavior by imposing rules from the outside without the consideration of what it really takes to change individuals, cultures and organizations. Corporate structure and expectations are important, but if you have a block inside yourself, it's very difficult.

H: *What do you like most about Havening?*

D: I see myself as a facilitator of the client's self-healing and staying present with them as they release long-held beliefs and memories is incredibly exciting and rewarding. I'm literally watching the rewiring of their personal story and it's the science of it that makes all the difference. Having insight and understanding of the neurological functioning that keeps people circling around the same issues means we can go deeper faster and the impact is greater. With this work, we break the cycle. For good. It's a creative process, it's about listening deeply and guiding, but it's backed up by this incredible scientific insight into the brain and how it works.

H: *Yes. Whether you're facilitating the Havening touch, or whether they're self-facilitating, it does tend to bring you really into the present moment. You can't drift or go anywhere else.*

D: When I'm teaching Havening, I often discuss the PC'S: Practitioner Preparation, Client-Centric and Safe Space. Before a practitioner engages with a client, they should ask themselves: Are you physically and emotionally well enough to see a client? Can you stay client-centric, putting their needs first for the whole session? Can you create a safe or sacred space to help facilitate a deep and far-reaching process?

H: *Yes. When you think about all of the different tools and techniques and interventions and everything that you've learned in a quarter century of coaching and empowering people from different walks of life, what place does Havening currently occupy in that larger repertoire? Is it one of your primary go-to tools? Do you work with Havening with most clients? What role does it play in the larger picture?*

D: It plays a major role, more and more. Other techniques began falling away, and Havening came more to the forefront of my practice. And it's something that you integrate, as well. So, it's not that I don't use my coaching skills. But Havening is integrated into the majority of everything that I do.

H: *This is something I am hearing over and over again. Whether the person starts out as a coach, or a psychologist, or a counselor, or whatever their focus, once they begin to integrate and use havening and really understand its power, it becomes one of their top three modalities or tools.*

D: Yes, absolutely. It's up there. It's not that I don't use other things, but it's definitely in the top. I remember when I put on my first Havening training here in Ann Arbor, one psychologist said to me, "I'm getting used to seeing miracles every day." And for me, that's really was such a key phrase. Another one said, "This is the missing link. This is what I've been looking for to help people change," and I thought, yeah, I agree.

H: *I love that. Seeing miracles every day. What are some of the most remarkable things you've seen and experienced in your own application of Havening, either with your clients, or in your personal journey?*

D: I've seen dramatic change happen, but in an integrated way. That is what is so key. It's not like the client has a quick and temporary high, feeling good and then two weeks later they're depressed. One client came to me to work on issues in attracting more money and getting a business off the ground. She was continually broke and fearful about making money. In one session, we ended up uncovering a traumatic event with a life-threatening link to money issues. After clearing the trauma through Havening, I was able to coach her on setting up a successful career and her business is thriving today. It's jaw-dropping to witness sometimes. And as facilitator, you walk away changed by that, as well. What's most incredible to me is how people are able to clear issues they've been working on for years and years.

It amazes me how creative people are, how we share a fundamental drive toward wellness. So often what people will come up with themselves to solve the problem is far better than I could ever interject or think of. That's a beautiful thing to see.

H: *Yes. I love that, when the client has that look on their face and their own answer comes, and it's a far superior answer than I would have ever been able to give them, because it's right for them, bubbling up from their own inner wisdom.*

D: When I was going through my certification, I called up Dr. Ruden. I had worked successfully with my first 20 clients, and on the 21st, I was puzzled, because the client didn't change in the first session.

I asked, "What am I doing wrong? I mean, everybody else did really great. What happened?" It seems funny now, and of course that was a powerful experience. I found it important to communicate, as a trainer, the appreciation of pacing and readiness of the client. Of course, sometimes you don't see immediate results. We joke about it now, but at the time, I was just getting very comfortable with things shifting in one session.

H: *You get used to the miracles.*

D: When you first learn the technique, you begin seeing things in a different way and you're inclined to embrace the bigger picture of helping the world by letting everyone know about Havening because the results can be so remarkable. That's just your immediate impulse and you don't want to come across selling something as 'too good to be true'. And as remarkable as Havening is, you want to be careful to communicate respectfully with your audience and not make unrealistic promises. Having said that, I'm incredibly passionate about what is possible with this.

H: *Many people are skeptical when they first hear about Havening. It sounds too good to be true. It also looks kind of silly. You're touching your face, your arms, your palms. You're counting from 20 to zero, humming a tune, and then, all of a sudden, your trauma goes away. So, were you skeptical at first? If so, what changed your mind?*

D: I don't think I was skeptical at first. I've used a broad range of different techniques over my career. So, I was more fascinated with learning and testing. I was definitely curious about whether the change could be permanent and really last. So, if there was any skepticism, it would be not that an immediate change couldn't happen, but that the change would really last.

H: *Yes. You are also a trainer. What have you discovered as you've been spreading the word about Havening within the professional community? How are people responding? What are you noticing?*

D: People respond much the same way as I did. They are very excited to learn any methods that will help them further their understanding and results. As a trainer, I can reach out to groups of people or professionals who have overlapping concerns with clients. For example, I just gave an introduction to a group of nurses from the Healing Touch Community. I'll be speaking in another week with a local practice of ten psychologists who are excited and interested in learning more about Havening.

I initially present Havening as an add-on technique to what they're already skilled at doing with the idea of enhancing or deepening their results. More often than not, Havening will become an invaluable resource in their tool-kit. For me, it went to the forefront. For others, maybe it will remain more of a powerful adjunct.

H: *How do you see Havening impacting the future of coaching, of mental health practice, of healthcare, and so forth, in the future? Ten, twenty years from now, what do you see happening?*

D: Well, I have my ideal, personal vision that as Havening grows and that more and more people become familiar with it, that it's widely accepted into, not just the alternative community, but also the mainstream mental health community. In time, studies more will be available that prove its effectiveness to a less receptive mainstream audience. As we know, there is suffering worldwide from events in the past that negatively affect so many aspects of our lives. And when you find something like Havening that is so effective with a relatively small downside risk, you can help so many people. But, I believe it represents a radical shift in how we think about healing.

And don't forget, there's much we're still learning about Havening. Collectively, we're learning from one another and the body of knowledge is being broadened. There's still more to learn and understand about how the brain works.

H: *Yes. And I think there's a place for that wildly expansive vision as well as the realistic pragmatism. My dream is Havening for humanity. Where every human being from cradle to grave has access to the tools both for themselves and for others.*

D: In the most basic sense, Havening has been biologically with us from the cradle. We comfort ourselves with touch, we rub our foreheads when we're worried, we comfort our children with soothing hugs. Now we are beginning to understand more deeply and scientifically how important sensory input our health and well-being. So Havening humanity and reminding people of the God-given gift that we already have these tools as part of our natural biology and now we can expand this to help our mind-body and brain connection .

H: *Yes. One of the ways that I talk about it is that Havening integrates these three elements that are commonplace on their own, but haven't been integrated in a specific way. There's the element of touch. There's the element of focused attention. There's the element of imagination. And all of these are innate to who we are as human beings and there are tools and techniques in each area. There's Reiki or healing touch or massage for touch. There's meditation and mindfulness for focused attention and there are also so many creative imagination tools. But it's Dr. Ruden's unique synthesis of these three for the purpose of healing emotional and physical pain that is groundbreaking.*

D: Well said; exactly spot on.

H: *I was speaking to a practitioner earlier today who had a conversation with a prenatal nurse who had attended a Havening intro. The nurse told her that she had observed babies, preemies, using* *three areas for self-soothing: the face, the arms, and the palms. How much more evidence do we need that this kind of touch is absolutely primal? I mean, imagine a tiny, little premature baby intuitively, reflexively soothing themselves through touching their face, the sides of their arms, and their palms.*

D: Yes. Brilliant.

H: *What advice, Donna, would you give somebody who is—maybe they're a coach, maybe they're a pastor or a counselor, maybe they're a therapist, maybe they're a nurse, maybe they're a doctor,—who is just looking into the possibility of Havening and adding it to their toolkit? What would you say to them?*

D: I'm not sure about advice, I may say or ask—Have you ever worked with people who seem to be repetitively triggered by a particular stimulus and pattern that doesn't change? Who have undesirable beliefs, emotions and behaviors that leave your clients feeling hopeless? How would it be for you to gain an understanding and technique that is consistently effective in these areas? Imagine giving them a tool that they can use with themselves, when stress and trauma arises to prevent undesired outcomes and strengthen resilience ? It's all possible.

H: *Thank you, Donna.*

CHAPTER 23

Even skeptics spread the word

Michele Paradise

Michele Paradise is wellness expert on Deepak Chopra's jiyo.com and founder of Change Your Mind For Good, based in Beverly Hills, California.

Harry: *Michele, how did you first discover Havening?*

Michele: I discovered Havening in London, where I was living at the time, through my NLP colleagues, who had been invited on a course with Paul McKenna, in 2013, the first UK Havening training. I couldn't make it to that training, but learning about it piqued my interest, and I started doing my own research. Everything I read engaged me more and more. I felt that this was something that would fulfill what I didn't realize at the time was a missing piece in my work.

I spoke to another colleague who said they liked it; Havening was changing their practice in a positive way. They were getting quicker results helping their clients to heal phobias and other trauma-related issues. I'd already trained extensively in hypnotherapy and NLP with some of the top trainers in the world, and I was open to anything that would help me help my clients.

I heard about an upcoming training in New York in October of 2014, and immediately decided to go. I jumped on a plane, attended the training, and it was probably one of the best decisions I've ever made.

H: *The October 2014 training. That's also the one that Kate Truitt attended.*

M: Exactly. That's where we met. I told her I was moving to Los Angeles and it would be great if we could do something together. And then we found out that we had a lot of parallels in our life. We had both worked as models, we both had suffered with eating disorders, and we both really saw the value of Havening and how it could and would do amazing things for clients. I wish I known about Havening when I was working with anorexics years ago.

H: *And you moved to LA a year later, correct?*

M: I moved here in November 2015 and Kate and I presented the first LA training of new Havening Techniques practitioners in November 2016.

H: *So who are your typical clients, currently?*

M: I don't see myself as a specialist. I treat everybody. I'm thinking about current clients as you ask me this question, and I've got a 16-year-old, a 75-year-old and everything in between. What they have in common is that every single client is stuck. Not broken, not diseased. I believe they're stuck and they need a bit of a push in the right direction, with the right guidance.

In my experience, that stuck-ness is connected to an emotional response to some sort of traumatic event or experience in their life, usually in childhood. And I can utilize this amazing tool to eradicate that, to melt that away, to delink, to decode that response, so that then the coaching, the growth, the empowerment aspect of my work with the client is even easier, and they get better results.

H: *How has learning Havening transformed your practice?*

M: I didn't know there was something missing, but now I incorporate Havening consistently. I call it the Havening sandwich. That's absolutely a beautiful metaphor for me, because I do the archeological dig at the beginning, using my NLP skills, which are great—metamodel questions, and all of that—and then I move into Havening.

The transition is seamless. I haven whilst I do some NLP techniques, as well. So, there is an overlap. And then we move onto hypnosis, or what I would prefer to call future pacing, so that we build a bigger, better future for the person. Havening has lifted my practice to another level. I work much more quickly and much more efficaciously. I get better results for my clients. Sometimes I see them for only one or two sessions and we're done.

H: *Do you tend to use Havening with most of your clients these days?*

M: Yes. Very rarely do I not use it. Doug O'Brien posted something last week about how he uses Havening, not all the time, but he uses it overlapping with NLP. And for me, that is super powerful. So I do this as well, and I'll also Haven while I'm doing future pacing or hypnosis or whatever.

H: *Thank you. Do you have any stories you'd like to share about things you've seen or noticed that have been particularly significant to you in your application of Havening?*

M: Probably the coolest thing that has happened to me on a personal level with Havening is this. I have low blood pressure—I'm usually 90/60—and I have a digital blood pressure cuff. I used to check myself from time to time, although I hardly use it anymore.

However, about five months ago, I got some really hard news, and I knew, I could feel, that my blood pressure had risen dramatically. I put the cuff on and I was 172/102, which is really high and very out of character for me.

I decided to do some self-havening. Let's test this and see how it works. I self-havened for about seven to ten minutes. I put the cuff back on and my blood pressure was 120/75. I was really pleasantly surprised and amazed by how quickly it shifted. I used Affirmational Havening, repeating "I am calm, I am calm, I am relaxed, I am relaxed, I am cool," to cool myself down. So, on a personal level, that was extraordinary for me.

Here's my next story. I've been doing a lot of intro evenings. The blurb before I arrive says I will be asking for a volunteer from the audience.

So, during one of the intro evenings, one woman attending was very skeptical. She raised her hand and came up. I told her that this could be absolutely content-free, which she preferred. And I asked for something fairly small. Nothing too big, because I didn't have a lot of time.

She sat down, got her to close her eyes, activated the memories. There were 38 people watching her, so that didn't help, either. She was shaking; physiologically, she was changing. Her breathing, her skin tone, all shifted. I'm thinking, "This is going to be interesting." So, I started Event Havening with her, and after ten to fifteen minutes we were done. She got down to a zero. I was sitting there thinking, wow! I didn't say that out loud, but I said it to myself. Wow. I thanked her and we exchanged email addresses, because I said I would like to check in with her to see how she's doing. She checked in with me four or five days later and said, "I just want to tell you that I was really testing you, because I didn't believe in any of this stuff. I'm quite skeptical of it. And I can tell you now what my event was: My cousin, at the age of seven, said something to me that sort of stuck with me." And it kept her in this bad place for years, and she was now 42 years old.

She continued, "I couldn't believe it, because it just cleared up. It was gone. When I think about it now, I laugh. When I think about the event, I laugh, and I walked out of there feeling lighter and freer." "I just think it's amazing, and I thank you very much for relieving me of the traumatic memory and the traumatic emotions around it for all that time I've been carrying it around." So, that, for me, was probably one of the most remarkable experiences, because of the circumstances.

H: *Yes, of course.*

M: There was another woman at the same event, and she said, "I wanted you to choose me." So, I got her to come up quickly, and we did a Transpirational, Affirmational one, because she was stuck in her career. I saw her recently, and she came up to me and said, "Oh my God, you're that woman. I just want to thank you. I've just broken through to the other side with my career, what was sticking me in place, and it's just amazing how quickly it worked." And I wasn't able to give that one a lot of my time and attention. I gave it everything I had at the time, but that was maybe five minutes. So I am continually amazed by how quickly Havening can work and how it lasts.

H: *As you're spreading the word what are you discovering and noticing about how people are responding?*

M: I do live in a very open-minded region out here in LA, in terms of spirituality. However, it's new, and I'm new, and I've got this British accent, so sometimes I see people with crossed arms, heads tilted, people looking at me skeptically. But they showed up, so they're obviously interested, and that's a very positive thing. They've come and they want to learn.

I frame this work as stress and anxiety management. So, just about everybody in the room is going to be dealing with something like that in their lives.

They're quite skeptical at the beginning. And then I tell stories like I just did about my blood pressure. And they begin to melt a bit and relax in their chair. And then, by the time I've done a demo, they're really on board. And afterwards, I get a lot of people coming up to me thanking me or saying, "I'm not sure about this and I'd like to know more," or, "Could I book a session?".

In one of my first intro/demonstration sessions, there were people there who knew me but didn't know what I did. But often, even the naysayers are taking it in.

For example, I was at a party the other day and this very bright and successful woman, who had attended an intro, but who also happens to be very anti-therapy said, "We were talking to somebody was really stressed out, and I told them to do some Havening!" That's what happens. It begins to sink in.

And then she admitted that she went for a job interview and she uploaded my video, which is a 12-minute self-havening process. And she havened along with me on the video. She told me, "I'm going to be really honest with you. I don't believe in any of this stuff, but I got a much better result. I was much more relaxed and I got the promotion. I'm not saying it's all due to Havening, but it certainly helped."

So, I now have disciples out there. Even if they're not coming to see me, they're out there spreading the word, and there's really nothing negative they can say about it.

And people frequently will say to me, "What happened to that woman? What happened to that woman that you Havened?" And, you know, I had permission to tell them, so I tell them where she is now and what's happening in her life.

H: *Beautiful. What advice would you have to somebody who's looking to at adding Havening techniques to their toolkit. What would you say?*

M: Do it. Absolutely, without question. Just do it. I also think it is an adjunctive tool, so I don't think that anybody who isn't trained in other areas should just learn Havening. And I believe the doctors would agree with me. Your other skills enrich your capacity to work skillfully with Havening and Havening can enrich and enhance your other skills.

H: *Yes.*

M: And it can take whatever you're doing to a whole other level.

H: *I had a conversation with Tony Burgess recently around this idea that Havening is a tool, not a therapy. How you use that tool depends on your own capacity, skill set, scope of practice.*

M: Absolutely. That's what's so beautiful about Havening. You can integrate it into your existing skill sets. And I discover something new with almost every client.

I've recently been exploring what I would call birth or rebirth Havening. I had a traumatic birth and I know that that influenced my childhood—showing up as nervousness and anxiety. What I'm finding is I'm asking every client about possible birth trauma. Because if you think about it, it's the very first trauma that you experienced, and if it's not healed, delinked, decoded, it's still there.

So, now I do a Havening process that takes them from the womb, down the birth canal, because on a cellular level, on a memory level, the trauma is still there unconsciously. And then we do outcome Havening to change the story. The results have been amazing thus far. That's one way I'm adapting it.

I'm also working with actors, because I don't think that actors should have to relive their own personal traumas in order to elicit the tears and anxiety and other emotions required by their craft. So, I'm working on a program with the owner of an acting studio here in LA and we're doing it differently. So, we're integrating Havening and NLP and modeling excellence and all that stuff.

H: *Wonderful tool. Adaptable pretty much infinitely.*

M: I love the creative aspect of treating clients. It's limitless. I'm evangelical about Havening, and I've never been evangelical about anything in my life. I know I sometimes might bore people to tears, but I just think they need to know. When I see people in pain, I know that I have this gift that has been given to me by the Rudens and the rest of us working in this field.

H: *Thank you.*

PART VI

Real Problems, Real Solutions

CHAPTER 24

Building the toolbox

Susan Cortese

Susan Cortese is President of Smart Business Communications and Discernys, both based in Paris, France.

Harry: *Susan, how did you first discover Havening?*

Susan: It just so happens that I am friends with Tony Burgess and with Julie French. Julie told me about it, and said, "Tony has discovered this thing. It's really cool. You should learn a little bit more about it." And I thought immediately of a good friend of mine who had been attacked, and she was really suffering from post-traumatic stress. She had been in a really bad place for over a year without being able to eat or go outside. So, I took her from Paris up to the UK, we spent the day with Tony, and I saw the effect.

She wouldn't be touched by a man. So I did Havening, while Tony guided her, so I participated fully in Tony's work, also coming up with some examples that would help her.

H: *Beautiful. And from that moment on, you knew it was something that you wanted to pursue and learn and explore and share with others.*

S: It's the share with others that was most important, because I'm not a therapist. I'm a coach.

H: *Yes. So am I.*

S: And I see that it heals. Nobody in France at that point had ever heard the word "Havening" before, and I just thought I want to bring this to this country.

H: *That is exactly the position I'm in. I'm not a therapist, but I see that the tool is just so incredibly powerful for relieving suffering, so we're very much on a parallel path. Thank you so much. So, as a coach, who are your typical clients?*

S: I'm an executive coach and business consultant, and I work in people skills, so I'm in companies.

H: *Do you integrate Havening at all into that aspect of your work?*

S: I do. If it's for the coaching, working with individuals, obviously we're working on an objective which often has aspects of managing stress. And so, I use Havening most for that: managing stress, managing emotions, and getting over past events in order to have better performance, or just better wellbeing.

H: *When you're working with a business client, how do you introduce the idea of Havening to them?*

S: Naturally, simply. I just explain it. You know, I haven't really changed what my business is in that way, in looking for coaching clients and working with those clients. It just often comes up in a session that I see that Havening could help. So, I say, "I know this tool. I can use this tool. I think it could help in this way. How do you feel about that?" And 100% of the time, they say, "Fantastic. Go for it."

H: *That's beautiful. What are some of the most interesting things that you have observed in your application of Havening with your clients? Any stories or examples you care to share?*

S: First of all, the most amazing thing is that symbiosis that happens with the client when Havening them. Seeing them voyage in their minds, and after the Havening, they're feeling so good, so relaxed. You know, some people say, "I feel like I've just come back from a long holiday." And then seeing the happiness on their faces and hearing how much better they feel, and then the next time we get together, hearing what kind of results it's brought about. It can often be amazing.

H: *Yes. Any specific examples of how that works in the business context that you'd like to share?*

S: Recently I worked with a woman who had a big event coming up, and she was very stressed out about it, and we did several Havening sessions to get her over what was holding her back. Then we used Outcome Havening for the upcoming event, having her feel really positive and self-confident about it, and getting her to a place where she could do what she had to do during the event without the stress. And she got back to me afterwards and said it was fantastic.

H: *Wonderful.*

S: Yeah. She just did a really good job.

 With another person, we were working on the anger that she often felt in different business meetings at a very high level in a big international company, and that anger was making her non-communicative, or speaking in a way that she shouldn't in those kinds of meetings. So we did the Havening on the anger, got her to spit it out, get it out of her system, and she felt absolutely fantastic afterwards. We followed that up with some Outcome Havening, also, so that she could imagine new ways of dealing with the different people problems she was having.

H: *Yes. And as a result, when she goes back into the business context without that anger, she has a great deal more freedom in choosing her response.*

S: Exactly, and she can say what she needs to say in a way that won't be aggressive.

H: *Yes. So often, the problems that we have in business are really not connected to the circumstances themselves, but they're connected to that traumatically encoded memory of some other pattern in our unconscious that we can't quite get a handle on. And having a tool like Havening allows, really, the transformation of those patterns. So, again, we can be more responsible, as opposed to reactive. That, for me, is one of the most wonderful things that I see with my own clients.*

S: I worked with a woman who had real self-confidence problems and self-esteem problems, and the Havening helped her overcome those, and in the same way, the practical application was thinking about her business communications and how she could deal with them. Her specific problem was dealing with certain direct reports and getting them to listen to her, being listened to. And overcoming those past obstacles, those things that had happened to her in the past, gave her that freedom, as you said.

H: *Yes. Many people are skeptical when they first hear about Havening because the possibilities just seem too good to be true. Were you skeptical at first? And if so, what changed your mind?*

S: I wasn't skeptical, and that's because of my faith and my trust in Tony. I just wanted to see it, and my first experience was one wherein seeing is believing.

H: *Yes. The quality of relationship and rapport that we have with the person who refers us is so incredibly important. I would say the same thing. I first heard about Havening through a friend of mine, who also is a coach, and he referred me to Dr. Ruden's book.*

I would say I'm an open-minded skeptic; I like evidence, but I won't necessarily just jump into something just because it's popular, because somebody else says it. But once I got the book and read the neuroscience and understood the background, I tried it on myself. In 15 minutes, I released a belief and a block that I'd been trying to deal with in a number of other ways for a couple of years. And first, I thought, how could this be? That propelled me to taking the workshop and becoming a practitioner and now sharing Havening with others.

As a coach, specifically a coach who specializes in communications, you have a number of tools that you use. What was most challenging or difficult, if anything, for you about integrating Havening into your existing work?

S: I'm not sure if it's a difficulty, but it's making a choice to ask the client if they would like to try Havening and feeling that this is what would be appropriate at this point in time. Sometimes, I have the feeling Havening could be very appropriate for the question that we're working on, but I'm not sure that the client would be ready to hear about that.

H: *Yes, I understand.*

S: And then it comes up later, and there I feel a greater readiness that the client will understand why and accept it, and we go for it.

H: *Yes. To what degree do you introduce the science when you're explaining or introducing Havening to a client?*

S: Almost always, as far as what's happening in the amygdala and what are the different electrochemical changes that happen in the brain.

H: *I'm finding, as well, that when I introduce Havening, more and more, I lead with the neuroscience and I lead with the story of Dr. Ruden and his research. I have a pretty wide range of clients, and I find, depending on the client's background and their particular propensity, sometimes the science, understanding the science, introduces a deeper quality of safety.*

S: I've gone through a process where, in the beginning, I always started with the science, because I do find it, as you just said, extremely important for the credibility of it and the reality that the changes are biological. And now, I start more with the innate aspects of touch, of feeling safe, of how we always do it, and that we're going to touch the arms of our friends or the faces of our children whenever they need comforting. So, we know naturally that that helps, and now we know scientifically why.

H: *Yes. That's a very elegant explanation. I like that. I will often have the client, or if I'm teaching in a group, I will have them simply experiment with self-havening, and then say, "How do you feel?" And inevitably, they will say, "Calm, safe, relaxed, peaceful," et cetera. And I'll say, "Well, there's a reason for that. We are biologically wired to respond to comforting touch with this increase in delta wave production, increase in serotonin, GABA, the decrease in cortisol and adrenaline and so forth. And people say, "Oh, that's why I feel better."*

How do you see Havening impacting the future as it becomes more and more well-known?

S: Havening for therapists to heal troubles is amazing, and I am fascinated by that and the stories of our fellow Haveners who are using it in that capacity. I think that is remarkable, and as I said, I would love for more and more therapists to know that they can add Havening to what they're doing and get faster results, and that it fits in so well. And then, for the self-havening, personal use, I see that also becoming something that could become a normal tool to use.

S: Gaelle du Penhoat is a practitioner here in France who wrote a book this year about stress management tools. I helped her out with that and wrote about a couple of the tools, especially Havening. So now there is this book, with all these tools for helping ourselves, and Havening is in there. It's part of the toolbox.

H: *Beautiful. One more question for you, and that is, what advice would you give someone who's looking into the possibility of adding the techniques to their toolkit? What would you say to them?*

S: First of all, the adding idea is the most important, that it takes a real professional to use it well, I believe, and that someone who already has their practice and has results and has rapport and knows how to work with people, will just find that they'll get better results with Havening, or at least quicker results.

H: *Yes.*

S: I don't think Havening does everything. I think that, when we're working with someone to go towards an objective or get over something from the past, that it's a lot more than the biological changes that we can effect. It also involves cognition and thinking about it and self-discovery. So, with other techniques, Havening gets them to where they need to be to advance.

H: *Yes. It really is a beautiful tool that enhances the effectiveness of anything else. I think of it as a kind of amplifier and accelerator.*
    Thank you, Susan.

CHAPTER 25

The root of the issue

Ira Scott

*Ira Scott is a Social Emotional Life Coach and founder of
LEAN INTO LIFE™ Inc., based on Long Island, NY.*

Harry: *Ira, how did you first discover Havening?*

Ira: It's an interesting story. I was in the corporate world for fifteen years. When the market imploded in 2008, it was time to make a decision in terms of what I wanted to do.

I decided, instead of chasing after the next big commission check, that I would pursue something that I have a passion for. For many years, I felt a life calling to help people, to do something that was more psychology-based. I also had an interest in self realization and human behavior. I had studied NLP on my own, then decided to formally train in NLP, hypnosis, Strategic Intervention and other modalities.

So, my dentist of over thirty years knew what I was doing and knew about some of the changes in my life. He used to drop hints that one day we might be working together. That always confused me because I had no plans to go to dental school. Little did I know what was going on behind the scenes! Lo and behold, Dr. Steven Ruden later would tell me and share with me about what is now referred to as the Havening Techniques.

H: *So Steven Ruden was your dentist?*

I: Yes. He invited me to a very small group presentation on Long Island, out near where his dental office is.

H: *So this was before he and his brother led the training in London and formally introduced it to the world.*

I: That's correct. There were maybe ten people there. I attended and met his brother for the first time. Steve Ruden did a demo with Kris Murphy who is now, as you know, a certified Havening practitioner. The transformation I witnessed was just unbelievable. From there I became really curious to understand more about it, in particular how and why it worked. I'm the why guy; I'm very analytical. I want to know the why behind the what.

Then in the Fall of 2013, I attended my first formal two-day training in New York City. Ron, Steve and Paul McKenna were there. I became a certified practitioner in the summer of 2014 and a certified trainer in the summer of 2015.

H: *Who are your typical clients?*

I: There really is no typical client. I don't limit myself by having a certain demographic that I target because I think that ultimately if we follow an orthodoxy, we limit who we can help. I once heard Tony Robbins say that whenever he runs into a therapist or a coach who says that they have a very difficult client what he's really hearing is a coach or a therapist who has run up against their own limitations.

H: *So you serve a wide range of people.*

I: Yes.

H: *How has learning and using Havening transformed your practice?*

I: It has expanded it. It's another modality, another tool, another resource. It is very rare that I will start a client with Havening. Yet, I almost always end with it.

H: *You mean in a single session or in a series of sessions?*

I: In a series of sessions. I would say with probably seventy-five to eighty percent of my clients, I end up using Havening at some point.

H: *So considering you have this really wide range of tools at your disposal, why and how do you specifically integrate Havening? What purpose does it serve within the larger context of your practice?*

I: I'm trained in NLP, Strategic Intervention and Neo-Ericksonian Hypnosis, based on the work of Milton Erickson. It involves indirect suggestion and conversational hypnosis. Havening as a bolt-on has been very useful. It reinforces the work that I'm already doing.

H: *A bolt on to the other tools that you already use.*

I: Right. Also vice versa. When I'm working with clients (we don't do this in trainings because we want to keep the process pure and clean, sticking to the protocols) within the Havening process, I may integrate conversational hypnosis. Or I may integrate some aspects of NLP into the Havening process which also makes it, in my opinion even more powerful. So it works both ways.

H: *In terms of this kind of integration, I really appreciate how powerful Havening, either self-havening or facilitated Havening, can be in evoking that state that you might define as trance or deep relaxation or greater receptivity to whatever else you want to do. Whether or not you're using Event Havening or one of the other Havening protocols, the touch alone is a powerful tool for state elicitation.*

I: Yes, absolutely. I teach my clients to self haven and also invite them to devote five to ten minutes to Affirmational Havening. I think the other types of Havening are better experienced with a skilled practitioner.

Ideally, this will be the first thing they do in the morning when they wake up and the last thing they do before their head hits the pillow, instead of watching the TV or news. People report great results from that.

H: *So many people are skeptical when they first hear about Havening. You were introduced to it in an interesting way from someone you knew for a long time. Were you skeptical at first and if so what changed your mind?*

I: I don't think I was skeptical. I approach life with an open mind and an open heart. I have a great deal of respect for Dr.

Ruden and thought if this is something that he wants me to witness and potentially be a part of, I should take a look at it.

I understand the skepticism of others, though. It almost seems like you can't believe it unless you witness it for yourself. I understand that, because there have been so many miracles within Havening so many stories that have been told about how people's lives have been transformed in just one session.

But for me, initially, I just had an open mind and open heart, loved what I saw and was hungry for more.

H: *Any Havening stories you'd care to share?*

I: Yes. More often than not the presenting problem is not the problem. It's typically a symptom of something else. Here's an example. This happened at a Havening intro at a wellness center on Long Island, with maybe ten people attending.

I did an intro to Havening, a bit of the history, a bit of the science and then asked for a volunteer to do a demo. Of course, I also mentioned that we can do this content free (another great attribute of Havening). The woman who volunteered was very eager. She sat down and I asked what was it that she wanted to work on.

She said, "I have this behavioral issue that I really need help with." For her it was what she called procrastination. She also seemed to imply that she would prefer to work content free.

I asked some questions, including asking her how long has this been going on. She said, "my whole life." She's probably in her fifties, and I'm in rapport with her, so I exaggerated her response. I said, "Your whole life! Really, you mean, from the moment you were born, you've been procrastinating? Oh my god; that's amazing." That did two things. It changed her state because she started laughing. It also was a pattern interrupt, interrupting the story she was telling herself, because of course she had not been procrastinating for her whole life.

After the laughter died down, I said, "Seriously, take a moment and think about when it started in your life." "When I was sixteen." "Okay. I know you want to go content free and that's absolutely fine. So tell me as much as you are willing or want to share as to what occurred when you were sixteen."

She took a few minutes to come up with an answer; I actually think she was thinking of a way to say it without directly saying it. Her answer was, "When I was sixteen there was something I wanted and needed to talk about, and my mother said no." Now I have a specific event.

I did Event Havening on her mom saying no to her at sixteen. Her physiology completely shifted. By the time we were done, she was in a relaxed state. She looked completely different. When we came back to the whole procrastination issue, it was almost as if that word had no meaning to her.

Afterwards, everyone left except for this woman and the person who owns the wellness center. We were talking amongst ourselves, and very matter-of-factly she comes out and says, "When I was a child I was abused." Of course, that was ultimately what she wanted to talk about when she was sixteen and she wasn't allowed to.

What is so interesting about this case is that not only did we de-encode a trauma from childhood, which enabled her to talk about something she'd been wanting to talk about for forty years, we also shifted her "behavioral problem."

What's really interesting is when she first volunteered, sat down and talked about this thing called procrastination, she had no clue (in her conscious awareness) that her procrastination as an adult had anything to do with something that happened to her in childhood.

That insight only came out through the Havening process and it was because she subconsciously was afraid. She lived in this fear that if she did something wrong, she would experience pain. Her past experience and current 'problem' were connected, but she had no conscious awareness of the connection.

With Havening we learn to listen both for what's being said and for what's not being said. We pay attention. We develop the sensory acuity to notice if what the person is saying is congruent with their physiology. We also consider that whatever they're presenting as a problem likely is a symptom of something else.

H: *I love that story because it illuminates something I've noticed, as I've learned about Havening, worked with more and more clients, and refined my capacity for history taking. I start to see so-called problems and behaviors very differently than I did before. I'm automatically looking for that traumatically encoded memory or that event or that other experience in the past that's showing up in the present in a way that's most likely completely unconscious to the person. They don't know where it came from, but they have this pattern of behavior that doesn't serve them. And for me, this ability to help a person liberate themselves from such a pattern is one of the greatest things on Earth.*

Any other stories or cases that you'd like to share?

I: Yes. This next story also took place at an intro, in New York City. We had a small group of five or six, and we're up on the third floor of a building—by New York City standards not very high up.

We cover a little bit of the history of Havening, a bit of the science and it's time for a demo. I was actually with a fellow trainer, Doug O'Bryen, and when we do intros we generally take turns doing the demo. This night it was my turn.

A woman volunteered. Her issue was claustrophobia. She said, "I have to be in a room with windows." Luckily, we were. She said, "I can't go in an elevator, I don't like confined spaces." So subways were also out of the question.

Before I continue the story, a bit of an aside. One of my trainers years ago said that in therapy and coaching work, it is best to remain as deductive as possible throughout the process. Only go inductive when absolutely necessary and if the client is stuck. And, if you are going to go inductive, to always do it in the form of a question.

One thing I tend to see with people in the therapeutic world is that they can tend to go inductive and they're doing it in the form of statements, introducing their own beliefs, their own values, their own opinions. Obviously, they can be way off base.

With this in mind, I stay deductive as best I can when I work with clients. However, on this particular night, I violated my own rule. In the back of my mind, as she was explaining her story of claustrophobia, I heard the voice of Dr. Steven Ruden say that often times people who experience claustrophobia have had drowning experiences.

So I went inductive in the form of a statement. I looked at her and said, "So, tell me about the time in your life when you almost drowned." She burst into tears, looked at me and could barely speak. I got her a Kleenex, calming her down and staying connected with her.

She was awestruck and looked at me, through her tears, saying, "How do you know about that?" I said, "Some very good training" (chuckles). And that also added humor and changed her state a bit.

Then she told her story. When she was seven years old, she was at the beach with her dad. Her dad would pick her up as a little kid, walk out into the ocean waves and swing her through the water. There was a moment when he dropped her, and she went under the water. She wasn't tall enough to be able to stand so the water was over her head. He was searching to grab her and pick her up, but in that brief moment she was traumatized.

So we did event Havening on this incident that happened forty-five plus years ago. When we were done, her physiology had shifted and she was in a relaxed state. When she went back and revisited that memory, it was like just another day at the beach. It didn't have the emotional charge any more. The best part of the story—when we left, she actually went down in the elevator.

H: *The symptom of claustrophobia had been healed at the root.*

I: That's right.

H: *I think that's the value of Dr. Ruden's emphasis on understanding the science behind traumatic encoding. The science behind unconditioned threat stimuli. The science behind how the amygdala fight/ flight/freeze system works in the first place. When you understand this, it gives you a kind of X-Ray vision. It allows me to see things that I otherwise wouldn't see as a result of it.*

I: Absolutely. One more point. We were only on the third floor, but when she arrived she walked upstairs. When she left she took the elevator and said, "I don't even remember the list time I was in an elevator."

H: *It's tough to be claustrophobic—especially in Manhattan!*

I: Yeah.

H: *Let's talk about the issue of touch. It hasn't been standard practice in the United States to use touch in this way. Any issues around that?*

I: No. We discuss it. By the time we get to that conversation we're already in rapport and there's already a certain level of comfort with the client. When I first meet and start working with somebody, ultimately it's about creating rapport and establishing trust. So when I get to Havening, we just have an open discussion about it . We discuss the fact that this technique does involve touch. I explain to them that I can apply the touch or you can apply the touch yourself. I demonstrate on myself what the touch involves so they can see it's non threatening. We're simply using the face, the arms, and the palms of the hands.

In the hundreds upon hundreds of people I've worked with, I have only ever had one person who said that they would prefer to apply the touch themselves. So we went forward with them self-havening and it was very effective and got the results.

H: *Any other reflections on this issue of touch?*

I: Yes. At its core, Havening is bringing to the therapeutic community this element of touch that is so fundamental to our well-being.A newborn baby has to be physically stimulated—touched—in order to live. We all know that if a newborn child is not physically stimulated the child will not survive, the child will die. This need to be touched is hard wired at birth.

H: *I think it's beautiful how this technique has been developed based on solid science that reinforces what human beings do naturally.*

How do you see Havening impacting the world in the next decade or two?

I: I think as it grows and expands and more and more people become aware of it, it's going to take on a greater role in the therapeutic community. I think we'll be moving away from the dominant medical model, because we both know, for the most part, pharmaceuticals are a band-aid. You put somebody on medications. They have all different side effects, some of which can be life threatening. And, frankly, you're managing symptoms and you never get to the root.

That's what I love about everything that I'm trained in, because whether it's NLP, hypnosis, Strategic Intervention and of course Havening, it's not symptom management, it's getting to the core cause, it's getting to the root of the issue and dealing with that, and then the symptoms go away on their own.

As Havening becomes more mainstream, which it will over time, I think there will be less emphasis on drugs and people will begin to realize that there's a better way. And we'll be able to more readily get people the help that they truly need that really serves them.

H: *What are you noticing as you're spreading the word about Havening within the professional community of therapists and coaches and others? How are people responding?*

I: In the therapeutic community, I think that you're going to come across people who were like me in the beginning. They have an open mind, they have an open heart, they're curious.

I think if you can just get people curious and get them exposed to it, Havening will speak for itself. And for those that are resistant, I think that they will come around in their own time.

They may have a set of beliefs that limit their ability to be open to the possibility of something so seemingly miraculous. With those people, I'm very gentle in my approach. I don't really attempt to force things on people; I think that people figure it out in their own time, their own space and their own way when they're ready.

H: *I think it's clear that many of the folks who are engaged in Havening right now are people who are open minded, curious, early adopters. Particularly because it hasn't been around for so long. Anything else you're noticing as you're conducting trainings and you're sharing this tool with people who will use it to serve others?*

I: The people who attend are people who have embraced the idea of something that can help them get results with their clients. They're curious by nature and they really want to have an additional tool to be able to help their clients and get the results.

It's ultimately all about getting results and impacting people's lives. What's even more valuable is that when you hear these amazing success stories and it seems like you've changed a life, the fact of the matter is that we haven't just changed a life, we've changed many lives. This person has family, they may have siblings, they have parents, they may have kids, they may have a spouse, they have friends, they have neighbors, they have co-workers, they have bosses.

It's the ripple effect. Others will experience transformation because this one person's been transformed. That's often overlooked. So the reach to one is ultimately the reach to many. That's another amazing feature of something like Havening.

H: *What advice would you give somebody who's looking into the possibility of taking the training and adding Havening Techniques to their tool kit?*

I: Do it. One of the greatest ways we learn is by experience. That's also something that's different with Havening: it goes beyond talk therapy. In my coaching work, I don't give people advice. What I do is I get them out of their own way. I get them to the place where they realize they don't really need me. Often it's about assisting them to have the experience of discovering their own answer. The same applies with Havening.

If someone was considering taking the training, I would give them a Havening session so that they could actually experience it within their own life and feel the power of it. Because ultimately, and I don't like to use the word sell, but for the lack of a better word, it sells itself.

H: *Thank you so much. As we're talking, I'm having this visceral sense of this ripple effect, one person touching another, touching another, until we one heart at a time help to heal the heart of this world.*

CHAPTER 26

What matters is what works

Doug O'Brien

Doug O'Brien is a Hypnotherapist and NLP Master Trainer with a private practice in New York City.

Harry: *Doug, how did you first discover Havening?*

Doug: I was introduced to it by my colleague, Ira Scott. About three or four years ago he said to me, "There's this new thing I learned called Havening. You really need to find out about it." I am skeptical, honestly, about a lot of things. So I told him, "Okay, if you say so. I'll try to keep an open mind. Let me see what it's all about".

I went to an intro and I was interested; it sounded like something that I could maybe get behind. Then I went to the full training with the two Dr. Rudens in New York City, met people like Tony Burgess and was impressed with what I saw. The demonstrations with Paul McKenna and Dr. Ruden just blew me away. This was in 2013.

H: *You have a really extensive background in hypnosis and NLP. So I can imagine you've seen many different methods and techniques.*

D: Yes. I've been doing NLP and hypnosis since 1985. For me to be so impressed by Havening is saying something.

I've seen a lot of things come and go and am by nature rather skeptical. I was skeptical about NLP when I was first introduced to it as well. But I tried to keep an open mind and like with Havening, I was blown away with it. My first teacher of NLP was Tony Robbins. And his take on NLP was that it doesn't have to follow the set rules. What matters is what works. What matters is you get the result that you're going for. So I always have embraced that principle.

H: *Since you already had a lot of skills, understanding and competency, has learning Havening changed your practice in any way?*

D: People don't come to me for Havening. They don't come for hypnosis or NLP. They come for an outcome. They want to stop suffering, or they want to get over a fear. They don't care how they get there. So I look for whatever tool is going to be the most effective one to get them there. And Havening has proven to be that in a lot a lot of cases.

When I learned Havening, I immediately starting putting it into that mix. So I still do NLP. I still do hypnosis. But now I often, probably sixty to eighty percent of the time, will include Havening in whatever session I do.

H: *That's beautiful. Something I love about Havening is the adaptability. Whatever your modality or your therapy or your philosophy, you can find a way to integrate it. Who are your typical clients? Do you have a specialty?*

D: I don't have a specialty. I've had my full time NLP practice since 1990, and I've got a solidly established reputation for getting results. Anything a person would go to a therapist for, of any kind, I've worked with. From depression to anticipatory anxieties, to sexual dysfunction or whatever.

I also worked for six years with Dr. Oz, at Columbia Presbyterian medical center, where I was the hypnotist in the department of complementary medicine. Part of the reason I was able to be there is that Dr. Oz and a few other open minded surgeons at the center were looking to see which alternative and complimentary therapies would be efficacious and workable in a hospital setting. We were being scrutinized to see if each technique would actually work and produce results. A variety of things were being tested.

One of the techniques being investigated was therapeutic touch. In therapeutic touch, there's actually no touch involved at all. It's an energy healing modality. Only nurses were allowed to be trained in it. It seemed very mainstream in many ways.

In therapeutic touch, the patient would sit in a chair or lay in a bed if they couldn't sit. The nurses would hold their hands five to six inches above the patient's body, scanning different parts of their bodies with their hands. They would feel the energy and determine where they felt an imbalance. Then they would bring a healing intention to that.

The technique seemed to be very good, people liked it. The nurses were even able to do this in the operating room. I wasn't allowed into the operating room because I'm not a doctor or a medical professional. I could only treat patients in their private rooms. But the nurses could go in there and do therapeutic touch while the person was being operating on, which is really wild! It was a widely accepted modality.

Then one day, a published report appeared. A sixth grader had done a science fair project, and had set up an experiment involving several therapeutic touch practitioners. She got a large refrigerator-sized cardboard box and cut two holes in it so that people could stick their arms through it without seeing what's on the other side.

She sat on the other side as they held their hands through these cardboard holes. Then, she flipped a coin. If it was heads, she'd put her hand over the person's right hand. If it was tails, she'd put her hand over the person's left hand. Then the person would say, "Okay. I can feel it on the right hand," or "I can feel it on my left hand." She conducted her experiment with ten or twelve therapeutic touch practitioners. Then at the end of the science fair project, she tallied the results. The practitioner's ability to feel the energy was no better than chance. In other words, they couldn't feel the energy.

I don't why this particular sixth grader's science fair project got so much press, but it did. If I recall correctly it was broadcast nationally on a show like 60 Minutes or something and reported in some newspapers. At any rate, virtually the next day, therapeutic touch was removed from the hospital. This is in spite of the fact that they were getting results... the patients subjectively felt much better, more relaxed. They could even see measurable factors indicating that the relaxation response was happening like their blood pressure being lower. They got tangible positive medical results from it, but because the science behind it was questionable, it was immediately kicked out of the hospital.

That's an important story for me, because it illustrates a critical reason why I like Havening so much. Dr. Ruden has done the research. When you apply the Havening touch you actually do make a neurochemical change in the brain. Delta waves are produced. You get calcineurin, you get GABA, you get serotonin. It really does work. That's one of the big reasons I'm sold on it.

H: *That's very important. I discovered Havening last Valentine's day, February 14, 2015. I was in a conversation with a friend of mine who's an executive coach. I was lamenting the fact that in the energy psychology world, the TFT, EFT domains, the science is still nebulous. They have some great studies including double blind studies, but they still don't have a mechanism of action that explains how and why it works. I've also studied NLP, I've had a private coaching practice for seven years. I've seen, as you have, virtual miracles happen with my clients, and I was really frustrated because I was searching for the science behind how these changes actually occur in the brain.*

My friend asked if I knew about Dr. Ronald Ruden. And everything changed from that moment on. I ordered the book, received it three or four days later. A month later I was in New York at the workshop. Six months later I become a certified practitioner, and now I'm actively engaged in the Havening community, writing this book and bringing a training to my home city.

My sense is that the specific neurobiological model that Ruden developed after his ten years of research opens up incredible possibilities and validates the experiences that we have that seem miraculous on a scientific, or literally a synaptic, level. Thank you for sharing your passion for the science.

What else do you like about Havening? What do you like about using that specific set of tools?

D: Numerous things. Number one, obviously, is that it works. That's the big thing. And it works for a variety of purposes. It works to set in new patterns. One of the things that we are striving for is to not only outgrow the old patterns but to grow into new patterns. With Event Havening and Transpirational Havening, we can outgrow old patterns, get rid of stuff that we don't want anymore. But with Affirmational, Ifformational, Outcome Havening plus the other protocols, we can help ourselves to set in place new patterns of functionality that are really important.

So I'm using this with, I said earlier 60—80%, it's probably more like 80—90% of my clients. It's pretty rare that I don't use Havening at some point with a client, even my executive coach clients. I've got clients who are not coming to me for a phobia or problem. They're executive coaches. I'm teaching them Havening and they're doing it. I've got a property developer in Florida doing Havening everyday. But he's doing Affirmational Havening and things like that in order to focus in on creating new patterns for himself. And it works!

H: *What was most challenging for you as you integrated Havening into your current work?*

D: You know what? I started using it with clients the very next day after the first two day workshop with the Rudens in New York. I've had no challenges with it whatsoever. It fit in seamlessly with what I was already doing.

H: *In your work do you do primarily facilitated self-havening, where the clients apply the touch themselves? Do you facilitate the touch?*

D: When I'm seeing someone in person, (I work with clients on the phone and on Skype and also in person), I almost always facilitate the Havening at first, then I teach them how to do it for themselves. So I start off doing it, assuming they are comfortable with that. Of course, they've completed an intake form that gives permission. I tend to do it for them at first so they get a sense of how it feels. I think it works better to have it being done for you.

H: *That's my sense as well. It will be interesting at some point for there to be some research around that.*

D: Yeah, that's interesting because it's a curious thing. There's a brilliant PBS series, The Brain by David Eagleman. In it, he talks about why it is that you can't tickle yourself. There's a reason for that. It's like with Havening or a massage. You can do self massage. It's okay; it works to get the knot out of your thigh muscle.

H: *But it's not the same as going to someone. Thank you. What are some of the most interesting, powerful experiences that you've had as you've used or observed Havening? Any stories you'd like to share?*

D: The one that I often go back to is the time I watched Dr. Ruden work with a woman who had been in the World Trade Centers during 9/11. That just amazed me because obviously she had been traumatized. Many people had been traumatized just from watching it on TV as I did. But she was actually in the buildings.

And to have her trauma be alleviated, basically, after ten minutes, was just astonishing. That's the one that I go back to when asked "what's the most amazing thing you ever saw?", because that was pretty much it.

When I work with people, every individual who has a phobia, who has a fear, who has a trauma, for them it's obviously huge. For them to no longer have that phobia or to no longer have that effect of the trauma is huge. I've done a lot of work with veterans, as an example. And to have them go from having regular nightmares and traumatic responses to not having them anymore is amazing. For them it is absolutely life-changing. I keep going back to my experience watching Dr. Ruden help this woman as the one that hooked me in the first place.

H: *It's amazing how one becomes more and more acclimated, but never less astounded, when you see these kinds of things happen.*

D: Very true. Well put.

H: *So from your perspective, how do you see Havening impacting mental health practice and wellness and coaching into the future, 10, 20 years in the future?*

D: I think that it really is something that's going to transform mental health. Freud was a seminal figure obviously in the world of psychotherapy, but he was also a Victorian. He was from Austria, growing up in a very patriarchal society. One aspect of that influence was that he actually sat behind his patient when he did psychoanalysis! They didn't even look at each other. And touching was just wrong—even illegal in some cases. You just didn't do that.

But it's such a human thing to have touch. When a child runs to his mother because he or she's afraid of lightning, the mother doesn't say, "sit down, let's talk about it."

H: *No, it's "hold me mommy, I'm scared!"*

D: It's just so human. So I think Havening is going to revolutionize things because number one, it's a natural human experience to touch and be touched, and number two, it works. So why talk about it for so many years in psychotherapy when you can literally get results in a season or two or three or whatever. I believe it will revolutionize psychotherapy.

H: *You are both a certified Havening practitioner as well as a train-er. As you've been spreading the word within your professional com-munity and your client community, how are people responding? I'm particularly curious about people who might be qualified to become practitioners and trainers. How do they respond to your sharing the work, the science, the experiences?*

D: Again, I have to give another shoutout to Dr. Ruden for the extensive research he did, because having the ability to say it has this science and research behind it, gives it backbone.

People are always intrigued by it. They're intrigued by this idea of psychosensory therapy, of being able to talk and touch at the same time. They're intrigued by the results that we get. They're intrigued by this process and by the fact that they can do it for themselves.

And when you add to it the discussion about how it works and the different components—the amygdala, the limbic sys-tem, the delta waves, the electrochemicals that are released, these electroceuticals, it's a pretty easy sell. People are excited about it. They want to learn it. When I reach people and I touch people, they're really intrigued.

H: *I worked with a really brilliant woman, a year or so ago when I was doing my case studies for certification. We did the session and she had a complete release of a significant long standing issue.*

She had this funny look on her face afterwards. She asked me, "Okay, so how did that happen?" When I explained it to her, I ex-plained the delta waves and the serotonin and the GABA and the calcineurin and the receptor sites and everything then she relaxed and said "Oh, okay, got it."

It's so fascinating how somebody can actually have the experience but once they have a cognitive understanding of the mechanism it seats it in an entirely different way.

D: Exactly.

H: *One more question, Doug. What advice would you have for someone who is reading these words who is looking into the possibility of adding Havening to their toolkit? What would you say to them?*

D: I'd say stop thinking about it and do it! It's the kind of thing that once you experience it, it flat out works. We have a body. We have an electrochemical system. We are an electrical and chemical mechanism. We get access to our brain, to our neurology, through touch and through the thoughts and ideas that we have. This—Havening—is the future, so do it now.

H: *Yes, this is the future. Thank you so much.*

CHAPTER 27

Get a taste of it

Olf Stoiber

Olf Stoiber is a psychotherapist in private practice in Munich, Germany.

Harry: *Olf, how did your Havening journey begin?*

Olf: I first discovered Havening about five years back, in 2011. I attended a Paul McKenna event in London with about 15 of my colleagues. It wasn't a therapist's training, but a huge event for the general public focused on improving your life.

Paul did exercises on stage, inviting people up to work on their own goals or to overcome something that bothered them. A couple of times, he invited somebody onto the stage and started rapidly rubbing their upper arms. We didn't know what he was doing. We knew his hypnotic work, and we knew his involvement in NLP—neurolinguistic programming—but this arm rubbing seemed a little bizarre at first. It went quickly and people after a very few minutes had a smile on their face and their issues were resolved. By some sort of miracle, people got better.

This amazed us. I took a lot of notes, and later some of us tried to emulate what we saw.I took one of my friends and I started rubbing their arms and palms. I think we worked on a particular phobia. And it worked.

At one point during the event, Paul mentioned the name Dr. Ronald Ruden, who taught him. I can still vividly remember going back home on Monday and googling that name. Eventually, I found a Ron Ruden who was a medical doctor in New York. I discovered a book he wrote on trauma. I thought, "That's probably him." So I sent Dr. Ruden an email telling him who I am, what I saw, what I experienced, and that I was really keen to learn what he has developed. I explained that I've tried it successfully on my colleagues here in Germany.

He was very appreciative, mentioning that I was the first person from Germany to reach out to him. He sent me several of his papers on Havening, but he told me there's no training available yet. I was sad to learn this. Being a practitioner in Germany, we are very keen on our certifications and professional qualifications.

I kept on bugging Dr. Ruden. I told him I could arrange a group of people if he would come over to Germany and teach us. I kept asking again, and again, and again. Finally, in 2013, the first training in London was offered; I knew I had to attend that one. I continued to attend many more London trainings after that. Then in 2016 I traveled to New York to attend a training, just to keep in the spirit and flow.

H: *Who are your typical clients?*

O: I get to work in many different areas, as a coach, a therapist and a trainer. My private clients are mostly people with more severe or profound issues.

For example, people who've gone through many, many years of psychotherapy with no results. People whose issues have been unresolved for many years or decades. People who wake up in the morning and go, "Oh, my God. Not another day."

H: *In treating your clients, how has Havening transformed your practice and your work?*

O: I cannot work now without using Havening, adding it into what I was already doing.

H: *What do you like most about Havening?*

O: The Havening community itself. There is an authenticity and compassion that you see when you meet people who are fellow Haveners. Having been to so many trainings, I've met a lot of people who might not have the best of intentions. When you deal with talk-based therapies or coaching modalities like NLP, you're bound to find the odd egg every once in a while, someone who is just trying to learn a technique so that they can manipulate others.

I haven't encountered a single Havener who wants to use this tool for anything else than making their lives better and their client's lives better.

In addition, obviously, there are the great results you achieve, as well as the scientific background, which is quite unique in many ways, evolving away from more esoteric terminology to a precise neurophysiological explanation.

H: *I've also noticed within the Havening community a beautiful balance between head and heart, between a high level of intellectual capacity and a deep sense of compassion and desire for service. I* *haven't seen that balance as well integrated in other professional communities.*

O: Yes, absolutely.

H: *What are some of the most interesting and remarkable things you've observed in your application of Havening Techniques? Any stories you'd be willing to share?*

O: Yes.

I remember this one female client who was victim to a multitude of traumatizing events—she had been taken hostage, raped many times, and also was pathologically allergic to touch. When she came for her initial consultation, she couldn't even shake my hand, because that would have triggered her trauma.

We discussed options. Obviously, my first impulse was to do hypnoanalysis, because this wouldn't involve touch and we could address the trauma without even exposing her to the very element that triggered reactions.

I also thought it might be a good thing to talk about Havening, because at the time I had just come back from a training, and I was very enthusiastic. So I told her about it. I told her how stupid it sounds to even consider using a touch therapy with her when that's the very thing that bothers her. I gave her the scientific background. At some point, she said, "OK. It's a leap of faith, but let's try this."

It became one of the most moving sessions I've ever had. She was in tears afterwards, but these were tears of joy, because she could really feel how the trauma was released, and how she could finally leave these horrible experiences behind her.

That was a good lesson for me. Not always going with my first thought, but really trusting the process. It was also a very beautiful experience for me and quite obviously so for the client.

When you put some trust in the process, as well as in yourself, as well as in the client's ability to heal, the results can be breathtaking.

H: *Thank you. Any other stories?*

O: Very early on, I was still trying to figure out a way to apply touch without it seeming weird. Ever since Freud initiated the development of talk-based therapies, touch has been completely erased from this work. Bringing back something that's actually very natural to an environment where it's been avoided felt like a challenge at first.

I had one client, a young man coming from a cultural and religious environment where males are very dominant. He was also very strong physically, one of these guys who you look at and get a little scared and don't want to look in his eyes for too long, because you're afraid you'll get beaten up! He showed up because he was suffering from a form of Hypochondriasis, always feeling like he had several severe illnesses although the medical check ups didn't provide any grounds for that.

At one point, after three sessions using hypnosis with little effect, I thought Havening might be really good for him. Especially transpirational Havening, starting with the feeling, seeing what transpires, and letting that process guide his healing. I explained it to him and he agreed on the process.

When I was sitting across from him, I still remember my discomfort. I was thinking, "Oh, whew, I have to touch him now. This is going to be weird." I could have facilitated his self-havening, but I prefer to facilitate the touch. We started. I touched his arms. I started touching his face.

I was thinking, "Oh, my God. I hope he's not going to beat me up. This is really weird." He began the transpirational process, with my continually applying Havening touch and him transpiring until the feeling vanished. It took a long time, maybe 40, 45 minutes. And the symptoms and emotional pain were finally gone for good. He was happy at the end.

That's when I realized for myself: the touch is not weird in an appropriate context, and, we have to leave our own presuppositions behind about what's acceptable and what's not. We have to consider that we are on the brink of a paradigm shift in this area. We need to trust the process. We need to explain why we apply touch. We need to take care that the context is right. Then we need to really just go for it and fully engage ourselves and our clients in the experience.

My client was able to get a really great result that I could not achieve using hypnosis. This was possible because I was able to address my own presuppositions about what's OK and what's not.

H: *That's a beautiful insight for you to have. Many clinicians who are traditionally trained also have a lot of hesitation around the application of touch, because their training is so contrary to that. I think it's a testament to your courage, your creativity, and your open mindedness that you were willing to explore it in the first place.*

Many people are skeptical when they first hear about Havening, because it seems just too good to be true. Were you skeptical at all? Did you experience any skepticism, even when you were learning from Dr. Ruden?

O: I wasn't skeptical at all, because in my first experience I didn't know what Havening was. I wasn't given any explanation. I didn't think of it as too good to be true because I got to experience it.

Bringing Havening to the German-speaking countries, and running trainings, I also haven't stumbled across much skepticism. Many people I've worked with have been able to directly experience or observe some form of Havening—in a group setting or in a demonstration. I think I will certainly be exposed to some skepticism and maybe criticism at some point, once Havening really takes off and becomes more popular.

In the second Havening training I led, I had a student whom I hadn't met before. He introduced himself as a university professor of biology. I thought to myself, "This is great. I get to explain applied neurobiology to a professor of biology." The first thing he told me was, "I found out about Havening. I saw Paul McKenna do it on YouTube, and I have to admit I'm very skeptical."

As I've already said, I like to give people a taste of it. The first demonstration we experienced together was enough to let him get a sense of what Havening is about. And nowadays, he's one of the biggest fans of Havening. He continues to study, apply, and use it every day.

H: *I've noticed that, as well. Once people have an actual experience, their perception changes. Since you have studied hypnotherapy, traditional psychotherapy, NLP, and other modalities, you have many different tools to work with. And, at this point in time, Havening is one of your primary tools, correct?*

O: It is. Although I usually don't just use one technique. I will mix and integrate. Perhaps beginning the session with coaching techniques and dialogue. Next, setting the stage for the healing process, perhaps using hypnotherapeutic language, then moving on to Havening.

Havening has become a technique I use almost all of the time. There's only one contraindication for me for not using Havening, and that is if the client cannot see any sense in it. If I explain it, and my client responds, "I don't like it," or, "I don't see how this can help me," I respond, "OK, that's not a problem. We can use something else."

Therapy should be about the client's needs. I can make recommendations. But it needs to feel right to the client. It's like going to a restaurant. You ask your waiter what's on the special today, and he says, "The fish is really good." You respond, "Oh, I don't eat fish. I'm a vegetarian. So, what else do you have?" He says, "No, no, no. The fish is really good. You don't understand." You repeat, "No, I'm a vegetarian. I don't eat fish. What can you get me?" He says, "Well..." and doesn't listen. 15 minutes later, you get served fish. That's what a lot of therapists do, and it's what I'm trying to avoid. They tell you they have the best technique, but they don't listen to the client's needs.

Having said that, it almost never happens that somebody does not like touch. Some people go into the experience and later, they tell you, "I never liked touch. I never like to be hugged. I don't like to be touched by people. I hate massages. But, you explained to me how the scientific background of Havening works, and it made sense. And, then, I discovered, I do like touch." It just needs to happen in the right context.

H: *How do you see Havening impacting mental health practices into the future, say the next 10 to 20 years?*

O: Two words—paradigm change. I feel like we're on the brink of a true revolution in the way we think about therapy and about the possibilities it gives us to assist our clients in improving their lives.

Freud started a revolution, introducing the world to psychotherapy. But, we also have to consider other processes beyond talk therapy that have been around for millennia. In ancient Egypt they used a process very similar to hypnosis. Many healing cultures, like in parts of Africa and in South America, have used many different processes, engaging the body and the imagination and ritual and more.

With Havening, we are simply rediscovering something that's actually very old, indeed. Touch is fundamental to human wellbeing. It's one of the most basic human needs. Havening uses its scientific background to reintroduce something very natural that has enormous healing properties.

H: *I agree. When I explain Havening, I describe it as comprised of three basic elements—the element of touch, the element of focused attention, and the element of imagination. Every one of these elements has been used in healing modalities for thousands of years, but they've never been combined in this particular way.*

You've got mindfulness and meditative practices to develop capacity for attention. You've got imagination, guided imagination as found in many modalities, from psychoanalysis to hypnotherapy to psychosynthesis. So much of Freud's work focused on exploring the process of free imaginative association.

You've got touch and so many touch therapies, from massage to Reiki to healing touch and more. But no one, until Dr. Ruden, thought to combine them together in this particular way for the depotentiation of traumatically encoded memories, and, to add the sol-

id scientific framework so that there is a clear neurobiological mechanism of action.

O: Yes. I agree. In 10 or 20 years, I cannot see a serious therapist working without Havening. Even if you use other modalities, like CBT, or psychoanalysis, or other forms of trauma therapy, we know that trauma is always also trapped in the body, in your physiology. We know if you don't work on the body, you cannot completely release all of the trauma. Obviously talk therapies can have a part in relieving trauma and its residual effects. But when we add Havening, we can finally fully liberate someone from the pain of their past.

H: *I love what you said about the revolution that's coming. I also believe that, in time, not a single therapist, coach, or person whose work involves the emotional empowerment of other people will be able to do without it.*

What have you discovered as you've been spreading the word about Havening within your personal and professional community? You're a trainer. In fact, you're currently the only Havening trainer in Germany. You're reaching out to people in different walks of life to inform them about this work. How are people responding?

O: I've never seen a Havening sales pitch, because people are just generally inspired by its possibilities. At this point, we haven't done any major promotion or advertising, so we're still in the luxurious position of only attracting the people who develop a true interest in the technique. At this point we've received a really positive response.

Just two days ago, on Saturday evening, we had a gathering of about 40 people. Many of them were former students of mine who have learned Havening. Every single one was excited.

Some are already certified. Some are currently in the process of completing their certification.

These student Haveners expressed so much exuberance about it, sharing how they now use it on a constant basis. So we are not simply telling people how great it is. We are getting direct feedback now from people who are using the tools over and over again. And those who haven't been trained in Havening yet are listening very closely.

H: *Thank you. I agree that there's no need for a sales pitch with Havening; it's just a matter of demonstrating how it works and helping people connect with that.*

What advice would you give somebody who was looking into the possibility of attending a training, adding Havening techniques to their toolkit?

O: If you're a coach, or a psychotherapist, or a medical doctor, or just somebody counseling people on a professional basis, it makes perfect sense to take Havening into your toolkit.

Get a taste of it. Find a good practitioner that you like. You can even work with them using Skype. Once you've tasted it, you'll want more.

When you've experienced the benefits of Havening first hand, you'll want to go into a training because it's so good, so effective, and so universal in the ways you can apply it to help your clients and yourself.

H: *Thank you so much.*

PART VII

A Safe Haven For Humanity

CHAPTER 28

Havening the world

Paul Emery

Paul Emery is developer of QEPR (Quantum Emotional & Physical Release) and co-author of The Soul Of Success.

Harry: *How did you first discover Havening?*

Paul: I discovered Havening through the internet. I'm a member of many professional Facebook groups, and I noticed several people suddenly started writing and raving about Havening. These were people like me that were qualified TFT practitioners. So I immediately did some research and discovered that Ron Ruden was doing a course in Ann Arbor. This was in 2013. So I booked myself for the course and flew from Thailand, where I'm based, to sunny Ann Arbor.

H: *Who are your typical clients?*

P: I work in health resorts a lot. So my clients are people who are doing health retreats. They go to spas and destination resorts, like the place I'm working now here in Thailand. Most of the people who come here are coming from outside Thailand. We get Americans, Russians, Chinese, English, Australians. People from over the world. They come to this place specifically to create more wellness.

Most of what's offered here is for the body—exercise, massage, facials, yoga. And I am here promoting my services. Many people don't expect me or the likes of me to be here because they're focused on the body.

H: *That must be a really exciting lifestyle. You get to meet all these different people and enjoy staying in wonderful places all around the world.*

P: Yes. Lots of different nationalities from all over the world. Today I worked with Russians, Malaysians, Arabs, and English.

H: *Wow.*

P: Many completely different cultures all in the same day. I've worked with almost every nationality in the world by now, including Mongolians. People from everywhere.

H: *Exciting. So what do the resorts say about your offering? How do they promote your services?*

P: People come see me to support their emotional health. Traditionally people come to a place like this for the physical stuff. Of course, their primary aim is to relieve stress. Everybody says, "I'm stressed. I'm gonna go to the resort. I'm gonna eat well. I'm gonna exercise. I'll have a massage every day." Their main goal is to relieve stress.

They don't really expect somebody like me to be available to help them deal directly with that stress. Sometimes they're reluctant to come see me because they think they've got to deal with some heavy duty emotional burdens. So they say to themselves, "I'd rather have a massage." Which in my view is a great thing, but its a temporary fix.

And they feel great after their massage. They feel great while they're here. They might feel good once they go back home for two weeks, three weeks, even a month for some people. They feel good, they go back home, they're relaxed, they have less muscle tension.

But then, of course, this can be like putting plaster over their issues. If they're still going through a divorce, or they've still got a phobia or they're still traumatized by something, then that emotional burden is always there in the background. It probably doesn't take much for that to come back up once they're back home.

So if they are going through a divorce, or a loved one died some years ago and they're still grieving about that, or they're dealing with some work conflicts, then it's good for me to be available to help them. Especially since, as you know, the kind of work we do is really thorough, because we actually address the core issue.

So they come to me, sometimes having no idea what they're in for. They may have never done anything like this before, this body-mind stuff. They might have seen a talk therapist, but nobody like me who does tapping or Havening. So it's quite unexpected. On the other hand, some people have never even seen a therapist in their lives and they've just been taking medication.

So it's really good to be here, as opposed to having an office somewhere where people know they're coming to see me and know exactly what we're going to do. Here it's unusual and un-expected that somebody like me is here.

When they discover me, they wonder if they want to deal with their stuff while they're on holiday. Some people say they don't want to because they're here to forget. Of course, you and I know that the best way to really forget about it is to come and see me and clear the issue for good.

H: *Yes, of course. Paul, considering your background in TFT, EFT and NLP, how has Havening transformed your work with clients? Do you use it most of the time?*

P: Right now I'm using Havening probably a good 80% of the time because I think it may be faster than the other modalities I've been using.

H: *What do you like most about Havening?*

P: I don't know if it's faster than the tapping and the TFT. But I like the fact that with Havening, you can put many things into the pot, so to speak. You can work with more than a single issue at one time, unlike with TFT where you have to do a different algorithm for each kind of issue.

H: *Paul, many people are skeptical when they first hear about Haven-ing because it seems too good to be true. When you first learned about it were you skeptical at all?*

P: No. I wasn't skeptical. I felt that I really must go and learn this. I was quite eager to learn. It was just something complete-ly different to explore.

H: *Do you have any interesting stories you'd like to tell around how Havening has worked for your clients?*

P: I had a client who suffered from war trauma. Severe PTSD for fifteen years and every night he woke up in terror. Nightmares, panic attacks, anxiety. He was on many medications. His life was a mess. He looked terrible. It was a little bit hard to convince him to come and see me, because he was Russian and spoke no English. So, as you can imagine, the language barrier was a challenge for us both.

I did three sessions with him. We worked with an interpreter. I knew that he woke up with these night terrors and that kind of thing. I told him, "Obviously you can't talk about the problem and it's too complex anyway." "Just think about what you would like to get rid of and the emotions behind it. The fear, the anger, the anxiety, whatever you're feeling."

It was completely cleared in those three sessions. No more terrors, no more anxiety, no more panic attacks, no more flashbacks. It was all completely neutralized. He was absolutely grateful, of course, and amazed that it just cleared.

I had no idea what the problem was other than it was severe war trauma and that he had these night terrors. So our work was completely content free. And we were able to clear fifteen years of war trauma. That was pretty impactful for both of us. You can imagine how grateful he was.

Here is another example. The day I finished my training in Ann Arbor, I had a client book time with me that very same evening for Havening.

He contacted me and he said, "Are you in Ann Arbor?" I said yes. "My mother wants to come and see you!" "Okay, how old is she?" "She's 83 years of age." He told me that she has a lot of regrets in life and a lot of emotions that she wants to let go of. We've only got an hour to work.

I told him to have her write down everything that bothers her because unfortunately I wouldn't have the time to just sit and listen to her talk about her life. I have to be direct and get the client to say what they would like help in and write it down, so I can read it. Then we can get to work.

She came to see me, this 83 year old woman. So she gave me the paper with everything that bothered her, and it was quite a big list, but there was nothing emotional on it. It was all physical stuff.

Now, I had just finished the Havening training and was keen to try the Havening, of course.

I asked her what was the main problem. She showed me her right hand. Her right hand was shaking violently. She said I can't put on my makeup and I can't write letters. I asked, "Have you been checked by your doctor?" "Yes, I have." "What did he say?" "He said we can't find anything wrong."

So that's actually a good indication for me as a therapist, since the doctors can't find anything. That actually gives me hope. Her hand had been like that for two years. She said "They gave me medication to try and stop it, it didn't help and it made me sick, so I'm off the medication. But I've still got this terrible shaking hand."

So we did Havening on the actual physical symptom, the shaking of the hand, and it did nothing. So I said how do you feel about this problem? She said, "I feel angry and frustrated." So we did some transpirational Havening on the feeling around the problem. And it didn't really do anything, either.

Her hand was still violently shaking. So I realized I've got to go a bit deeper. I asked her if there was anything in her life that she felt angry about. Anger can be a main component for physical symptoms.

She said yes, she was still angry at her ex-husband for leaving her 50 years ago. She wanted to write him a letter and tell him what she really thought and felt about him. This raised a flag for me. I said, "Okay. Let's focus on your anger that your husband left you fifty years ago. He abandoned you. I want you to repeat angry, angry, angry." So she repeated angry, probably for about 20 minutes! Angry angry angry, very angry, very angry, angry. Twenty minutes. I thought, "Oh my gosh, she's got a lifetime of anger!"

Anyways, eventually she stopped and lifted up her hand. No more shaking. And that was my first Havening session! Amazing, isn't it?

H: *Yes, that was like a trial by fire for you the very first time.*

P: I know. In the hotel in Ann Arbor. And it was such a visual thing to see. The shaking and then afterwards, no more shaking.

H: *Yes and it's also a tribute to you as a detective to really continue to look beyond the surface to find the core of the issue.*

P: I went for the physical symptom. Didn't work. I went for how she felt about it. Didn't work. So I went for the biggie. I said why are you still angry?. She didn't even blink! "Yeah, fifty years ago my husband abandoned me and I wanted to write him a letter." So she held that anger! Obviously not on a daily basis. It wasn't on her conscious mind. But that was the first thing she said, without blinking. So that was amazing that she just went there straight away.

H: *That's a beautiful example of the power of Havening. One more question. What advice would you give somebody who is looking into learning this, who is thinking about adding Havening to their toolkit?*

P: I would say go ahead and do it because it will transform your practice. It will make life easier and simpler for you and of course much better for your clients and patients. It's based on solid science. It can be content free. The client feels good having it done to them. You feel good as you're doing it. You can teach them; they can do it themselves. I'd say it's transformed my practice and of course especially as a therapist we like to learn new things and grow. I know I do.

I know many therapists like to stick with one thing. But for me, if they want to grow and become more effective, to be more efficient, to help their clients, to serve their clients better, then Havening is the thing.

H: *Paul, it has been wonderful to connect with you. You have a delightful, enthusiastic and passionate presence. I'm sure your clients feel that as well.*

P: Yes, they do. I do my best to put the Havening word out there. I've co-authored two books, as you may know, one with Jack Canfield and one with Brian Tracy. I write about Havening in both. It's one of my passions.

H: *Thank you.*

CHAPTER 29

A Community of Healers

Michael and Louise Carmi

Dr. Michael Carmi is a General Medical Practitioner (retired) and former Professor of Primary Care and Associate Post Graduate Dean at the University of London.

Louise Carmi is a former Senior Nurse Manager and Child Safeguarding Specialist, Havening Trainer, UK Chair of Veterans Havening, and coordinator of the London Havening Practice Group—currently the largest practitioner support group worldwide.

Harry: *Michael and Louise, how did you discover Havening? I met you last year in New York at a Conference and you both were quite experienced at that point. How did you learn about it?*

Louise: Michael has known Paul McKenna for a long time and he has become a friend. Paul talked about Havening and was thrilled with the results, and said to Mike, 'You really must come to this event in May 2013 in London and see what it is about'. He explained that his friend, Dr Ronald Ruden , had been working on Havening Techniques® for more than a decade and was about to hold the first international workshop , although prior to this there had been smaller workshops in New York.

Our daughter Debi, an acupuncturist and healer, had already signed up for the event and went with Michael. I could not attend as I had childcare responsibilities that weekend. I can only say they were absolutely bowled over by the experience of those initial two days. I would go as far as to say that it was life-changing for the complete family in terms of impact, in ways that could not have been imagined.

After the weekend, Michael explained his experience, and Debi demonstrated Havening to me, and taught me how to do it. It seemed too good to be true. From that time—this was May 2013—it was almost as if we had a conversion. We are all highly skilled health workers, and Michael and I had many years experience working in the National Health Service, in challenging roles. The impact of that weekend brought us both out of retirement mode because of the powerful effect and simplicity of Havening. As I was keen to use it, I did the first available training after that event to join Michael and Debi in becoming some of the first Certified Havening practitioners.

I would also say that because I had spent three decades working with families in really difficult situations: complex health issues, domestic violence, child abuse and neglect, and many years working with families who had experienced 'cot deaths' (crib deaths), the headline for me was: if only we'd had this technique then, how many lives would have changed for the better, patients and staff alike. It is a remarkable self-help tool to reduce stress.

Michael : Absolutely.

L: That set us off on the road to Havening, from that beginning, the three of us —'the Carmi Army'—wanted to share Havening with the wider community, and with the medical community, so it is rather a passion! I think that this is because it has made such profound changes with people. It changes them, it changes us. It is such a wonderful seemingly simple tool—but one which has a scientific basis .

H: *Yes , both you and Michael were retired. Do you actually see clients now, or do you help people more informally as volunteers? How does this work fit into your lives ?*

L: Michael sees clients / patients on a pro-bono basis, many of whom he has known from his previous work as a family doctor: former patients and people who are referred by local contacts. I work in Central London and locally and see a mixture of both paid and pro-bono clients . As a trainer, I get great pleasure in introducing Havening to interested groups, and supporting the development of skills.

Havening has rather taken over rather than fitted into our lives! We have recently returned, as a family from being invited to help lead the Havening training in Australia. This was an amazing experience and is leading to some super, talented practitioners 'down under'.

H: *What are some of the most remarkable changes that you've seen in people as you have worked with them with Havening?*

L: You know this brings tears to my eyes. One word that reflects the changes: transformational. You see people coming in, maybe slightly anxious, a bit unsure of what they are letting themselves in for, sometimes skeptical . When they go out, they float home, in terms of their physiology, their composure, and their state of wellbeing. They often look taller, and feel lighter—as if a physical burden has been removed, as well as the burden of phobias, emotional trauma and grief.

H: *Do you have any stories you would like to share ?*

M: Very early on after I had been on the Havening Training course, I went to visit a friend who was complaining bitterly of dental neuralgia and had a dental abscess. I said, 'Well, let me try this'. I got rid of the dental neuralgia using Havening and to my amazement, I also got rid of the dental abscess.

This really started me thinking: What is happening here? I now have a much better understanding that we are affecting the nociceptive area in the amygdalae, and it appears that we are also affecting the immune system, and that really interests me as a doctor. And certainly to speedily and permanently get rid of an abscess without antibiotics, without surgery is incredible. It doesn't belong in conventional medicine, it is inconceivable. So when this happened it was very reinforcing for me as a practitioner to say, this is a very powerful tool .

Another example: We were in a Veterans Meeting with Malika Stephenson (Veterans Co-ordinator) and after about 4 hours we were leaving the building when a veteran came in using crutches. His colleague asked if we could do anything to help him.

He had been shot in the ankle 20 years previously by a member of the IRA, and had been in continuous pain virtually all the time since then. He had recently been seen by an Orthopaedic Surgeon for an opinion, and the Surgeon had given him two options: either have his ankle fused so that it was immobile or have his foot amputated. He had said that he would probably go for amputation. I was horrified at this.

At the end of a 15 to 20 minute Havening session, this man was standing, without crutches, with a smile on his face , exploring the movement in his legs, and pain free. Then he said, 'I can't do squats', and he started doing squats. I will always remember that! It is imprinted on my memory now.

This was a total revelation. After a brief Havening session, he was able to be pain free after 20 years of agony. This meant that he now had options and choices that he did not have when he walked into that room.

L: I had one client who was referred by a doctor, who had psoriatic arthritis, deformed hands, severe pain, highly medicated. This person had been more or less stuck at home for 7 years. Within 2 sessions of Havening over 4 weeks, the pain medication had been reduced by 50%. We had three sessions altogether, and I taught self-havening as a take away . Within a short time, this person had gained not only in physical health, but also in confidence and had applied for, and been accepted into, a Volunteer post in their local area. I check in with some clients over time to see how they are getting on, as we know that Havening has long lasting effects. A year later this person said they were applying to go to University. That's a big life change.

H: *Remarkable.*

L: Yes; there are lots of remarkable happenings with Havening.

H: *As you are spreading the word about Havening, what are you noticing as you share it with more and more people? Particularly peo-*

ple who are in the medical profession, or who are therapists, coaches or whatever ?

L: Initially disbelief, intrigued. In those that are willing, and we have had quite a few that are willing to dip their toe in the water and invest some time into learning Havening, amazement, absolute amazement. It is great watching the transformation during the 2 day Havening training and seeing the difference just 2 days can make to people, understanding some of the science underpinning Havening and gaining confidence in doing the technique.

H: *Thank you. Any more stories?*

M: I tend to work almost totally content-free because I think it enables people to get to where they need to get to more readily. Very often I find that after Havening they will tell me what the content was, as it has lost its grip on them. I have treated people who are totally skeptical about Havening. One guy, a PhD in Pharmacology who works for a big Pharmaceutical company, had a limiting knee problem for a few months; resolved and pain free in one session. He was certainly a non-believer, so it is even great if you don't believe!

H: *Thats a wonderful thing, and I think as we learn more and more about the neuroscience, we gather more cases and more and more research.*

L: Yes, there is research happening in different areas. It's an exciting time to be involved at the beginning of Havening. We have been involved in some research in the UK too.

Also, as we support the London Practice Group with a great group of Certified and emerging Practitioners, we have a wealth of anonymous anecdotal information emerging when we explore information on the impact of Havening.

But we also occasionally hear of the cases where Havening doesn't work, and this is interesting too. Because of our experiences we come from a position where we know that , in the main, Havening will get the expected result. When it doesn't it's an opportunity to look more deeply. I wonder where this trauma is buried, I wonder why, in this situation Havening is not having the result I would normally expect. Over 3 years plus in practicing, I have had no more than a handful of clients out of several hundred where we did not get the anticipated results. Intriguing.

At the Practice Groups, we also discuss interesting cases of all types. This one seems quite simple and doesn't on the surface seem exciting—but the implications are. One of our Certified Practitioners works with mothers with very young babies, and gives postnatal advice and breast feeding support. There was one mother who was very troubled with breast feeding, and even though the baby seemed to be latching on correctly, her nipples were so red, inflamed and painful that she had only been able to feed for 2 or 3 minutes at a time over the previous week. Our colleague havened the mother whilst she breastfed. The baby fed for 30 to 40 minutes, and the mothers nipples were remarkably changed post feeding—looked normal and not inflamed and painful. Something physiologically interesting going on there—as well as resulting in a calmed mother and a well fed babe! Another story from the treasure chest of information that we are discovering.

H: *This is exciting for the future of health care and mental health-care. And, as you know, although obviously there are hurdles to overcome, in terms of research and skepticism and so forth. How do you two see, coming from your extensive experience in healthcare, Havening potentially changing the future of how we are able to help people with these problems ?*

M: I would like every pregnant woman to be taught self-havening. This would not be expensive and would have a fantastic effect on the fetus and on the mother, promote bonding, reduce anxiety and open the pathway to a healthier future for the next generations.

H: *One more question. What advice would you give to someone—a medical professional, lay person or a coach—someone who is interested in Havening and thinking about adding Havening Techniques to their own toolkit. What would you say to them?*

L: Don't hesitate!

M: Yes , it is interesting your should ask that. I have been Skype-Havening with a friend of a very good friend who lives in Switzerland. This person is a psychologist and said after the last session, 'You know, I would really like to take on board Havening as part of my toolkit'.... I said, 'That will be fantastic, just let me know when you are ready for it'.

L: In terms of adding to the toolkit, I would say it changes the way you practice. I know we have both mentioned clients with physical pain a lot in this conversation. When we look at psychological pain due to traumatic life events, I have had clients who have previously gone to therapy or counseling for years and years, and spent thousands of pounds (or dollars) who have phoned me saying, 'I need 2 appointments this week, 2 next week'. I have said, "I will see you, and leave space for you, but in my experience I don't think that you are going to need so many sessions. Let's go with the flow".Two sessions later :resolution.

Havening is truly life changing, and could save Health and Social Care Services a fortune.

I would say to people who are interested in learning more about Havening that it is transformative in both ways. It is transformative to the patients/clients. It is transformative to the practitioner because you work in a very different ways, and you are Havening yourself as you Haven, so it is protective to some extent. It is also very much about empowering people, building resilience and helping people learn self-havening as a take away. Working sensitively with clients so that when the main issues of trauma that have been holding them back have been released, you are then in a position of helping them build the blocks for a better future for themselves, and supporting them in that direction. I think the speed and efficacy of Havening absolutely changes the way that many conventional therapies have worked in the past.

H: *Thank you.*

CHAPTER 30

From inner peace to world peace

Kathryn Temple

Kathryn Temple is founder/CEO of The Happiness Foundation and Managing Director at the Lifelong Learning Company, based in Lowestoft, United Kingdom.

Harry: *Kathryn, how did you first discover Havening?*

Kathryn: A client of mine, who'd trained with me to the highest levels of NLP and EFT that I offer, asked me if I had heard about Havening. I had not.

I looked it up. I thought it looked intriguing. I watched some videos, observing different people doing it, then I decided to get trained. So I came to New York in 2013 to train with the Rudens. It all began with a chance conversation with my client.

H: *Who are your typical clients?*

K: I have commercial consulting businesses in the UK and Gibraltar and I also operate the Happiness Foundation, a non-profit. They're very different, serving different categories of clients.

In my business I work with leaders in major corporations, places like Deloitte, Credit Suisse, Bassadone Motors. I also have a private practice.

The Happiness Foundation serves vulnerable people in the community. Children, families, people who've been abused, raped, assaulted. Crime victims. People with anxiety and depression. Kids with behavioral problems.

Through the Happiness Foundation, I teach classes designed to help enhance wellbeing. I always show my students self-havening techniques. I also share Ron Ruden's quote: "If you do hopeful havening one minute every day in the mornings, it will change your life." So I recommend that they do this, because it sets the day off in the right style.

I also get them to do grateful havening in the evening, before bed. I always say that which we appreciate, appreciates. And what a beautiful restful way to go to sleep. And it can change the quality of their sleep, because if there was cortisol around, they now have waves of serotonin and oxytocin going down those neural pathways.

Changing the quality of their sleep will change the quality of their dreams, which will have a positive impact on their belief system (since beliefs are often laid down in our sleep), which will effect the way that they wake up the next morning. I think doing grateful havening at night is basic maintenance for good mental health.

H: *Yes. This reminds me of something I noticed when I saw you speak at the Havening training last year. You have a truly comprehensivist* *viewpoint, in that you are not simply thinking about Havening as a tool for helping somebody depotentiate a traumatic memory or feel a bit better in the moment. You're thinking 360 degrees; exploring every possible application of this toolkit to enhance well-being. Tell me more about your experience of Havening.*

K: The thing that I love about it is it's very gentle and soothing.

The name itself—Havening—is just glorious, isn't it? To me, it is like being cozied into yourself, like comforting yourself.

In my experience, Havening has significantly shifted the impact of abuse and ongoing trauma for children or young people who have had that going on in their lives for years. That's probably the most remarkable shift because, as we all know, those patterns of abuse can be passed on from one generation to another like some unwanted family heirloom, which is absolutely tragic.

Havening massively relieves people and it actually continues to make a difference even beyond the session. They sleep better. It also shifts their relationships with their loved ones. As we know, PTSD can come out as anger; it can make people snappy and ratty. So Havening can make a massive difference in their relationships. It can have an impact, a ripple effect, right across their lives, professionally and personally as well.

I also love the fact that it changes the way people relate to their children in particular, because then it's having an inter-generational effect.

It's as if Havening helps to restore the deep inner-peace circuitry of that right mind. And a right mind is a good thing to have.

I've worked with a lot of the military. I work with Special Forces. I've trained some of the police welfare officers. I tell them all about Havening and encourage them to do the training.

I've also applied it with our emergency service workers who've seen some terrible things. Sometimes, our policeman have discovered bodies that have been there a long time. It's not very pleasant. They have all of the smells and so on associated with discovering bodies in very unpleasant circumstances and in unpleasant states. And Havening has helped them.

H: *Thank you. Many people are skeptical when they first hear about Havening, because it seems just too good to be true. Were you skeptical at first? If so, what changed your mind?*

K: I'm always open to things. There's always innovation in the kind of work I do. I was open with a little skepticism.

Of course, before you apply it to anybody else, you apply to yourself. I thought about an issue that I had. I thought on the scale, it might be about a five or a six, but actually when I went into it and focused in on it, I thought, "Oh, my gosh! It's an eight," which surprised me a little.

I went through that basic Event Havening protocol as it was, as it stood then, havening myself. The feeling went to a zero. I couldn't believe it. I was shocked that it could go like that right down to a zero. It surprised me starting at an eight. Didn't expect it to be as high as that, but it was. Then, you look. I could see that I was looking for it. What happened to that feeling?

That was what I noticed. So then I said to different friends, "If you have anything to clear, let's play with this tool." I started out with friends and family first of all. And I noticed the same thing about them all. At the end of it, they're looking around, looking for it...where is it? I love that.

H:. *You've trained to the very highest levels of NLP and EFT. How does Havening fit in with the larger repertoire of your tools?*

K: It very easily integrates with everything, and there is not one client session where I haven't used it. As far as tools are concerned, I use a very eclectic, integrated mix. I use what works. I use what that particular client needs. And Havening easily integrates into whatever I use.

H: *Thank you. What are some of the most interesting, powerful experiences you've had as you've used this tool with your clients? Any stories you'd like to share?*

K: There was a story of a young girl who disclosed at the age of 30—this was through the Happiness Foundation—that she'd been abused by her stepfather from the age of four, bless her. The stepfather was no longer in that family.

I did some work with her over an elongated session. About four hours doing all kinds of different work, including forgiveness work for her mom, etc.

She chose to go to the police and report the abuse. The case went to court. He was given a 21 year sentence. She gave her story away to a national newspaper in the hope that other people would not feel embarrassed about coming forward and would have their chance for justice. She let people know that the work with the Happiness Foundation made the most enormous difference.

Through that, Jeremy Vine, who's a BBC radio presenter got in touch with us. Her story was published in two magazines, in the London Metro as well as a national newspaper. The BBC and the ITV are the main TV stations in the UK. ITV came and did a news item on us, a mini-documentary with us and the girl. I talked about Havening in that as well.

The other story that has been really interesting is working with children with autism and Asperger's to overcome various kinds of overwhelm, including overwhelm over food. One was a little boy who would only eat rice, bread, white bread, pasta and drink milk.

I thought, "Well, the common denominator is white. He likes white, but there's no color in his foods." We got him to be able to tolerate color. That was the real issue. It wasn't food groups. It wasn't that it was mostly carbs. It was that things were white. He didn't like color. Havening helped him to tolerate other colors and to overcome the overwhelm. That was cool.

Here's another story. There was a chap I was working with in a business. He had served in the Falklands War in '83. We were doing some work on leadership and on influence.

Over a cup of tea, he says, "Can I share something with you?" I said, "Sure." He told me about when he was in the Royal Air Force, and had flown over the Belgrano, which was the ship that caught fire. He said he still had flashbacks, including the smell of human flesh burning and so on.

I said, "Well, I can easily help you with that." And we did; with Havening, it cleared very rapidly for him. That fire was in 1983, and he'd struggled with that for all this time.

Another one is a funny story. Not really a funny story at all, but it begins in a funny way. I have a photocopier for the office. It needed service. This young man came in to repair it. He says, when he came in, "You know, I don't agree with what you do, don't you?"

I thought, I've never met him before. I just said, "It's OK." I left it at that. No problem.

He said, "What is it you do?" I said, "I'm a psychologist." He said, "So, can you help people like me then?" I said, "Who's people like you?" He said, "I killed my uncle when I was eight."

Quite a disclosure when he doesn't agree with what I do! I said, "I reckon that's on a farm. Am I right?" He said, "That's right." He says, "How do you know that?" I said, "My auntie had a farm. There's a lot of accidents can happen on farms."

He said his father had put him on a tractor, and was asking him to reverse. Remember, he's only eight years old. The father's showing him what to do to reverse it. Of course, the boy goes forward and kills his uncle with the tool that was on the front. His father had never forgiven him for that, even though it was the father's decision to put him on the tractor.

I said, "Would you like to have an experience of what it is that I do that you don't agree with?"

He agreed and we havened. It probably took 12 minutes, 13 minutes. He rang his father that night. They went out for a drink. They hadn't been on speaking terms for a long, long time. He disclosed it to his wife, who he hadn't told about it.

One more. The daughter of a policewoman was here yesterday. She has been struggling on medication. Very easy to see she's on medication, because the pupils are dilated, with a lot of anxiety.

I used a lot of Havening, and it brought a lot of peace into her system.

H: *How beautiful.*

K: I've got another one for you. About four or five times, I've used it with couples but I've had them Haven each other.

It was beautiful to watch. I nearly wanted to go, "Here's the keys. Get yourself upstairs." [laughs] Because you're thinking, it is ages since they've ever had that level of eye contact over that extended period of time. Other than perhaps when they were first falling in love. It's beautiful and they open like flowers to each other. Absolutely gorgeous. I love that.

The eye gaze is very powerful in the Ubuntu philosophy as opposed to shaking hands, like we do in the West. They hold each other's hands, and they gaze very deeply into each other's eyes. One of them will say, "I'm here to be seen" and the other will say, "And I see you."

With Havening, you look so deeply into someone's eyes when you're doing it to each other. It's absolutely beautiful. When you truly see someone, it's very difficult to do them harm. It shifts the perspective of the couples.

Those have been some of the interesting cases that I've really enjoyed a lot.

H: *Thank you. You spoke eloquently when I saw you at the New York workshop about the larger picture of the possibilities of Havening. What do you see happening a decade or two from now in terms of how Havening could change the world?*

K: I think it is a great tool for peace. If you think about peace, the Native Americans believe the first peace is self-peace. It is our piece of peace that changes the world.

I see Havening being used as a proactive tool in schools, even in antenatal classes. It suits us from the cradle to the grave. That's truly what I believe, Harry. It's a tool for humanity to promote inner peace.

With inner peace, we relate to everybody, including ourselves, very differently. It changes the way that we interact with people in the world, because our mental health and our resilience is better. We know about the power of human touch. If that's on the antenatal agenda, can you imagine?

We need to teach it at many, many levels, starting with mums as a way of managing their state. They're either raising that baby in the stormy waters of cortisol, and it's thinking, "I don't want to get out of here. My mother's terrified half of the time." Or that baby's swimming in a sea of serotonin, thinking, "This is a good world. It's a peaceful world."

Given that we're forming babies' nervous systems and neural networks, that has to be a glorious thing to be teaching Havening in nurseries. We know that in psychology, children who can self-soothe do the best. They have the best outcomes.

If we can teach the moms, if we can then teach the little ones in nursery, in primary schools, and all the way through school, so that we catch the generations coming up that are the future of our world, what is possible? I feel really excited at the possibilities for Havening!

The Dalai Lama said, "If we could teach children mindfulness, we would change the world in a single generation."

I think that's an ambitious, but laudable aim. What I would like to see is us teaching Havening in school as a way of building children's resilience, as a daily habit, like brushing their teeth. Then it becomes part of a daily maintenance program.

It should also be part of the undergraduate program for teachers, and for doctors. It could be on all professional trainings. HR professionals should be able to use it and take it as a tool into the workplace.

Also when there are traumas and difficulties, it can make a difference. We had big floods in North Norfolk a couple of years ago. Some people lost everything. They can't get insurance for their houses. The government did give some money for a relief fund, but when I went up there to help, it was like Beirut. I've never seen anything like it. There were sand dunes, sewage, dead sheep that had drowned, washing machines in fields far away. It was unbelievable.

Being able to use tools like Havening in this kind of situation makes a difference. It's such a soothing and gentle tool to use. It's also very empowering, because every single person that you share it with can easily do it for themselves. That's one of the great benefits and boons of Havening. It becomes a tool for the world.

H: *Thank you. What advice would you give somebody who's looking into attending a training or learning about Havening for themselves? What would you say to them?*

K: The process is very easy to learn. It is easy to integrate into a toolbox of tools for coaches, for therapists and change agents, like teachers. But in addition to that, it is so, so effective. Effective in changing minds.

CHAPTER 31

Havening, healing, and humanity

Ulf Sandstrom

Ulf Sandström is co-founder of the Peaceful Heart Network that works with scalable First Aid for emotional and traumatic stress and a therapist in private practice based in Stockholm, Sweden.

Harry: *Ulf, how did you first discover Havening?*

Ulf: It was through a number of coincidences a couple of years ago. Like now I was working with Gunilla Hamne, my colleague in the Peaceful Heart Network. Since 2007, we have been using a somatic brief intervention technique called Trauma Tapping Technique or Tension Tapping Technique in a lot of different places like Rwanda with genocide survivors, and in Congo with liberated child soldiers, victims of gender based violence, orphans and other survivors of traumatic incidents.

Before Gunilla and I met, I was mainly using hypnosis. But I was also looking for a way of working without using words because hypnosis is so language dependent. So I was Googling "wordless anxiety treatment," and I stumbled across Gunilla. I had no idea she was from Sweden like me. I didn't know anything about the treatment she was using.

I contacted her and I said, "Wow. You're also Swedish. That's cool; can you teach me this stuff?" She came to Sweden, I learned the technique, and we officially founded the Peaceful Heart Network. We've been working together ever since. We focus especially on wordless first aid for laymen, spreading First Aid techniques that can be scaled from one individual to another, turning survivors into empowered healers.

H: *Yes. I love your book Resolving Yesterday.*

U: Thanks.

H: *It's a beautiful book that describes the process and some of your journeys.*

U: It really is a journey. During this journey, I have been and still am very involved in hypnosis. I've co-founded the International Hypnotists Guild, and the Hypnobirthing Association of Sweden. We bring people to Sweden from all over the world to do workshops and we brought Dr. Bhaskar Vyas from India to teach us about Indian hypnotherapy. We brought over Katherine Graves who's a great hypnobirthing teacher. And we brought over Doug O'Brien.

H: *Yes. Doug is a master hypnotist, NLP trainer and also a Havening practitioner and trainer.*

U: Exactly. You know those movies, like '24 Hours' where parallel things are happening? Where all these interconnected things are happening at the same time? This is what it was like meeting Doug and learning about Havening.

One part of my life involves going with Gunilla to Rwanda, Congo and other places, building up different ways of teaching and explaining tapping. We want to take this to a national level; we want to be part of Rwandan national health care for example. To do this we need to present the technique with scientific basis.

We're on this activist road. We're looking for people who understand that healing is possible and that these treatments don't have to be complicated, that seemingly simple somatic therapy with touch can actually make an enormous difference if done properly. So, we're constantly doing research into the mechanisms and efficacy of the tapping technique.

Another part of my life involves moving forward with hypnosis. I run into Doug. We bring him to Sweden and he teaches sleight of mouth, advanced NLP techniques and other cool stuff. On the road of hypnosis Doug and I get to know each other and he meets Gunilla.

At the same time, these two roads are running parallel. They have nothing to do with each other. So Gunilla and I start reading up on the literature about trauma, we start doing scientific training and we run across Peter Levine and Waking the Tiger, his book about how trauma can be stuck in the body.

You know, there are many different theories. So we're looking at different explanations and models to determine what makes tapping work. At that time many years ago, on one side you had most of the energy psychology people claiming that it was all based on energy meridians, and on the other extreme you had the skeptics saying even that is doubtful and the intervention can't work because these meridians haven't been proven scientifically beyond doubt to exist.

And, Gunilla and I are activists, we really honestly don't care if there are twenty explanations or five or two or if it's a combination of all of them, because for us, at the end of the day it's about making real change here and now. If what we use works, we will continue using it.

At the same time, we need the scientific explanations to open doors. Waking the Tiger was good but it was still focused on a meridian-based explanation. So then somebody tells us about Dr. Ruden's book, *When the Past is Always Present*. Anytime somebody tells me a book seems good, I read it, I check it out, I see for myself, I try out what it describes.

And that's what happened. So for almost a year or two we were using *When the Past is Always Present* as one of the possible explanatory models for how and why our tapping is working. What impressed us was the way Ron had created a complete hypothesis about the actual neurochemistry involved. Havening appeared on our radar but we already had an efficient technique in action and didn't bother to indulge in it at the time.

A year later Doug happened to be back in Sweden and the three of us were chatting; him, me and Gunilla. We were talking about *When the Past is Always Present*, and Doug says, "Havening! You guys should check out Havening." "That rings a bell, what about it?" "Well, you know, that's Ronald Ruden's work." Then Doug mentioned that he had just attended a training with Dr. Ruden.

So he showed us Havening in a demo. He introduced us to Ronald over email, we struck up a Skype conversation with Ronald and from there he generously invited us to take a look at Havening. That's how we ended up in London attending one of the trainings.

H: *That's fascinating. I know your work involves not only this activist work, where you teach self-care tools to people in these areas. You are also a professional musician, plus you have a private practice. Who are the clients you work mostly with in your private practice?*

U: Everybody. When I started out with hypnosis long ago I thought I was going to be helping people lose weight or quit smoking for the rest of my life. That didn't appeal to me because at the time I thought of these issues as self-inflicted habits or symptoms. Now I realize they can be symptoms of self-medication for stress and traumatic experiences, which bring them into a different light.

Today I like working with any type of symptoms. I think it works this way: you get more of the same type of clients that you actually help because word travels and people talk about it to other people in the same situations. So, I usually get a lot of people who have trauma in one way or the other involved. As we both know, with the DSM-5, traumatic experiences or attachment issues can contribute to many of the symptoms of most diagnoses in that manual.

H: *So having already had hypnosis and the tapping therapies and a number of other tools in your toolkit...*

U: I usually say the three legs of whatever I do to help a client are based on understanding how language affects us, how hypnosis can reinforce that and reach beyond the rational mind, and then sensory therapies like Havening or tapping.

H: *What role does Havening play in your practice now?*

U: A big role. I took the training and was very impressed by a couple of things. Attending a Havening workshop like the one in England was an experience. I'm also an NLP practitioner, and just the year before that, John Grinder had kindly invited me and Gunilla to London to check out new code NLP, which has a lot in common with sensory therapies because it's about changing state. It felt like a second blessing to be invited to the Havening workshop.

It's also amazing how different therapies attract different people. With Havening, I found a room full of people with a lot in common. Hypnosis often attracts musicians because musicians work in a state of flow and tend to understand it easily. At the Havening training, there were a lot of hypnotherapists as well as a lot of other open minded people from different backgrounds. I guess that the science aspect attracted people that I felt had more things in common with me. I liked that.

Science is a pragmatic approach, but you still have to be open-minded when you're doing something new and cutting edge that hasn't yet passed through all the hoops. So these are people who like to be on that frontier. I like that.

We had great meetings, great discussions. It was excellent to hear the high level of attention to detail by both Steve and Ron. I was mesmerized by it. I was impressed.

Ron was generous in discussing the science of trauma and Havening separately with me and Gunilla, and a lot of pieces fell in place about how trauma's encoded and why our work works. So I decided to go on and complete the Havening certification.

It's a certification that requires effort. You need to do the work. You need to read up on the science. You need to understand it. You need to be able to explain it to somebody else, which means you actually need to really sink into the technical part of it. You also need to report a large number of sessions and present video recordings.

I really enjoyed that. I thought it was a process well put together. It made me a better hypnotist. It made me a better NLP practitioner. It made me a better tapper.

H: *How so?*

U: The structure. The way Ron structured Havening. I can't help looking for patterns in anything I do, so when I got back I was trying Havening everyday, on every client. Then I would compare it to tapping, then I would compare it to hypnosis. Then I would combine all of them. Then I would pick them apart, just because I was curious to see what happens. And I could use the actual structure of a Havening session for a hypnosis session, intending to do the same thing with hypnosis instead of Havening. The result wouldn't be the same because they all have different uses, but it was very interesting.

So I think the structure of Havening is excellent. Understanding the structure and science has transformed everything I do. Plus, I added another powerful tool. It seeped into everything. I had science before, but not that specific science. I had structure but not that specific structure. Every new structure adds value.

H: *Yes. What would you say has been your most significant discovery? As you learned Havening, if there was one discovery that allowed you to impact your clients more fully regardless of the modality, what was that? Was it the understanding of the mechanism of depotentiation? Was it some other aspect of the structure?*

U: I would say it's the combination of several elements. The depotentiation process, the actual window of opportunity, once you activate that neurological circuit, and the short amount of time necessary for depotentiation. Knowing that there is a chemical process happening 'under the hood'. I don't even think it is necessary to understand all of it exactly. Having this model in the back of my mind makes it easier for me to focus on what is important in a session.

H: *Absolutely.*

U: I was listening to a great Ted Talk about this guy who analyzed 85,000 brain scans.

H: *Daniel Amen.*

U: He was saying that the one domain in all the medical sciences that never knows what's actually going on and never really looks at the organ they're treating (the brain) is psychology. With Dr. Ruden there is an electrochemical and mechanical model.

Also in Ruden's model (and in other models as well), we're dividing the stimuli that can trigger traumatic memory into different areas. There's the direct threat and then you also have secondary content and context. By understanding just the way that content can be linked to traumatic memory and trigger it, you realize it doesn't necessarily have to be the gun or the fist or the bridge or whatever. It could be the time of day, or a smell that has nothing to do with it. It could be anything like that.

There is an example that Ron usually cites on trainings which is a woman with a wrist that was hurt in an accident in a London cab, and the pain was re-triggered by moving back to

London at a later point in life and alleviated with Havening. It illustrates how stuff can be seemingly illogically linked so that you don't go down the road of linear cause and effect. Instead, you're just trying to activate the circuit and depotentiate it. That really changed how I work.

H: *Thank you. In terms of your private practice, what percentage of the time do you end up using Havening with your clients?*

U: I would say that goes in periods. For a while I was doing only Havening because I was having so much fun with it. If you know other modalities and you have a lot of clients, one way to stay on your toes is to mix it, to do it or not to do it and see what you missed. If I were starting over, Havening would absolutely be one of the tools I would learn. I would not be able to work as efficiently without it. I would say I use all or parts of it more than 60% at this time. The cases I do are very, very different. For some clients, Havening is not appropriate, and touch is not appropriate. For other clients it's perfectly adequate.

H: *Yes, and in your sessions do you allow clients to do self-havening or do you facilitate that yourself or both?*

U: I facilitate, usually. It is more powerful in my experience, and Gunilla and I have had a lot of discussions about the importance of touch with American therapists because we've been presenting TTT in California and in prisons and in a lot of different places where this is debated.

So, does it work just as well as if somebody does it on themselves? Our bottom line is that these interventions work better when somebody facilitates. This is what we hear from all our clients when we compare.

We think there is an element of actually being helped by somebody, as well as other elements of actual healing involved such as the healing of touch. On only two occasions in the thousands of sessions I've conducted, has there been an issue of somebody not wanting to be touched.

H: *How about your work with refugees and survivors and so forth and when you're teaching people self-care, do you integrate Havening into that now?*

U: Absolutely. When we teach self stabilization or self regulation as we call it, we present a number of grounding techniques. We try to give people a toolbox that works in whatever culture they're in. Some cultures allow touch, some don't.

For some people, it's easier to remember a more complex sequence of treatments. For some people it's easier to remember a simpler one. What's good with Havening is you can do it so simply for yourself just with the hands or just with the face or just with the shoulders. It also ties into a lot of other modalities that people have heard about like the butterfly hug of EMDR Self Help (Eye Movement Desensitization and Reprocessing) and other tapping techniques.

I use Havening very often when I do Skype sessions. The place where it beats everything else so far is when I do a phone session where I can't see the other person. Even though tapping is extremely simple, talking them through thirteen points of tapping is more complex than just asking them to rub their hands or rub their shoulders and just keep the rhythm and keep going as you speak to them.

H: *What are some of the most interesting cases that you have seen Havening prove it's effectiveness with?*

U: I did a session over the phone a while back with Havening. It was a person who was very anxious, had some suicidal senti-ment. They focused on the feeling, the Havening calmed them down completely and they felt really good after.

Just today I received mail from a person that I have treated over Skype, who was greatly helped. She said she was going to chemotherapy and another person was getting radiation thera-py. This person had to put on some kind of mask and was freaked out by it. So my client taught the other patient self-havening and gave her a video I had recorded with self-havening. And she managed beautifully.

H: *Was there anything that was difficult for you as you integrated Havening into your other work or was it a pretty seamless integra-tion because of your understanding of the neuroscience and your therapeutic experience?*

U: Completely seamless. Absolutely. I can't even say there was an effort. I also think that it is different from many other tech-niques that you can learn, because Havening is very hands-on. It's easy to measure the effect, it's easy to see what's happening. It's easy to know now that after ten minutes have passed I will see a difference in the SUD of this person because if there isn't, we probably need to focus on a different aspect of the issue.

H: *Many people are skeptical when they first hear about Havening because the possibilities seem too good to be true. I'm guessing you probably weren't skeptical at first, especially because you learned about Dr. Ruden's book before talking to Doug. Did you have any skepticism at all about the tool?*

U: No. Also I had been using brief therapy techniques like tapping for some time, and had already experienced "incredible" results. So for me it was more like, "Wow, this is a new way, with a slightly different explanation, a different structure. This is really cool. I have to check this out." Also, for me, if somebody I didn't know had said, 'you should check out Havening, it seems to have something in common with what you do', I might have put it on a wait list. When I heard from somebody that I knew and respected like Doug, it was a no brainer. If he said it, I knew I should give it a chance.

H: *How do you see Havening impacting the treatment of trauma and mental health practice in general, say five to ten years in the future?*

U: Ah! I'm in two worlds on this question. I'm an activist. I'm trying to spread emotional first aid techniques for laymen despite what people think about that. There are people who ask if teaching laymen to treat people is the right thing to do or not, but in the areas where we work people have no choice. So Havening, tapping, all of these are beautiful ways of creating peace in these situations.

At the same time, I would love for normal healthcare, primary care, to use these techniques because they are so efficient. Ruden is preparing the way. Both doctors are doing scientifically-based work, moving forward slowly, being careful about the results, having a certification process that makes sure people actually know the technique and are doing it in the right way. This is activism inside the system for me. This means that they are creating a chance for therapies like this (and this is a very efficient one) to eventually be used by the system, in primary care, which it should be. I think it's simply a matter of time now.

The third author of trauma books, beside Peter and Ron, that we really like reading and listening to is Bessel Van der Kolk. His book, *The Body Keeps The Score*, and his research supports what is going on with Havening as well. And now people here are using similar techniques for the crisis and trauma centers that treat refugees who have experienced torture. We hear that techniques we're sharing like Havening are being spread to people who deal with refugees. So I think Havening's going to have a big impact because it comes from the medical arena and it's presented in an effective and clear way.

H: *Yes, I just did an introduction a couple of weeks ago for a group of therapists, social workers, counselors, who work specifically with survivors of torture. They were very interested and receptive to the idea of Havening and many are going to participate in a demonstration a little bit later. So you're absolutely right.*

U: I love Havening. I use it all the time. I wouldn't be able to work as well as I do without it. At the same time, I hear myself saying, "But I'm also using these other techniques." That's not because you need them in combination with Havening, I just want to make that clear. The reason I use them is because I knew them before and I'm a curious guy. If something comes up I'm gonna check it out, no matter how good the stuff I have is.

H: *Yes, and the thing that's nice about Havening is by itself it's a tool not a therapy. So you can use it and integrate it with whatever you do and whatever models work for you and whatever already works.*

U: I've listened to Bessel's lectures. He did a presentation at Heidelberg at a convention where I also did a presentation, where I showed the use of tapping and Havening together with hypnosis for taming the amygdala. What he says is, "If you come to me and say that you have this one solution for everything, I'm not going to listen, not because it doesn't work, but because my experience is that only once you know at least five (I say three) different modalities or interventions, whatever they are, then you're able to say that something actually helps because you actually know of and can compare to others."

H: *Yes.*

U: So I think everything else I do helps me understand the power of Havening. I can tell, it works! It's working, it's doing wonders.

H: *That's a wonderful argument for having people who already have solid tools in their toolbox incorporate Havening as an additional tool that they can use to become more effective. You're also a Havening trainer, training professionals as well as lay people. What have you discovered as you've been spreading the word about Havening within the professional community and among those who you train?*

U: It seems to me that there are three main categories of people when it comes to finding and evaluating help for mental and emotional challenges.

There's the 'research' people. They're interested in research and research results and they don't always have practical experience, which means they focus on science without necessarily having much of a foothold in the real world. So the discussion about what may or may not work is constantly at risk of becoming completely hypothetical. It doesn't help those people when I say, "Well, I have over a thousand client cases. I have good empirical experience," because that doesn't count in their world.

And then you have the people who have trained in some other intervention technique that is extremely science-based or claims to be scientifically validated, and in Sweden a lot of that is cognitive-behavioral therapy (CBT). There is a lot of research about it and the therapy can therefore be said to be evidence-based, but there's a big misunderstanding of what this actually means because the evidence does not always say it is the most efficient method, only that it is one of the most thoroughly researched methods. There is growing evidence that CBT is less efficient than somatic approaches and sometimes even counterproductive when treating traumatic stress.

There's also a catch twenty-two. How do you bring new therapies to people if you only allow interventions that people researched twenty years ago?

So for both of these groups—the researchers and the evidence-based-skepticism-loyalists—it can be a challenge to get them to even look at something like Havening and similar interventions.

Then you have the practical pragmatists—people who have lots of practical work experience and a curious mind. They get the principles of these body-based interventions in less than ten minutes. They try it in the next five and they go, "Cool. I've gotta check this out." I've run into this with psychologists, doctors, psychotherapists and psychiatrists. They give an honest shot and check it out. Some of them have trained in Havening, and now they're using it.

H: *What advice would you give somebody who might be reading this interview who's looking into the possibility of adding Havening Techniques® to their toolkit?*

U: My advice is for them first to think about why they would like to explore a new technique. Is it to prove it or disprove it? Is it to be able to help people help themselves? Is it to be able to deal with whatever they're doing better?

The why matters. If you come from a position of actually wanting to help people, then it would be unwise and unfair to these people to not look at Havening. If you swore the Hippocratic Oath and you're supposed to help people to the best of your capacity, it would be unethical not to check this out when there are so many people who can vouch for the results.

I also think it's a tool that allows you both to help people and help people help themselves, which is where the activism comes in. If you come to a place where there are a lot of people in need and you can get twenty of them to start doing self-havening, and then you can tend to the ones that need other kinds of attention, you're actually helping more people than if you're waiting to get them all one by one in a room to sit down and talk to them.

H: *Absolutely.*

U: I think the whole area of psychosensory treatments, working as Bessel says from the bottom up, from the body to the mind instead of from the mind to the body, is fascinating and also extremely efficient.

As a reference, I work as a product designer as well. I've been designing lighting control systems as a consultant for many years. So it's a high tech industry, it involves a lot of people and we are always embracing new technology and techniques if they add something. Whenever somebody says, "Hey—there's this new technology!" everybody goes "What, what is it?" "Well, it supposedly can help you do x in y time." And everybody in the team will go "Yeah, let's check it out!"

Then we would say it sucks or it works, now let's look at the next one! I can't grasp why everybody isn't like that in every other industry, like mental health for example. I mean, that's the most productive, pragmatic and result-oriented way to approach something, isn't it?

H: *Yeah, let's try it, find out if it works, great. If it doesn't let it go. If it does, let's go for it. I look forward to a world in which everyone has that kind of compassionate pragmatism as their approach!*

U: And I must say, if you are a lay person reading this, if you're a seasoned mental health practitioner, if you're a doubter, if you're a skeptic, no matter what you are, giving this at least an hour of your time and checking out how well founded it is and how well it works is something you will never regret. I can totally vouch for that.

H: *Thank you.*

PART VIII

An Idea Whose
Time Has Come

CHAPTER 32

Tracking a global movement

Feliciana Tello

Feliciana Tello is Chief Operating Officer of Havening Research.

Harry: *Feliciana, how did you first discover Havening?*

Feliciana: I lost my job in 2008 and I was working as a dental assistant temporary. The agency sent me to Dr. Steven Ruden's office for a three month engagement. That was in 2012. When the assignment was over Dr. Ruden asked me if I was interested in a project; he needed a website built. I said yes and built the first havening.org website back in September 2012.

H: *Now you've been part of this emerging Havening movement for a little over four years. What have you noticed about how the word is spreading and how people are responding to this very new and innovative, idea?*

F: A lot of people, when they first hear about Havening, they're taken aback. They can't believe this really works. In fact, it took me nine months after I first learned about Havening to even try to haven myself. But once I did, I realized how effective it was. The same thing happens with other people. The moment they try it, they get excited, like I am!

So now, just four years after building the very first website, people from all over the world are reaching out to us every single day in three to four different ways. Either someone new is following us on Twitter or Instagram, or phoning, or asking me a question via e-mail. I'm also hearing from our practitioners, from our trainers, from people who have seen a video on the web.

Each month we have over 4,500 people come and visit our website. Two-thirds of those are brand new, and they're staying on an average of 3.5 minutes each! This is tremendous and we've really only been sharing Havening with the public over the last three years.

H: *This movement is clearly growing and spreading. Whats next?*

F: We're sharing it with more and more people in different venues. Last week, Dr. Ruden presented Havening to a group of dentists and he was able to give them continuing education credits, sponsored by the Queen's County Dental Society. So now dentists are discovering how to use havening to help their patients with dental phobias. We're doing a program in December with veterans, with Community Strong. Dr. Ron Ruden recently did a presentation along with trainer Adam Vane at a conference for coaches. Another one of our trainers, Ira Scott, presented Havening at a conference on Brief Therapy that was attended by many of the top psychologists, clinicians, and coaches in the world. Dr. Daniel Amen recently interviewed Dr. Ron Ruden on Facebook Live and the video has been watched over 12,000 times thus far!

So we're sharing with more and more groups. More research studies are on the way. We're not spending a ton of money on advertising; right now the word is spreading person to person, by word of mouth and by sharing Havening with different groups of people.

H: *How about your own personal Havening story? I know you are also a certified Havening Techniques practitioner now. What inspired you to go through the certification process and begin working with your own clients?*

F: I was inspired to start working with Havening after the first nine months. As I mentioned, when I first started I really didn't believe it or try it. But once I tried it for myself, that all changed.

When I lost my job in banking in 2008, I lost my identity. I lost who I thought I was, and that trauma manifested itself physically. I lost the nails on my fingers. I had cracks on the corners of my mouth. If you're with me, you'll notice that I'm often smiling and my mouth is open wide. I couldn't do that for years. For years when I opened my mouth, I was bleeding and in pain.

I tried medicine. For years I tried internal approaches, external approaches, going to doctors. Finally, I havened it. I havened away the trauma that hurt me so badly!

Then I realized, this trauma that I thought had changed my life for the worse, had actually changed my life for the better. My nails and mouth began to heal. Then once my nails healed and my mouth healed I was 150% on board with Havening! I have been fully on board every single day since then. Every day, I have spoken about Havening in one way or another.

H: *That's wonderful. It seems miraculous that this single tool was able to transform so much for you. How about your clients? What are you seeing in terms of the people who you're now working with as a practitioner?*

F: The best part about it is that I see the change so quickly. I'll begin the process and their face and eyes will be cloudy and dim. And then at the end, 20 minutes or a half hour later, their eyes are glowing, their face is shining, they're smiling. That kind of result is blowing people away and it makes me feel like a rockstar. They feel amazing and then they go and tell somebody else.

H: *As you know, many people are skeptical when they first hear about Havening because it sounds too good to be true. Were you skeptical at first when Dr. Ruden introduced it to you?*

F: Absolutely! I really thought it was mass hypnosis! For the first nine months I could not believe that it worked, why it worked, how it worked. It took me nine months of watching people time and time again, seeing the results and hearing the results until I finally tried it myself.

    I always say the same thing to people who are doubters or if they're worried or concerned. "Well, it can't hurt and you really don't know until you try." Every single person that has ever tried Havening that I know of has had some degree of success.

H: *That's wonderful. What are some of the most interesting things you have observed, either in your own clients or watching the doctors work with different clients?*

F: I remember one time Dr. (Ron) Ruden was presenting in front of a bunch of veterans, talking about PTSD and how we could help. This one guy begins to describe some of the horrible things he had seen and experienced. Dr. Ruden said, "We can take care of that." The guy says, "You can't help me. Nobody's helped me in forty years. I've tried doctors and therapists and not one person's helped me."

Dr. Ruden turned to him and says, "You wanna bet?" He invites the guy up, and Dr. Ruden begins to haven him. Twenty minutes later this man says, "I can't believe what you just did. I cannot believe after forty years, I'm not in pain about this anymore." He's now one of our biggest proponents.

H: *What advice would you give somebody who's kind of skeptical, and they're looking into the training, but they're not really sure yet. What would you say to them?*

F: I would say to them that nothing happens by accident. If you've bumped into this website or you're reading this or if somebody's mentioned Havening to you, there's a bigger reason. If what you've done in the past hasn't gotten you where you need to be, then try something new.

H: *Thank you so much Feliciana. That's a great testimony. You have a wonderful bird's eye view of everything that's going on.*

F: Thank you! It's exciting and I'm blessed and thrilled to be part of it all.

H: *Me too.*

CHAPTER 33

Curiosity, Patience, and Persistence

Dr. Ronald Ruden

Dr. Ronald Ruden, M.D., Ph.D., is a primary care physician practicing in New York City. He is developer of the Havening Techniques®.

Harry: *Dr. Ruden, I'd like for you to share the story behind Havening's discovery. How did you get interested in this subject in the first place, and what specifically awakened you to the possibility that has now become the Havening Techniques®?*

Ron: Back in 2001, my colleague and friend Paul McKenna was visiting me in New York. We were walking along Central Park West. He asked me if I had heard of a technique called tapping, whereby you tap on acupoints. I had not, but was curious. The technique was described in the book, *Tapping The Healer Within*, written by Roger Callahan. I bought the book, read it, and I thought, "This is a bunch of silliness. How could tapping on someone's face produce a change in the brain?" It made no sense to me.

I decided to experiment. I had a doctor in my practice who had a severe phobia of cats. I showed her the book; I showed her the algorithm which Callahan described for this phobia, and I said, "Okay. Let's do this. There's nothing to lose. I'm just curious. I don't think it's going to work." So, we performed the technique described by Dr. Callahan. Lo and behold, her ability to bring up a fear response when thinking about cats completely disappeared, literally within minutes. That was really interesting to me.

Over the next week or so, I asked every patient who walked in the door, "Do you have a phobia?" And about five people had significant phobias. I used the same algorithm, and sure enough, I cured every one of them.

I decided that there may be something here, but the model that Dr. Callahan had put forth was based on an Eastern model of the flow of energy through meridians. According to this model, illness occurs because these meridians are blocked, producing what he called a perturbation in the brain, in what he described as the thought field.

I'm an allopathic physician. I wanted to see if there's actually a neuroscientific point of view which we could use to explain what's going on, because I was fascinated by how rapidly and completely these simple phobias were removed and dissolved. You have to understand, I had absolutely no idea how this could possibly work; this idea that tapping fingers on your forehead or under your armpit after the person had activated the thought process could cure the phobia.

Around the same time, there was work coming out of Joseph LeDoux's research lab here in New York City by a Dr. Nader. Dr. Nader found that encoded trauma could be dissolved by interfering with protein synthesis after activating the memory of that fear. And he called this inhibition of reconsolidation. A whole new field opened up, exploring the mechanisms by which reconsolidation could be blocked by using specific chemicals or drugs like Anisomycin, which inhibits protein synthesis.

I got really excited, thinking, "That's how this must work! We must be interfering with protein synthesis." I spent the next two years reading every article there was, (and there were lots of them) on inhibition of reconsolidation. And, I kept on conducting, in my office, phobia treatments.

H: *Continuing to use the same tapping protocols?*

R: Yes, the same protocols, with a modification. By that time, Gary Craig had recognized that the wide variety of specialized protocols Dr. Callahan put together were unnecessary. Craig found that one simple protocol could be used to fit the full range of the various conditions. Yet he still worked from the same underlying model, this idea that tapping on the acupoints allowed the chi to flow more properly through the meridians and thereby would remove the thought field perturbation. I still couldn't wrap my brain around exactly how that would work. So I'm getting excited about this concept of inhibiting protein synthesis, thinking that this must be the answer.

Then I made an observation. One of the papers I read noted that the removal of the reconsolidation took about six hours. For example, suppose you set out to train an animal to fear something. Let's say you associated a light and a shock. You show them the light and then give them a shock. They freeze. Show them a light, give them a shock, they freeze. Do it a couple of times, show them the light, then they freeze, in a typical Pavlovian model. Next, you show them the light and then inject a protein synthesis inhibitor like Anisomycin. Sure enough, when retested, researchers found that the previous response to the light no longer existed. However, it took six hours for this thing to kick in.

I realized, of course, that when using this tapping protocol, the tapping instantaneously removed the response to the stimulus. There was a six-hour delay by using protein synthesis, and essentially no delay by using the tapping protocol. So, the whole idea of inhibition of protein synthesis to reconsolidate the memory was obviously incorrect, in terms of how tapping worked.

I broke out in a sweat. I thought to myself, okay. I have two choices. I can throw up my hands and go, "Oops," or I can realize that this is an opportunity. There must be another mechanism by which this works, because the results were so clear.

So I went back to the literature. I needed something that could be very rapid, and the only thing that could be this rapid based on my reading of the literature was synaptic depotentiation; the removal of receptors on the post-synaptic neuron.

In this model, when a signal would come through, there would be no receptors on that neuron to propagate the signal, so that signal—stimulus—would no longer produce a response. And, of course, that was my 'aha' moment.

The issue did not involve protein synthesis. In fact, it rather involved synaptic depotentiation of the post-synaptic neurons along what we call the thalamo-amygdala pathway. So, the thalamus would send the signal to the amygdala, and on the amygdala side, which is the post-synaptic side, the receptor would then be depotentiated, which means that it is removed from the surface and then internalized, so that when the signal from the thalamus came along, there was nothing available to propagate the signal.

From there, I began to look at different ways tapping could produce a signal to depotentiate these receptors. This was a big mystery. I initially thought that it was serotonergic. In fact, in the first paper I wrote, published in 2005, the metaphor I used was that activation of the memory by imaginal recall was like opening up a pathway—imagine a pathway comprised of indentations—holes—on a beach. And then, as a result of the tapping, a wave of serotonin comes in and fills the holes so that the pathway is no longer visible. The holes represent the receptors which have now been removed from the surface of the post-synaptic neuron, no longer available to propagate the signal.

As it turns out, that simplistic metaphor was correct. We now know, from the research, that it is the AMPA receptors which are the transmission process by which an intermittent stimulus is transmitted from the pre—to the post-synaptic receptors, which allow for the signal to be converted into a response.

Once I had this fundamental idea that AMPA receptors were needed, then I had to figure out the details of the mechanism by which touch produced the depotentiation. This led to about a decade's more literature review and experimentation, eventually leading to the current thinking about how this works.

I began to look at Mel Harper's work. He also looked at this process of synaptic depotentiation, and his idea was that a delta wave, which he was able to generate in the brain by using vibrating pads on people's hands, could depotentiate the AMPA receptors on the post-synaptic neuron of the amygdala. I wondered if there was a better way of generating delta waves. Harper had studied this. He put vibrating pads on the cheeks, on the palms, on the arms. Then by measuring simple EEG, he was able to see how it increased the delta waves.

I didn't have that equipment, so I decided, instead of tapping, to use simple soothing touch. I also looked at the work of Tiffany Field. Working in the area of massage therapy, of touch therapy, she showed that both serotonin and dopamine went up and cortisol went down by using therapeutic massage.

And so, I began to think that maybe a specific stroking used in therapeutic massage, called effleurage, which is a soft, gentle stroking, might work instead of having to apply electrical stimulation via vibrating pads to the face, to the arms, or to the palms. I began to look at this as a possibility, and to explore this hypothesis with hundreds and hundreds of patients, experimenting with exactly where and how to apply the touch.

I noticed over time that this simple stroking of the arms, under the eyes, the forehead, and the palms was very effective. I am now convinced that this manner of touch generates significant delta wave production in the brain, and that this, now referred to as Havening Touch®, is what allows us to depotentiate the post-synaptic neuron.

As I continued to look at how delta waves in different parts of the brain interact differently with memory systems, I, along with my team of early collaborators, eventually produced a systematic process, not only encompassing the removal of an unwanted emotional experience, but also the introduction and incorporation of a desired emotional state.

As I began to search out the mechanism by which positive outcomes could be enhanced, it became clear that, during slow-wave sleep, the memories of the day are consolidated into the brain. During daytime, when you're awake, delta waves do not normally occur. So, it was obviously a paradox that although we were awake, the brain perceived us as being asleep and thereby was open for consolidation of new memories.

Once we understood the role of delta waves in these various neurobiological processes, we were able to produce a comprehensive, system that we now call Havening Techniques®.

FIFTEEN MINUTES TO FREEDOM

Beginning with Event Havening, the system now includes Transpirational Havening, which helps to clear the traumatic encoding of entire memory networks, organized around the experience of a specific emotion, such as fear, anger, sadness, or rage; Outcome Havening, which helps the client to actually change their memory of a traumatic event so that they can experience a feeling of empowerment instead of victimization; Affirmational and Iffirmational Havening, which activate and install positive patterns of thinking and feeling; and Role Havening, which allows for an internal experience of resolution of relationships that have previously triggered emotional distress. There are also numerous variations on these core components that are used for building resilience.

H: *Thank you. Would you speak a little bit to your discoveries as a physician in relationship to the mind-body connection? That is, how something presenting as disease or chronic pain, could actually be connected to a traumatically-encoded memory?*

R: That was another one of the surprises. Robert Scaer, one of my colleagues, had written a book, *The Body Bears the Burden*. He noticed that even simple, minor injuries could produce pain far out of proportion to the event, and he concluded that this had to happen in the brain. He recognized that there had to be a place in the brain where these things were stored so that stimuli that would, on a subconscious level, activate the memory when the pain occurred, would then produce the pain response. And, in fact, that's exactly the case.

My first example of this—I remember it vividly—was a woman who came in presenting with pain in her right hand. 100% of my colleagues would have sent her for an MRI, or sent her to a hand surgeon. They would have not known what to do. But, using the model that this pain may have been encoded during trauma, in my history taking I asked the question, "Did you ever injure your hand?" This was because when you looked at her hand, there was no obvious source of the cause of the pain. And she told me her story. Fifteen years ago, she had traveled to London, where she was in a cab accident. The cab flipped over and her hand slammed against the door. I said, "Well, you said the pain began three months ago. What happened three months ago?" She responded that three months ago, she decided to return to London. Interesting. So, I said, "Do you still remember the car accident?" She says, "Like it was yesterday." I said, "Bring it up." We brought up the event. We applied Havening touch to the event and brought the SUD (Subjective Unit of Distress) down to zero, and instantaneously, the pain and the problem disappeared, never to return.

H: *What other conditions have you seen resolved and healed through proper application of Havening Techniques?*

R: We've seen over the years, with close to 100,000 Havenings done worldwide, some astonishing results, results which were untouchable by pharmacological or psychotherapeutic means. In addition to the many examples of emotional healing that have taken place, we've seen removal of chronic back pain, treatment of reflex sympathetic dystrophy, removal of PTSD, treatment of what we call idiopathic neutropenia, where white count is low.

H: *Dr. Ruden, please speak more about the difference between Havening and other modes of physical and emotional healing.*

R: Havening represents a paradigm shift. We're not using pharmaceuticals; we're not using talk therapy. We're using a delta wave, which we define as an "electro-ceutical"—using the electrical part of the brain. The advantage I think Havening has is that we have a solid neuroscientific understanding of how this works. Of course, these models and mechanisms of action remain speculative. We can't yet get in the brain and directly observe these processes. But in vitro work in petri dishes confirms many of our hypotheses. Thus far, we have not identified a single example of something that did not fit the model we are proposing for how Havening works. Not one. So we're pretty confident that this model accurately explains what's going on.

So we hope that the science itself will support our commitment to move ahead. My goal is to spread the word, to get Havening to people who can use it for themselves. There are caveats to all of these things. Sometimes people have such significant traumas that self-havening may not be enough. These are concerns that we have, so when we teach self-havening, we suggest that if you have a history of trauma, that you find and engage a practitioner who can help guide you.

H: *Yes. One of the conversations I've had with Tony Burgess, who, of course, is one of your primary trainers is that Havening is a tool, not a therapy. For example, if you think about lasers, you can use lasers for lighting at a party, or you can use lasers to help perform the most intricate surgery. The tool can be applied in a multiplicity of ways depending on the scope of practice, the ethical guidelines, the level of skill, and so forth.*

R: I think that's true. That's why we call it Havening Techniques as opposed to Havening therapy.

Something else that is really wonderful about Havening Techniques is that the practitioner doesn't have to know what the problem or memory is. As long as the individual can bring the emotions into awareness, we can treat them. This is completely different from existing allopathic approaches, where you have to make a diagnosis. We don't make diagnoses. We deal with emotions and physical disturbances.

The idea that we don't need a diagnosis; rather, we simply need to find out the root of the issue, actually comes from Freud, who looked towards hypnosis to find the origin of the individual's problems. Although he had words that described the problems, he didn't make diagnoses. This is another reason why I think our approach is very different from the Western psychiatric or psychological community which relies on diagnostic criteria to begin to treat the patient. And, in fact, the whole of psychopharmacology is also based on the diagnostic paradigm.

We choose not to look at it that way. We don't like to focus exclusively on symptoms or label people diagnostically. We look at people from a different perspective, seeing them as the consequences of the events that happened in their life. Then we take those events which were encoded traumatically, and attempt to remove that encoding so that the consequences, the downstream effects of that encoding no longer cause chronic, inescapable stress. Then the brain can return back to its normal homeostasis and the body can heal.

H: *Thank you. That was a beautiful summation of the process. One more question. What is it like for you to recognize that your research, discoveries, and work are poised to change the face of how we think about emotional, physical, psychological dis-ease and healing?*

R: One of the advantages of being my age, nearly 70, is that there's no need for me to look at this as a discovery which makes me feel important. I look at it as an offering to the world; a new way of looking at things. This is never going to be about myself. This about the technology which has been created.

I stand on a foundation of all the great scientific research which was done before me. This discovery was only made possible because of millions of hours of brilliant thinking, research and diligent effort which led to hard-won knowledge. I'm just another piece in the puzzle. I have a neuroscience background. I'm a physician. I have, by temperament, an intense curiosity and persistence. From my point of view, I was the right person at the right time. This work represents the sum total of the discoveries which were made beforehand. I simply put them together in a different way.

I am personally very excited. I continue to explore and learn. But Havening belongs to the world. And so we are not here to compete, we are here to share, and so if we can do that, we have accomplished what we set out to do.

H: *Thank you so much. As you stand on the shoulders of those who've gone before you, many will stand on your shoulders as this discovery touches, transforms and helps to heal the world.*

R: Anyone who learns and uses this technology that we call Havening Techniques is excited by its power. Previously, the ability to treat some of these conditions would take such a long time. Now, through this technology, we can rapidly alleviate suffering that in many cases, has been considered untouchable.

What makes me happiest is the fact that other people have joined us in this work. Not only have they joined; they are engaged, they've contributed ideas, they've created new techniques. This is probably the thing I am the most proud of, that this technology now inspires people to find new ways of using it. You are correct: people will stand on my shoulders and create new ways to help others along the way.

H: *Thank you.*

CHAPTER 34

Changing the world

Dr. Steven Ruden

Dr. Steven Ruden is the educational director of Havening Research.

Harry: *Dr. Ruden, you have been part of the journey of Havening since your brother's initial research and experimentation. What have you discovered?*

Steven: As we began this journey more than ten years ago, we really didn't understand very much of what was happening, both in terms of the process as well as the outcomes we were observing. Even though we noticed that people were losing fears, feeling better, acting differently, the deeper understanding of what we're doing was not yet clear; we weren't sure what was working and why.

So we set out to discover and develop protocols that work well to address people's problems and that were also based on a sound scientific understanding. As we continued our research and exploration, new science was coming out all the time, which we incorporated into the model.

We came to a point where we were using a very specific type of Havening—Event Havening—as our model. Then we discovered we also could do other things as we understood more about the impact of touch in the generation of delta waves. This emerged as we applied the insights contained in Mel Harper's article, Taming the Amygdala.

As a result, we expanded our menu of protocols to include Transpirational, Ifformational, Hopeful, Affirmational and Outcome Havening. Each of these protocols, although it incorporates Havening touch, works differently than our original Event Havening protocols.

We now understand that activating new possibilities operates by a different mechanism than de-potentiating traumatically encoded memories.

H: *Thank you. So Havening Techniques developed through this iterative process of research, practice, experimentation, discovery. You continue refining both as new science emerges and as you would experiment more and more with the protocols, embracing this continuous process of improvement.*

Most people are somewhat skeptical when they first hear about Havening, because the results seem too good to be true. I went through that phase myself and later, as I met you and your brother, went to the workshops, experienced Havening myself, and explored the techniques with my own clients, what seemed to be too good to be true very quickly became almost commonplace, in terms of what you expect.

When your brother first started talking about this were you skeptical? What were some of the things that went through your mind as you were beginning to discover this new paradigm of healing?

S: First of all, I'm still amazed. Ron and I used to talk about it. "What are people going to say when we tell them to hum a tune, rub their arms and do a visualization and then their life long problems will disappear?" So, in our initial presentations, we were very selective in choosing who we would bring this to. We knew we had something extraordinary, but we were challenged on how to share it with the public, because we expected the skepticism you mentioned.

We also devoted a lot of time to discussing the science that we felt was the underpinning, because what we saw clinically and experienced ourselves was so different than anything we had seen. We felt we had to talk about the science to convince people that this kind of rapid permanent change was even a reasonable possibility.

Of course, if one looks at the history of healing, going all the way back to the shamans, to surgical techniques, to germ theory, to psychopharmacology, to psychology, all of these things evolved out of a single idea. And all were controversial in their time.

H: *Clearly with Havening, you're operating out of a new paradigm. Whenever a new paradigm, like germ theory, is introduced, at first it seems illogical, or perhaps too good to be true. Then, once the new paradigm begins to be accepted and there's an understanding of what underlies it, then there's a greater degree of acceptance.*

S: As Arthur Schopenhauer is reported to have said, "When a new idea is introduced it is ridiculed. Second it is violently opposed. Third it is accepted as self evident."

People suffer needlessly because at the present time there's not an optimal way to treat their suffering. Maybe psychopharmacology helps. But I think this new paradigm without medication, without long psychotherapeutic or talk therapy, may be another way that we can help people achieve their preferred outcomes in life.

One thing that's nice about Havening, as compared to other modalities, is that not only can we remove barriers that keep people held in their past, but we can also introduce new ideas and hopeful ideas and compelling values and passion and purpose that allow them to move forward in their lives. It really does provide a complete circle of well-being.

Havening is also one of those innovations that is emerging from a new understanding that creating well being requires addressing both physical AND emotional dimensions, whereas historically these elements were separated. But we know that physical and emotional healing are totally intertwined with each other. One begets the other.

H: *That's interesting. I appreciate the point that you are making about physical and emotional well-being being linked. The neurobiology of Havening and its application both in terms of removing emotional residue of painful memories, as well as enhancing outcomes, speaks to that beautifully, because the physical and the emotional are intertwined. When you first discovered the power of this tool, did you work with your own patients who had dental phobias?*

S: Yes. In fact, I still use Havening in my dental practice. If the patient's in the chair and they say, "I'm really anxious," I ask them if they would mind if I use a procedure called Havening to help. And I briefly describe the process. And, of course their emotions are totally activated in that moment. So I haven them. Usually, in about five minutes or so, we're able to help them get comfortable enough to proceed with treatment. The anxiety or fear that was there before is no longer present.

I use Havening everyday. I don't necessarily do a full-on Havening process but certainly I'm able to modulate a lot of emotions, especially with children who are scared. And I have their mothers help me out, and haven the children while I instruct them.

I also use Havening with my staff. When someone on my staff is having a particular problem, I may come in and work with them. So I use it everyday in my dental practice. It makes my life, the lives of my staff and my patients lives more comfortable.

H: *Have you spoken to other dentists or hygienists about using Havening in their practice? Have you shared this tool with your dental professional community?*

S: I have. I was invited by my local dental society to talk to other dentists. The presentation was well-received. I've done demonstrations of these procedures with dentists observing and they're impressed. And, of course, there's a big leap between seeing something and doing something. Anyone who wants to use Havening professionally needs to be trained properly and go through the certification process so that when they want to use it in their practice, they are adept.

H: *Thank you. How do you see Havening eventually impacting mental health practices, particularly in terms of treating traumatic experiences? 10 or 20 years down the road, what is your vision or your sense of the impact that Havening could have on that larger context?*

S: My hope is that Havening will become the default approach. Our primary goal right now is to maintain the integrity of our trainings, the integrity of our certified practitioners, the integrity of how our trainers go out and train so that we maintain a consistent message and consistent quality. In this way, we know that the new people who are going out into the world as ambassadors for and representatives of Havening Techniques will be able to produce the same outcomes that we do at this present time.

H: *Can Havening be used and learned affectively by lay people, people who are not counselors, therapists, psychologists, coaches and the like? And if so, how might a lay person use Havening, for example for self care, or is Havening something that really exclusively should only be used within that professional context?*

S: We've recently been exploring that question. My personal view is that people can use Havening in a wide variety of arenas. So, for example, if people are having difficulties in their marriage or if they have children that are ill or if they have things that cause them distress, people should learn how to self-haven, just as people should learn how to meditate, or practice mindfulness, or exercise. I think Havening ultimately will be one of those tools that will help improve everybody's well-being.

H: *Thank you so much. You're out in the world and involved with many trainings. You touch everybody who is either training in or personally benefiting from Havening because of your role in Havening Research. What are you seeing as Havening spreads around the world? What's most encouraging? As I recall there are now 15 or 16 countries that have certified Havening Techniques® practitioners, or where trainings have taken place. What are you discovering as this idea, and this new paradigm of healing spreads around the planet?*

S: I think it's pretty universal. What I see for the most part is that the people who haven other people are thrilled and they enjoy their work and it gives them great pleasure to be able to help another individual. I think anyone who discovers Havening or is introduced to it in the proper way is astonished. Then they get to a point where they want to try it on everything that comes along!

What we see globally is how exciting it is that Havening can used in conjunction with other skill sets that they have already. People are using Havening with their psychotherapy, with their NLP, with their hypnosis, with their massage, with their Reiki, with the other modalities that they have spent perhaps a lifetime practicing and perfecting. And they take Havening because it's a wonderful adjunct and use it in a way that's appropriate for that person at that moment.

What we see globally is that people are beginning to use Havening earlier on in the process of healing, then bringing in their other tools and procedures as needed.

And what we're seeing already for those people who have been working with Havening Techniques for a year or more is that they're using Havening more frequently as their go-to procedure and then bringing in other procedures as needed.

Others who are new to this tend to stay with their existing ideas and understanding and introduce Havening over time. Either way, we are getting positive feedback from all of the people who are participating.

The other day on the Facebook page I saw a post in Norwegian and sometimes there are posts in German and sometimes Italian and I chuckled to myself. How global we've really become after only a couple of years since Ron and I introduced Havening to the world community! And we are growing in the way we are without any large marketing, mostly by word of mouth.

It's very encouraging to us. People are drawn to Havening who want to do projects and research. We have people doing projects with veterans, actors, school children, hospice workers, nurses, educators and other healthcare professionals. Havening seems to being viewed globally with great excitement.

One of the challenges we face as we bring this new paradigm of healing into the world, is that every country has it's own rules, regulations, and restrictions. Some are more flexible and some are less flexible in terms of how health care providers are allowed to serve their clients. So in some countries, only trained psychotherapists are able to do this work. In some countries, until the work is evidence-based, meaning a critical mass of peer-reviewed research has been completed and published, practitioners cannot use techniques that might produce outstanding results. In some countries, the guidelines are much more flexible. So we are navigating this river of regulations carefully.

H: *It must be exciting for you, having been part of this since the very beginning, to see this idea whose time has come beginning to spread in so many ways. Are you and your brother continuing to do new research and develop new protocols and possibilities? Are you also involved right now in creating those more traditional research studies so that eventually Havening has the reinforcement of publication in academic journals? What's happening in that arena?*

S: Well, to your first question, it's always evolving. It's always evolving and we are always learning new applications. So, for example, Gina Pickersgill is working with Second Life, which is a online virtual world in which people adapt avatars and interact with other avatars via the web. She is havening people as avatar to avatar on the website successfully.

H: *Virtual havening in other words.*

S: Yes! I've experienced it!

H: *And the results are equivalent or comparable as in person?*

S: I can only give my experience. I actually felt I was there. I'm sitting in front of my computer screen and I'm self-havening along with the avatar.

H: *Fascinating.*

S: Fascinating stuff! So, virtual Havening via avatar is cutting edge and may be useful in very specific circumstances. Ron and I are also looking at how Havening can help address specific challenges.

For example, we're working to see if Havening is valuable in obsessive-compulsive disorders. We're looking at best practices for working with veterans, and best practices with other specific populations. So, this simple concept regarding use of delta waves and activation/depotentiation of a memory is proving to be applicable and useful for a wide variety of issues.

I'm also moving more towards the idea that helping improve resistance to disease and build resilience are going to be the future keys of well-being. Havening is the ideal tool to do this.

If one were to look at an optimal modality, it would contain the following items. It's easy to learn. It's transportable. All you need are your hands. You can treat large groups of people at the same time. You could use it over Skype or virtual media, so you don't have to be present. It would have zero side effects. These are characteristics of what an ideal health treatment would be.

And we are also learning that our emotional history is the precursor to our adult well-being. As you know, the child is the father to the man. As we have experiences in our childhood, how we experience life through the prism of our perceptions allows us to be resilient or vulnerable, allows us to develop emotionally stable behaviors and responses, or not.

If you have too much trauma and are unable to regulate it, the allostatic load is increased. That is the amount of energy the body needs in order to remain in homeostasis. And eventually the stressors of this high allostatic load allow for permissiveness of disease presentation.

What we see in Havening is once the allostatic load is reduced, the outcomes or consequences of this load also disappear.

So, I don't talk about Havening in terms of treating a particular diagnosis. I facilitate an individual being able to self-heal. As compared to the medical model in which the physician takes the role of healing the patient, I do not heal my patient, my patient heals himself or herself.

The paradigm of physician trying to heal a patient in the United States today has created the most unhealthy population in the history of this country. In spite of the fact that we have all of these superior technological models, people are more obese, have higher rates of diabetes, autism is 1 out of 68 new births, depression is at all time high, autoimmune diseases are increasing. One must ask, "Why?"

My view is that the adaptive capacity of the individual is being stressed and that stressor is the traumatic events that have been encoded in their brain that increased the allostatic load and caused the stress response to be unable to be turned off.

We want to help people understand that this trauma creates suffering, and this suffering creates a desire to remove the suffering, and this desire is at the root of all addictive behaviors and cravings.

I take exception to the fact that in current thinking people who treat suffering think it's the drug that's the problem, that heroin—that's the problem, or cocaine—that's the problem, or the over-eating—that's the problem, or the alcohol—that's the problem. That's not the problem! Because brain scans that are taken of people who are drug addicted, alcohol addicted, food addicted, shop addicted, work addicted, all show the same basic pattern.

H: *And that pattern is the increased allostatic load, the traumatically encoded memories, creating a permissive landscape.*

S: Yes, and it looks the same for all of them!

H: *Thereby demonstrating the value and efficacy of a tool like Havening, which not only works to reduce the specific emotion connected to the traumatic memory, but also helps to build a more resilient landscape.*

So what you're saying is the emerging paradigm that you're operating out of is about well-being, and as I understand it, you're implying that the cause of the lack of well-being shows up in all these different ways, in obesity, in health problems, in addiction, etc. But at the root, that cause is having too many traumatically encoded memories impacting brain chemistry.

Is that right?

S: The cause is suffering, and the attempt to alleviate that suffering. And people suffer, express and assuage their suffering in different ways.

H: *And through the practice of a tool like Havening, we get to remove the root of the suffering in the first place?*

S: Yes.

H: *That has profound implications for humanity as a whole.*

S: I know.

H: *Because we are really talking about the cause of disease, discord, distress being this neurobiological response to trauma. And the cure for disease, discord, distress, being the reversal of that.*

S: Correct. And there has been no down-regulatory mechanism in the human system to remove an encoded traumatic event up until now.

H: *Yes. The hope of humanity lies in our hands, literally. Right in our hands.*

We've come a long way in this conversation integrating specificity on the neurobiological level, with the removal of the cause of both emotional and physical symptoms, with the implications for the larger picture of humanity. Any other thoughts or reflections you'd like to share?

S: One of my greatest mentors, when he trained his students, would just stand up in front of the classroom and speak. But the depth of sincerity with which he spoke his words allowed the students to truly understand the message.

When I talk about Havening, I hope that people can sense my deep sincerity in having something here that I believe can change the world. And it's where I come from that I think wins the day, rather than what I say. Because unless you've experienced it, or seen it, it's hard to imagine.

We know that people who experience this or are comfortable enough to share this with other people in a therapeutic manner will find it astonishing and they will within themselves feel a great sense of accomplishment and excitement about how they can help people.

And they will want to share and will continue to share it.

This excitement cannot be generated by Ron or I.

Ron and I put out the information. Now, people are taking this information and are using it for the benefit of themselves and others and taking initiative and pushing the envelope forward, and they are doing this simply to be part of something that can possibly help humanity and change the world.

I am always grateful that people pick up the mantle and bring it forward and we have some wonderful people out there. They are all over the world.

And sooner or later, hopefully in my lifetime, Havening will become more and more well known.

H: *What else is ahead for this Havening movement that is expanding each day and reaching more and more people around the world?*

S: Peer reviewed research will be available in 2017, published in well-respected journals. Also in 2017, we are going to be looking at altering our course of approach a little bit.

We're probably going to be creating two training tracks, one for licensed healthcare professionals and another for the non-healthcare-licensed individuals such as life coaches, teachers, and parents, since the criteria and competencies for using Havening in these different contexts are not always the same.

H: *When you were talking about how this is spreading without so much of your initiative, except putting it out there, it reminds me of the Victor Hugo quote "Nothing is as powerful as an idea whose time has come." I do feel that this is the time for the idea called Havening to spread and to reach the world.*

Thank you so much for your reflections, your comments, your insights, your stories. I'm very proud to be part of the growing Havening community and have been astonished, with what I've experienced in my own Havening process, what I've observed by other skilled practitioners, including yourself and your brother, and what I've experienced with my own clients.

It is clearly a new paradigm. It looks so simple and seems so unusual, just as the introduction of the germ theory or the discovery of some other paradigm that shatters everything before it and says, "Wait here's a new way to look at this!" Grounded in neuroscience. Grounded in neurobiology. Grounded in a deeper understanding of how the brain processes memory. Grounded in a solid understanding of psychosensory therapy, the use of touch and sensory stimulus to transform the brain.

From this simple set of ideas, within our own hands, we have the capacity to help humanity heal. So thank you for your important role in that and your continued work in that. It's an honor to interview you and to be part of the team.

S: Thank you Harry! I wrote a long time ago that one of the greatest gifts I have are the people I meet along the way. It's truly my pleasure to share these moments with you.

H: *Thank you.*

Postscript

Over a decade ago, around the time Dr. Ruden was beginning the research that would lead to the development of the Havening Techniques®, I participated in a week-long conference, convened around the theme of 'Transforming Fear Into Love'.

It occurs to me that this is precisely the promise of Havening and the other psychosensory modalities. What if the pathway from fear to love, both on the individual and the collective/societal levels—was essentially a process of de-traumatization—unhooking, delinking and depotentiating the encoded patterns of defensiveness and fear that have been wired into our collective neurology for millennia?

What if these simple yet profound tools held a key to the co-creation of a more peaceful, just, and sustainable world?

Thank you for joining us for this introduction to the power and promise of Havening Techniques. I hope you have been inspired to, at the very least, look more deeply into these remarkable tools for transformation. The global Havening movement is changing the world, one person at a time.

Please join us at **havening.org**.

Getting the help you need

How to find a Havening Techniques® Certified Practitioner

The best way to discover the power and promise of Havening is to experience a session with a Certified Havening Techniques Practitioner. Practitioners have undergone a rigorous quality control process to assure that they have the mindset and capacity to assist their clients in skillfully applying Havening Techniques to reduce stress, boost resilience, enhance wellbeing, and heal the pain of the past. To find the practitioner who's right for you, go to www.havening.org and click the 'Locate a Practitioner' button.

Helping others heal

How to get trained in the Havening Techniques®

If your work in the world involves helping others heal, and you've been inspired through these interviews to consider adding Havening to your toolkit, consider attending a Havening Techniques training which is the first step in the certification process. To learn more about the training, including content, schedules, locations, investment, continuing education credits and certification options, please go to havening.org.

About the author

Harry Pickens is an award-winning musician, educator and life transformation strategist. A Certified Havening Techniques® Practitioner and Trainer, he is Founder/Director of Havening Louisville and Havening For Humanity.

He is also developer of Emotional Empowerment For Personal Mastery™, a step-by-step protocol that helps his clients release the pain of the past, fully embrace the miracle of the present moment, and consciously create their best possible future.

Harry earned his Certificate in Applied Positive Psychology from the Flourishing Center, and also holds practitioner and trainer certifications in EFT and Spiritual Technology, including the Pro EFT™ Master Practitioner certification.

Based in Louisville, Kentucky, USA, he works with clients throughout the world via Skype, phone, and in person.

Contact Harry at haveningforhumanity@gmail.com.

Made in the USA
Middletown, DE
23 July 2018